Restoring the Flow

Restoring the Flow

Confronting the World's Water Woes

R.W. Sandford

RMB
Victoria Vancouver Calgary

Rocky Mountain Books
#108 – 17665 66A Avenue
Surrey, BC V3S 2A7
www.rmbooks.com

Rocky Mountain Books
PO Box 468
Custer, WA
98240-0468

Library and Archives Canada Cataloguing in Publication
Sandford, Robert W.
  Restoring the flow : confronting the world's water woes /
Robert William Sandford.

Includes bibliographical references and index.
ISBN 978-1-897522-52-3

  1. Water conservation—North America. 2. Water quality management—
North America. 3. Water-supply—North America. 4. Water conservation.
5. Water quality management. 6. Water-supply. I. Title.

TD222.S25 2009   333.91'16097   C2009-903727-0

Book design by Frances Hunter
Cover design by Chyla Cardinal
Front cover photo: Mikael Damkier

Printed in Canada

Rocky Mountain Books acknowledges the financial support for its publishing
program from the Government of Canada through the Book Publishing
Industry Development Program (BPIDP), Canada Council for the Arts, and
the province of British Columbia through the British Columbia Arts Council
and the Book Publishing Tax Credit.

BRITISH COLUMBIA ARTS COUNCIL
Supported by the Province of British Columbia

Canada Council Conseil des Arts
for the Arts   du Canada

Mixed Sources
Cert no. SW-COC-001271
© 1996 FSC
FSC

The interior of this book has been produced on
100% post-consumer recycled paper, processed
chlorine free and printed with vegetable-based dyes.

This book is dedicated to Ralph Pentland and Jim Bruce, respected and prescient pioneers in understanding the importance of water to the way people live in Canada.

Contents

Invocation

Rivers within yearn for rivers without

Though water tends to repel organic compounds, it is strangely attracted to most inorganic substances, including itself. Water likes to be around other water. Its molecules, in fact, cling to one another more tenaciously than those of many metals.

You can observe water's remarkable qualities of self-adhesion if you sit by a river. Water sticks together. Water draws water with it. Sit on a riverbank long enough and you might observe that water also likes to sing. The faster it moves, the louder it sings. Still water barely whispers; falling water roars.

There is a reason we feel different when we are in the presence of large volumes of water. Water reacts to almost everything, and almost everything reacts to water. The feeling you get standing at the edge of a river or lake or beneath a thundering waterfall may be aesthetic but it is physical too. Your body is aligning itself with the molecular attraction of the water and the water is aligning itself to you. The effect can be even more pronounced when you stand by the sea. Ankle deep in surf, we feel the water of our cellular seas within yearning for the salty sea without. The water inside us feels the tug of the tide. We know water, but water also knows us.

Go to the kitchen. Turn on your tap. Let the water run. Feel the cool moisture of wind and the wetness of cloud and rain. Feel the cold of snow and the hardness of glacier ice. Hear thunder. Feel the river flow through your hands. Feel the water within you yearn for the water without. Fill a glass. Bring it to your lips. Search with your tongue for water's memory of faraway seas.

Taste distant mountains. Feel the fissures in deep limestone tingle on your tongue. Hold the glass up to sunlight. See our star burn through the sparkling lens made of the most amazing of all liquids. Drink.

Repeat daily until fully and finally restored.

A Meditation on Population

Imagine yourself in a stunningly beautiful open-air restaurant, which you discover, to your utter astonishment, comfortably seats three billion people. This restaurant is so amazing that it is impossible not to reflect upon how lucky you are to be able to dine there. You know that no one is naturally entitled to live this well, which adds to your feeling of good fortune. But then six billion more people suddenly show up at the already comfortably full restaurant. It does not take long before there is little room to move. Most of the new customers can't even sit down. There are not enough servers, so most people have to wait. In the end not everyone gets served and soon it becomes apparent there isn't enough to eat. Many don't even get a drink of water.

You soon notice that the beautiful furniture, appointments and natural surroundings are being destroyed or stolen. The washrooms are overwhelmed and toilets overflow. People start fighting with one another because they are hungry and confused and because there is no one with any credibility that can tell them what they should do. Soon the magnificent restaurant is in ruins and everyone is on their own to fend for themselves. The kitchen is looted for what is left and now there is nothing for anyone to eat except for what they can find in what remains of the landscape that surrounds them.

It doesn't take long to realize that such a restaurant is not likely to exist again for some time, for the climate in which it was created – environmentally, socially, economically and demographically – has been altered beyond recognition and may not appear again for some time unless we exercise uncommon restraint now and for many generations to come.

ACKNOWLEDGEMENTS

This book would not have been written without the support of a great many of people. Since the publication of *Water, Weather & the Mountain West* in the fall of 2007, the success of the United Nations Water for Life initiative in Canada has been predicated principally on the support of three organizations: Unilever Canada, the Max Bell Foundation and the Walter & Duncan Gordon Foundation.

I am particularly indebted to Catherine McVitty of Unilever and to Tim Morris at the Walter & Duncan Gordon Foundation for their advice as well as their support. I am also greatly indebted to Dr. John Pomeroy and Dr. Julie Friddell of the University of Saskatchewan for their ongoing contributions to my understanding of how the hydrological cycle manifests itself, particularly in the cold regions of Canada, and for all the contacts in the research community they have encouraged me to make within the IP3 cold regions research project. I would also like to acknowledge a debt of gratitude to Dr. Edward Johnson, who not only encouraged the relocation of the Canadian Partnership Initiative in support of the United Nations Water for Life Decade to a new "research home" at the University of Calgary, but also offered a fellowship at the university's Biogeoscience Institute in support of further public policy scholarship efforts.

For mentoring me on matters relating to public policy and water in North America and around the world, I will never be able to repay the debt I owe to Henry Vaux, a retired vice-president of the University of California system who is presently the chair of the Rosenberg International Forum on Water Policy. Related to the Rosenberg Forum, I would also like to thank Helen Ingram of the University of Arizona in Tucson, who continues to unselfishly share a lifetime of experience and wise insight into water policy issues. It is through this high-level forum that much of the content of this book came into existence. Other members of that forum who have also contributed greatly to my understanding of water include Canada's Margaret Catley-Carlson, Dr. Alberto Garrido of the Universidad Politécnica de Madrid and Kimberly Beaird, who administers the activities of the Rosenberg Forum through the University of California at Davis.

This book owes a great debt to a number of other prominent scientists. I am much indebted to Dr. Michael Demuth of the glaciology division of the Geological Survey of Canada for all the encouragement and information he has shared. I would also like to thank Dr. David Schindler of the University of Alberta for his refreshingly candid perspectives on the state of contemporary knowledge of water resources in Canada and for the valuable information he has shared. For sharing his profound knowledge about how to translate science into effective public policy, I once again owe a great debt to David Eaton of the Lyndon Johnson School of Public Policy at the University of Texas in Austin.

I would like to thank my colleagues at the Alberta Water Research Institute, particularly David Hill, Dr. Lorne Taylor, Dr. Alexander Zehnder and John Thompson for the inspiring learning opportunities they have shared.

I would also like to thank my colleagues at the Forum on Leadership on Water (FLOW), centred in Toronto, for their enthusiastic endorsement of this and all other projects related to improving public understanding of water in Canada.

I continue to owe a debt of thanks to Kindy Gosal, Josh Smienk and Garry Merkel of the Columbia Basin Trust for their unflagging support for the UN Water for Life initiative and for sharing their science and knowledge about the history and nature of their remarkable basin.

For their willingness to share information on water in relation to climate change I am indebted also to the members of the Western Watershed Climate Research Collaborative science advisory committee, including David Sauchyn of the University of Regina, Dr. Shawn Marshall of the University of Calgary,

Dr. David Rodenhuis of the Pacific Climate Impacts Consortium and Dr. Henry Baltes of the Swiss Federal Institute of Technology in Zurich.

For their sharing of information and perspective and for the sheer commitment they make to water management I would also like to thank Michael D'Andrea of the City of Toronto and Oliver Brandes of the Polis Institute in Victoria.

Once again I owe a great debt of thanks to Don Gorman at Rocky Mountain Books for taking up the cause of water in Canada and for believing so wholeheartedly in this book. I also owe a great deal to Joe Wilderson, also of RMB, who offered not only valuable and patient editorial advice but also continues to possess a lively and witty interest in many of the issues this book explores.

Finally, I must especially thank my wife, Vi, and my children, Reid, Amery and Landon, for their sacrifices during long periods of uncertainty associated with the conception of the United Nations Water for Life initiative in Canada, the subsequent birth of the Western Watersheds Climate Research Collaborative and the writing of this, my third book on water. Without the unconditional support of my family none of this could have happened.

While all of the above, and too many others to name, offered information and support that was ultimately expressed in the form of this book, none is responsible for any errors or omissions that may exist in this manuscript. For these and for all interpretations of current scientific knowledge stated herein, the author alone must take responsibility.

Converging Global Water Trade-offs

North America

This book is about the global water crisis and how it will affect us in Canada and thus the United States as well. Canada and the United States have historically been a good team in terms of shared responsibility for our continent's water resources. In these difficult times, when our countries appear to be growing apart, we should remind ourselves of past successes. What is happening elsewhere in the world may demand we return to past co-operative effort.

We have been so very successful in the past. In 2009 celebrations took place to mark 100 years of co-operation between Canada and the United States on managing the two nations' shared waters. The jubilee culminated on June 13th with the official centennial commemoration of the birth of the International Joint Commission.

A great deal has been written about the history and function of the IJC. The relationship between Canada and the United States has been defined for almost a century by the Boundary Waters Treaty signed between the two countries in 1909.

This treaty addresses a broad range of transboundary water issues, including definition of boundary and transboundary surface waters and the joint study of these waters with reference to their potential use.

The treaty establishes mechanisms for the approval of certain uses and permission for obstruction or diversion of transboundary waters that may affect flow volumes in either country. The treaty also contains provisions that prohibit pollution that may result in injury to health or property on either side of the international boundary. The treaty is widely considered to be an exemplary model of an international transboundary agreement.

The IJC performs two essential functions. It approves remedial or protective works, obstructions or dams on transboundary waters and sets terms and conditions for the operation of such works. It also investigates and makes recommendations on questions relating to operating rules or disputes that are referred to it by either or both governments. The key point here is that the IJC has to be *invited* by one or both federal governments to investigate disputes and to collaborate with conflicting parties in the interest of creating durable solutions to transboundary water issues.

While the International Joint Commission has enjoyed legendary success in the resolution of such issues, concerns have been growing over a perceived decline in its effectiveness. There is no single reason for this, but the biggest factor appears to be that neither the Canadian nor the US government is supporting the commission – and utilizing it – to anywhere near the extent they once did.

The main issue is that the powers under the Boundary Waters Treaty to refer water matters to the International Joint Commission are no longer being employed the way they once were. Put simply, important transboundary water issues are no longer being referred to the IJC to be resolved. We have begun to rely upon unilateral action instead of teamwork.

Instead of utilizing historically successful institutional approaches to dispute resolution, the federal governments in both Canada and the United States are choosing to address these issues in the political domain. Scholars of the calibre of Ralph Pentland and Adele Hurley state the problem simply: "The International Joint Commission can only be as successful as American and Canadian governments want it to be."

The IJC is, by world standards, a truly successful institution. At a time when many of our most trusted institutions are failing us, we should hang on to the ones that work. We are going to need outstanding international co-operation to address some of the problems we presently face.

The whole world will be watching to see what we in North America do in reconsideration of the Columbia River Treaty, a process that will begin in 2014. The whole world will also be watching to see how Canada and the United States together will help the rest of the planet deal with the growing global water crisis.

The world at large

The global water crisis is real. Worldwide, approximately 16 per cent of agricultural soils are currently degraded, with significant impacts on food production, rural incomes and national economies. Unfortunately, the potential to expand the global cultivated land area is nearly exhausted and the Green Revolution has already optimized its potential to increase global food productivity. There is also a growing global water crisis, which is affecting supplies of both surface water and groundwater.

On a planetary basis we are converging simultaneously on both water scarcity and food shortages. It is highly unlikely that we can prevent these global threats from backing up into the North American context from beyond our borders. The impacts of water scarcity and food shortages abroad will affect us economically long before the millions of people directly affected by them elsewhere clamour to emigrate here. They already are affecting us.

There are at least four threats.

Growing global water scarcity is associated with increased human demand and more pollution, which limit the number of uses to which water can be put.

Global food production decline is associated principally with groundwater overdraft, non-sustainable agricultural practices, loss of productive soils leading to expanding aridity, and increasing intensity and duration of drought.

The growing realization of nature's need for water revolves around new understanding about how ecosystems generate, capture, purify and release water. This understanding could become a foundation of a practical new definition of sustainability.

Converging public policy trade-offs with respect to food production and water supply are the result of continued population growth and economic development that does not properly take into account the real costs of damage to the biodiversity-based planetary life-support function. As there are some rather terrifying developments associated with this trend, it is one that bears further examination.

"Peak water": Facing up to some terrifying trade-offs

Currently, global human population growth is highest in places where there is the least water. (Think of the Middle East and Africa, but think also of Alberta and southern BC in Canada and the Sunbelt in the United States.) Thus we find that globally a third of humanity is now competing directly with nature for water.

Unfortunately, there are now so many of us, and our dietary expectations have risen so dramatically in the past 50 years, that we are approaching the limits of how much water is available to grow all the food we want.

It is estimated that to meet the food demands that are projected to exist in the world in 2025, we will need to put an additional 2,000 cubic kilometres of water into irrigation. This amount is roughly equivalent to 24 times the average flow of the Nile River.

Given current water use patterns, the population that is projected to exist on the planet in 2050 will require 3,800 cubic kilometres of water per year, which is close to all the freshwater that can presently be withdrawn from the surface of Earth.

Maybe we shouldn't just be worried about running out of oil. I for one don't think we will make it to the projected global population of 9.4 billion. There isn't enough water. What we are talking about is *peak water*. We don't have enough to meet both agricultural and urban needs while at the same time providing enough water to ensure the perpetuation of natural ecosystems.

As a consequence of growing populations and increased competition for land and water, humanity is converging upon the need to make uncommonly difficult public policy trade-offs that have never had to be made on a global scale before. Think about this:

If we provide to nature the water it needs to perpetuate our planetary life-support system, then much of that water will have to come at the expense of agriculture, which means that many people will have to starve to meet ecosystem protection goals.

If, on the other hand, we give agriculture all the water it needs to have any hope of feeding the populations that are projected to exist even in 2025, then we must expect ongoing deterioration of the biodiversity-based ecosystem function that has generated the conditions our current society depends on for both its stability and its sustainability. I don't want to sound gloomy, but this isn't good. Who among us would like to have to make such decisions? But in fact, we are already making them, every day that we perpetuate the status quo.

In tandem, these two global trends – growing water scarcity and limits to further food production capacity – have huge implications our economy and our North American way of life.

The first implication is that as our population continues to grow we should expect the same kinds of water supply and quality issues that are appearing elsewhere in the world to make their presence known in Canada. This is already happening.

The second implication of converging global food and water scarcity relates to the role Canada already plays in producing the world's food. The good news – if there is good news in all this – is that limits to worldwide food production capacity will affirm North America's already important place in the global food and water economy.

Virtual water export

Increasingly, the response to global water scarcity will be defined not by direct transfers of liquid water between regions and countries, but by how much water is traded among nations in the form of water embodied in food. When Canada exports wheat to China, it is sending the water in that wheat with it. As of 2000, about 1000 cubic kilometres of water annually was being traded from nation to nation in this way.

Water savings from virtual water transfer can also take the form of water use equivalents employed in the production of food. For example, if corn can be grown in Nebraska with just 500 litres of water per kilogram of product, while cultivating corn in the Middle East requires twice as much water, then Middle Eastern purchases of us corn will save some of the Middle East's always limited irrigation water, which can then be reallocated to higher-value crops such as vegetables, nuts or fruits.

Models predict that by 2050 some 53 per cent of the population of the world will be facing one form or another of water scarcity. If this happens, then countries that need to make up for inadequate water supply by having to import water virtually, as food, will require a virtual global transfer of 7500 cubic kilometres a year.

This represents more than a doubling of food and virtual water trade internationally between now and 2050, which is no minor proposition – especially for Canada. Some experts have predicted that as a result of that trade, agriculture will ultimately become more important to the economy of Canada than oil and gas.

To take advantage of this opportunity, however, we need to recognize new pressures that are emerging with respect to competition for increasingly limited water resources. Even in Canada, water supply in urban areas is becoming more expensive to assure. The reasons for this include higher costs to develop more distant sources, more complex and therefore more expensive source development, the greater need for higher-cost treatment facilities and the lack of co-operation of low-cost water users such as the irrigation agriculture community.

If what is happening elsewhere in the world is any indication of what will happen as our populations grow, it is reasonable to expect that in the future there will be greater tensions between cities and surrounding agricultural regions over water allocation and land use. In Canada this won't just happen in the dry West, but it will be there that the problems appear first.

As a result of this tension we should anticipate challenges to the existing water allocation doctrines upon which current water rights have been established. This does not mean, however, that we should necessarily be rushing to take water away from agriculture to put it to higher economic use.

As has already been pointed out, rising food prices globally and threats to food production capacity caused by groundwater overdraft in other parts of the world are likely to make Canada's food-producing capacity central to the stability of international food supply – provided once again that agriculture can become sustainable. The whole matter of sustainability, however, remains up in the air.

The small but crucial matter of sustainability

Sustainability is an important issue. Sustainability is defined as "development that meets the needs of the present without compromising the ability of future generations to meet their own needs." The consensus of the 2008 Rosenberg International Forum on Water Policy was that contemporary discussions about sustainability were largely irrelevant because we as a society cannot agree on what sustainability means on the ground. Many experts lament the superficial way in which the term "sustainability" has been appropriated by so many public and private interests and manipulated to their own ends. There was a sense that, in the absence of a common understanding of the meaning of the term, we have adopted by default a consensus view of what we want sustainability to be like that doesn't reflect reality.

Seen in this light, a common definition of sustainability becomes the bedrock upon which all future possibility must be built.

The emerging world of ecohydrology: Nature needs water, too

Perhaps the most unsettling scientific discovery concerning sustainability in contemporary times relates to nature's need for water. New understanding about how ecosystems generate, capture, purify and release water could become a foundation of a practical new definition of sustainability.

The central tenets of ecohydrology are breathtakingly simple. Nature is of survival value to people, and much of its survival value is established through the supply of fresh water. In order to provide water and other benefits to people, nature needs water, too. Thus it follows that nature should be a legitimate water customer in its own right.

The unfolding ecohydrological principles associated with this emergent worldview demand that we ask what may well be the question of the century. The issue at stake, in this context, is not how much water we need to allocate for nature at the expense of people so that nature is somehow sustainably maintained. The really important question is how much water can be allocated for driving current trends of global population and economic growth without reducing and degrading ecosystem services to the point that they can no longer support either people or nature.

What ecohydrologists are claiming is that in many places in the world the sacrifice of important and valuable water supply, regulation, self-purification and biodiversity-enhancing ecosystem services to the single purpose of agricultural food production is not sustainable.

What the emerging science of ecohydrology is discovering is that agri-monocultures and urban monocultures in dry areas reduce water quality and quantity in the same way. Both reduce the amount that can be absorbed by soils and captured and made available to surrounding vegetation. This is a shocking realization. Agricultural and urban monocultures dry out adjacent areas by reducing the sponge capacity of once diverse plant communities that surround them. They suck up all the water for their needs, which leaves less for surrounding areas, which affects both water quality and water quantity.

This suggests that simplifying dryland ecosystems like the Canadian prairies has no less of an effect on the global climate than deforestation in more humid regions. It suggests that we need to improve our understanding not just of fundamental ecohydrological function, but of the expanded services that our natural, agricultural and urban ecosystems might be able to provide in the future, and engineer toward the realization of that potential. While this is no small order, there is some urgency to it, in that as a civilization as a whole we are converging on some very troubling circumstances.

To address and then take advantage of these circumstances, we need to create the public policy foundation for the Canada we want to exist in 2050. Given that the world will likely be relying upon us more heavily than ever to meet increasingly challenging global food production goals, Canada's future economic success – at least in terms of agriculture – may well be defined by how carefully and productively we manage our water resources. That suggests we have to get our own water management house in order.

Getting our house in order

Before we can begin to realize opportunity in what is happening elsewhere, we need to solve some of our own problems. In the context of water resources management our future economy could be defined in increasing measure by continuing improvements in at least a dozen areas.

1. Dispelling the myth of limitless abundance

The first challenge we need to address relates to self-perception. We have to dispel the myth of limitless water abundance in Canada or we will continue to make public policy choices based on false assumptions that could have undesirable ecological, social and political consequences in the future.

We may have 20 per cent of the world's fresh water resources, but much of that is water in the bank left after the last ice age. We have only 6.5 per cent of the world's renewable water resources and most of that is found in the north.

We spend far too much time in Canada worrying about water exports and not nearly enough time thinking about the damage caused by our own management choices. If our US neighbours want our water, or if we want more in the south, we are going to have to go north to get it, and that will be very, very expensive.

The lesson here is that we have to be careful not to make ourselves vulnerable by making political decisions based on false assumptions about how much water we actually have. We have to solve our own problems first before we satisfy the thirsts of others. This suggests that another myth we have to dispel is that we are world leaders in the management of water resources. We are not. We could be – and we will be if leading thinkers and water management practitioners have their way – but at present we are not.

If we compare ourselves to other developed nations, we haven't done anything particularly special or unique. That this is so is belied by the kinds of problems we are presently facing.

2. Integrating management of groundwater and surface water

The alarming state of our country's groundwater resources was put into relief in a 2009 report by the Council of Canadian Academies. This report evidences the fact that while some groundwater situations in Canada, such as the Oak Ridges Moraine region in Ontario, are being managed sustainably, contamination of groundwater aquifers is widespread all over the country. We are even contaminating aquifers we share with the US.

The panel composed of this country's best hydrologists also pointed to long-term problems we have created for ourselves by denying the seriousness of groundwater and surface water issues related to projects like the oil sands. All of these problems can be resolved but not without much strengthened and better-integrated public policy.

3. Improving monitoring, forecasting and prediction

Every time there is a federal or provincial budget cut, one of the things usually axed first is the long-term monitoring of our water resources and the related interpretation of what the data we have already collected means.

In the meantime, we have continued to develop at a furious rate, and now, when we really need that data to make wise decisions about the future, it is not there.

Now, because of climate change, the hydrology of our entire country is on the move. There is an especially crucial need for groundwater monitoring and for enhanced hydrological and meteorological observations and associated predictions in the high mountain headwaters of western Canada. It is at these elevations that climate change impacts are expected to be felt first and where they are expected to be most pronounced in their impacts on water supply.

To be of greater use, interpretations derived from such monitoring have to be shared far more effectively between researchers, water management agencies, major water users, policy-makers and the public. Proposals to do exactly this remain unfunded.

4. Making the link between water and energy

Most Canadians have yet to make the link between water use and energy costs. It takes a lot of water to produce energy and a lot of energy to move water. Water is heavy. It takes a great deal of energy to abstract, treat, distribute and retreat it for further use. Leaving your tap run for five minutes costs the same as letting a 60 watt lightbulb burn for 14 hours. And that calculation does not even account for the downstream cost of greenhouse gas emissions.

5. Instilling a conservation imperative into our society

Is there a water crisis in Canada? No. But in parts of Canada – and especially in southern Alberta and parts of BC – we have all the makings of one.

Because our population is growing, there is greater pressure on our water resources from agricultural and industrial use and more of our water is unfit for other uses because we pollute it. We can avoid a water crisis, or put it off for decades while at the same time saving billions in infrastructure costs, if we make conservation a habit and concentrate fiercely on protecting the quality of our water resources.

In order to make room for the future and for those who will populate it, water conservation anywhere, but particularly in the dry West, should not be optional. We also have to recognize nature's need for water.

6. Recognizing nature's need for water

If we do not recognize nature's need for water, there will not in the end be enough water for cities, agriculture or nature. We need a thorough reassessment of the role ecosystems play in water supply and quality in the Canadian context. We also need to identify and agree upon the optimal and minimal water requirements of each of these ecosystems in order to secure the sustainable provision of their services.

7. Improving agricultural practices

Though it remains something of a heresy to say so, we also need to improve our agricultural practices. The biggest problem relates to agriculture's impact on water quality. Agricultural water use is becoming an issue globally because contemporary industrial-scale food production practices inevitably result in reduced return flows to nature of water of poor quality which diminished and often water-starved natural systems no longer have the capacity to purify.

Unless we reduce the nutrient loading of our western rivers and aquifers, we may not be able to take full advantage of our opportunity to serve the world by exporting water virtually to water-scarce countries elsewhere. Agricultural and water policy have to be linked.

8. Reversing eutrophication

Eutrophication is the over-enrichment of rivers, streams and lakes with fertilizers and manure carried by runoff. In 2008 David Schindler and John R. Vallentyne published a book called *The Algal Bowl: Overfertilization of the World's Freshwaters and Estuaries.* The title is a tribute to John R. Vallentyne, who published the first edition of this book in 1974. As Schindler explains in his preface, Vallentyne argued 35 years ago that we had to stop dumping fertilizer and pesticide residues into our lakes and streams.

If we didn't, Vallentyne predicted we would find ourselves in an Algal Bowl in the Canadian West that would be more destructive of our ecosystems and our economy than the Dust Bowl that preceded it.

Unfortunately, Vallentyne's prediction has come true. Thousands of Canadian lakes and watercourses are now suffering from varying degrees of eutrophication. This is not a minor problem.

What we have done to Canada's fifth largest freshwater body, Lake Winnipeg, is an international environmental scandal. Experts around the world are astounded we would let this happen in North America. It will take at least a generation and millions and millions of dollars to reverse the damage we have done there. If we have any hope of restoring our waterways to their original health we have to start this work now.

9. Resolving the biofuel issue

Taking more and more land out of agricultural production and requiring more and more water for non-agricultural purposes will create a vicious circle of food price increases that will make it more difficult if not impossible to meet future global food production needs.

Current biofuel policy is now widely seen as "an excellent example of how to do the wrong thing with enthusiasm." One recent estimate argued that if we increased the fuel efficiency of North American cars by only 10 per cent we would save the cost of everything that is presently being invested in biofuels in the United States. Then fuel production would compete less with cities, agriculture and nature for water. But that would just be a start.

The problem is not the desire to create alternative energy sources. The problem is the failure to integrate public policy with respect to biofuels across linked domains of water supply, land use policy, energy security and food production.

Biofuel and other energy policies cannot be developed in isolation from water supply policies or agricultural water use and practices policies. If they are, expect conflict in the future between sectors over water allocation.

10. Drought preparedness

The current situation in Australia and the US Southwest offers deep insight into the kinds of difficulties western Canada in particular will inevitably have to address in the face of prolonged droughts.

We now know from paleoclimatic records that decade-long droughts are part of the current natural climate variability of the West. We are not talking here about what global warming will bring. We are just talking about dealing with droughts of a decade in duration that we know have occurred within recent history.

We need to ask ourselves now how we would deal with, not six years of moderate drought such as we experienced in the 1930s, but ten years of water scarcity followed by a drought that was half again as severe as anything our country has ever experienced before. This means we have to take climate change far more seriously than we currently do.

11. Taking climate change seriously

Many Canadians still misunderstand the climate change threat. As Nicholas Stern noted in his 2009 book *The Global Deal: Climate Change and the Creation of a New Era of Progress and Prosperity,* the danger from climate change does not arise only, or even primarily, from heat. Most climate change danger is from water. On one hand there is too much water, in the form of storms, floods and rising sea level. On the other there is too little water, which manifests itself as drought. As we have seen in Australia you can have both extremes at once.

The current situation in Australia also offers deep insight into the kinds of difficulties western Canada in particular will inevitably have to address in the face of prolonged droughts that occur within or are projected to occur on the prairies under all current climate change scenarios. In parts of Canada, rising temperatures could quickly push our agricultural sector beyond its current capacity to adapt, with devastating impacts on our regional environment and economy.

It may be wise to be proactive in the reform of our institutional arrangements so as to enhance our adaptability to climate change effects. We may wish to act before unforeseen events make our society vulnerable to the same kinds of problems that befell Australia. This will likely mean the creation of water markets or exchanges. There are opportunities here, but – as we have seen with biofuel policy – to be of use, markets have to be created with broad outcomes in mind or they will create more problems than they solve.

12. Establishing the right kind of markets

You can tell that the global water crisis is real because James Bond knows about it. In the most recent Bond movie, *Quantum of Solace*, the bad guys aren't after gold or diamonds. They are after the control of water markets.

While there are many who are very upset about the potential for market commodification of water resources, international example suggests that water can be at one level a human right and at another a market commodity. Water can perform these two functions simultaneously, a fact proven by every human civilization that has existed in recorded time.

The problem is that privatization of water utilities and the creation of water markets cannot function in the presence of corrupt governments and inept institutions. As water scholar Helen Ingram points out, well-operating markets and effective water utility privatization depend for their success upon strong regulatory frameworks and functioning oversight.

As we have witnessed recently, markets can, in the absence of oversight, collapse under the weight of their own self-interest. Still, despite what just happened, we remain market crazy on this continent. What is being missed in North America, however, is that markets are not a panacea.

Bottled water is a good example. The market supplies reliably clean water, but the profits thus generated are not employed in the restoration of upland watersheds, which would make bottled water unnecessary. As in the case of biofuels, the market has been permitted to serve itself without linking to other policy domains leading to sustainability.

As we have seen, markets are excellent servants but poor masters. Water markets will remain imperfect tools until they focus as much on sustainability and intergenerational equity as they do on short-term profit. We have to be particularly wary of unpriced externalities and imperfect information. In order to produce sustainable results, markets have to be directed toward appropriate ends by thoughtful public policy.

What I am saying is that before we once again let markets suck all the air out of the room, we need a complete reform of water governance in Canada. Sooner or later, governments are going to have to decide how our water resources will define the future of this country, and then determine how the economy should be directed to achieve the desired ends.

The Urgency of Water Policy Reform in Canada

There are real risks associated with not considering water policy reform at this time. Just as surely as water scarcity and decline in food production are converging toward the diminishment of the quality of human life in many other parts of the globe, it is not inconceivable the same problems could arise here.

Without policy reform we could very well reach a point where remediation of the damage we are doing to our own surface water and groundwater will be more expensive than we can afford or beyond our technological capacity to address. Without broader policy reform, water quality and availability problems will very likely limit future economic and social development in parts of Canada.

The failure to properly account for nature's need for water will further exacerbate water availability and quality issues, making us more vulnerable to the impacts of landscape and climate change.

Without water policy reform, we risk waking up one morning

to discover that we are no longer any different from the rest of
the world. We will have all the same water problems our neighbours have.

What Canada needs is a new water ethic that harmonizes federal and provincial water resource management aspirations with the
need to change the country's economic system so as to make true
long-term sustainability possible. So why can't we create that ethic?

Ralph Pentland, who has been part of concerted high-level action on water policy in Canada for more than 40 years, recently liste
in this country respond more effectively to the kinds of concerns
that have been troubling experts for a generation. All failed. Why?

In response to this question, the chair of the Rosenberg International Forum on Water Policy, Dr. Henry Vaux, referred to the
work of two scholars who examined the same problem in the
United States. Max Bazerman and Michael Watkins believe that
crises related to issues such as water quality and availability qualify as "predictable surprises" in that leaders know in advance
that problems exist and are likely to get worse over time.[1] Some
problems, from injury to the human body to damage to natural
ecosystems, can repair themselves eventually, but when scientific evidence suggests that a problem is not likely to solve itself, a
predictable surprise becomes likely. A third feature of predictable
surprises is that fixing the problem is likely to be expensive in the
near term, while benefits will not likely accrue until much later.
When faced with such matters, leaders recognize that solving the
problem will be expensive both politically and economically and
that the prospects of receiving credit in the short term are very
small. Every experienced politician knows that such issues are
fraught with risk.

A fourth characteristic of predictable surprises is that the cost
of addressing such issues must be balanced against what the cost
might be in the future of not acting on the threat – which may
be much higher. Water and climate change issues both fall into
this category. We know it will be expensive to fix the problems

we face today and likely more expensive in the future if we don't. Unfortunately, politicians recognize political danger in not being recognized and rewarded for disasters they help prevent. For this reason, as Bazerman and Watkins point out, it is easier to cross your fingers and hope for the best rather than act.

The fifth characteristic of predictable surprises is that decision-makers, governments and corporations often fail to prepare for them because of the natural tendency of human beings to favour and maintain the status quo, if only because so much has been invested in it. In complicated areas such as the management of water resources, business and government feed one another's bias toward doing things as they have always been done. As long as the system continues to limp along, there is nothing to catalyze action. Bazerman and Watkins further report that in such circumstances there always seems to be a small, vocal minority that benefits from inaction and is motivated to subvert the actions of leaders for their own benefit. While a whole society can be desperate for its leaders to take decisive action on an issue like water, special interests such as irrigation districts, water utilities and cities that benefit from the status quo will fight hard to block reform. And that is how predictable surprises happen.

Nobody in Canada wants to wake up one morning with a predictable surprise on their hands. There doesn't appear to be any reason why a province like Alberta couldn't lead Canada out of the reform rut. This may be a good time to do so for at least two reasons. The first reason is that options for reform exist.

Potential avenues of reform

There are at least three potential avenues of reform. We can revitalize the current system by activating unexercised jurisdiction and harmonizing federal, provincial and municipal oversight with respect to the management of our water resources.

Revitalization of the existing system will demand improved

monitoring, forecasting and prediction capacity tied to better enforcement of existing laws. It will also demand the introduction of new regulations that protect water quality and recognize nature's need for water.

Alternatively, water policy reform in Canada could emerge from the example of others. One immediately wonders if it might not be worthwhile considering implementing programs in Canada similar to those undertaken by the European Union and its member states by means of the Water Framework Directive. Though it is not perfect, this policy instrument enables the EU to define water quality standards and parameters of aquatic ecosystem health, and individual nations are then charged with meeting those standards by whatever means they feel will work best in local circumstances.

Certainly, if the EU, with its 27 member states and population of 500 million people speaking 23 official languages and occupying a territory of 4,324,782 square kilometres can create a continental water framework, it is conceivable that a single country with only 33 million people spread through 10 provinces and three territories with only two official languages should be able to do something comparable even though, at 9,984,670 square kilometres, that single country is more than twice the size geographically. Without question we have the capacity to create a similar groundswell of change. All we have to do is want to.

Not only is the European Union Water Framework Directive a model worth examining, it may even be something we could consider applying on a continental basis, which would mean working as a team again with our US neighbours.

No matter what policy instruments we ultimately employ, however, the institutional challenge of freeing more water for natural ecosystem function demands we do more than simply insist that nature compete with past precedents in water allocation. It demands ensuring that water for the environment ranks high enough among new claims for water allocation to attract the attention of policy-makers. While this has yet to happen in the US, where the precautionary principle has yet to be adopted widely in cases where science is unclear about the actual and potential impacts of further large-scale water withdrawals, there has been movement in this direction in Europe under the Water Framework Directive.

As we learned at the 2006 Rosenberg Forum in Banff, Canada, the European Declaration for a New Water Culture provides four broad categories for ethical action with respect to water resources management. The first category is "water for life," both human and non-human. This is interesting in that it places water for people and water for nature on par as the foundation of a new European water ethic, whereas our water ethic in North America does not grant water to nature until all human needs have been met.

The Declaration also stands on the foundation of a citizen-based water ethic which aims to ensure that water becomes an instrument for maintaining not just adequate supply and sanitation for health, but also for well-being, social cohesion, social capital and capacity-building. The Declaration further recognizes the "water industry" as an essential element in economic growth, but this is a third level of priority. Unlike in Canada and the US, it is considered unethical under the terms and conditions of the European Water Framework Directive to allow business concerns to interfere with water for life.

Finally, the Declaration takes a firm ethical stance against crimes against water, which include destructive withdrawal practices, toxic spills and other actions that threaten the planet's precious and irreplaceable water resources. This is radically different from the water ethic that presently informs water management decisions in North America, where, in the absence of adherence to the precautionary principle, the burden of proof for demonstrating why ongoing water allocations or operational practices threaten the sustainability of water resources is placed entirely upon those who would oppose them.

A third avenue of reform might be to allow regions to reform water policy on a large-scale watershed basis. The premiers of the western provinces and northern territories have created the Western Water Stewardship Council, which aims to resolve potential conflicts in the management of all the river systems that have their origins in Canada's western mountains. Perhaps something similar might emerge in the St. Lawrence and Great Lakes areas and in Atlantic Canada, which again would demand co-operation with the US.

Perhaps Alberta's Water for Life Strategy could be the model for a more integrated regional water policy design.

The second reason why now may be a good time to press for water policy reform is that the public has begun to take an interest in water issues and may well support leaders who would press for change.

Canadians are ready for change. Early in 2009, the Canadian Partnership Initiative in support of the United Nations Water for Life Decade was pleased to be involved in a national Ipsos-Reid poll sponsored by Unilever and RBC that for a second consecutive year explored the attitudes of Canadians toward the value of our country's water resources. The poll found that Canadian concern about water has not diminished in the face of our current economic woes.

The poll also confirmed that the majority of Canadians consider water our most important natural resource; even more important to our future than oil. This is a heartening sign.

Unlike so many other places in the world, Canada still has room to manoeuvre in how we manage our water resources. If we can balance the water availability and quality needs of nature, agriculture and our cities, everything else we need to do to become sustainable, including addressing climate change, may very well fall into line.

Then we *really will* be leaders with something new and useful to share with the rest of the world.

CHAPTER ONE

The Drying Out of the Interior of Our Continent

CONFRONTING DROUGHT IN BRITISH COLUMBIA

Drawing a mental map of the drying West

Imagine in your mind a map of western North America. Focus in your imagination on the top left-hand corner, on the western provinces and northern territories of Canada. You will notice that hard up against the Pacific Ocean on the far left is British Columbia. Move your attention inland to the centre of the province. Mark a mental line from the desert that spills over the US border at the bottom of British Columbia northward through the centre of the province into southern Yukon Territory, which, you will remember, is adjacent to Alaska.

Trace a line from the southern Yukon eastward until you find the Northwest Territories, an immense, sparsely populated region that drains into the great Mackenzie River. Continue to trace that line south into northern Alberta to just below the oil sands town of Fort McMurray and then eastward into northern Saskatchewan. Continue the line south out of the lake region, then eastward until you get to the prairie city of Brandon, Manitoba. Then arc your way back to where you started, in southern British Columbia. Notice that the line you just traced covers nearly half of Canada. But notice, too, how dry much of the land is in the space you have identified and how dry the American states are that lie adjacent to the line you traced from southern Manitoba back to where you started in southern British Columbia.

Now draw the line again starting in southern British Columbia, but this time imagine dragging with it the most serious pine bark beetle devastation known to have occurred in the forests of western North America since Europeans arrived. As you trace your mental line up through the centre of British Columbia, drag in its wake a total of 10 million hectares – some 25 million acres – of dead pines. Then drag this death up into the southern Yukon, eastward into the Northwest Territories and back down into northern Alberta until you reach Fort McMurray. Then go back and draw this same line again, and as the pine forests die, replace them not with the forest type that existed before but with bush and grasslands that are better suited to the hotter temperatures that brought about the pine bark beetle infestation in the first place.

Once you have redrawn the biogeography of central BC, southern Yukon, the Northwest Territories and northern Alberta, retrace your imaginary line from southern BC back to Fort McMurray and stop there. Watch as oil sands operations rapidly expand from 400 square kilometres to twice or three times that size, creating a desert growing in all directions from the open-pit wound at its centre. With your mental finger on that site, look northward, where you will see warming temperatures descending from the pole, melting the permafrost and drying out the tundra. Watch as this warming advances steadily southward. With your mental finger still on Fort McMurray, look the other way, due south, where you will notice that rising temperatures are marching northward as the prairies spread in advance of rapidly rising temperatures on the central plains. Watch even as precipitation rises as the two advancing fronts of increasing warmth collide in northern Alberta. Watch as these rising temperatures expose vast regions of sand dunes from earlier drier periods in the West.

Now, if you can, mentally animate all of these processes so that you can imagine their cumulative effect being fast-forwarded simultaneously over the next 30 years. Watch as the forests of central British Columbia are replaced with grasslands. Watch bush land replace much of the southern boreal forest across southern Yukon, Northwest Territories and northern Alberta and Saskatchewan. Watch as northern permafrost disappears and the boreal wetlands dry up. Watch as thousands of northern lakes evaporate into history. Watch as the effects of tar sands exploitation expand far faster than reclamation can keep up. Watch as the prairies warm and their dryness radiates northward toward the expanding desert created by the bitumen mines. Watch as the benefits of anticipated increases in rainfall are lost to longer, hotter summers. Watch as prairie aridity expands westward into the front ranges of the Rockies. Watch as the old deserts of the past are brought to life again by the wind and the sun. Look south and see something very similar happening in the US West. Notice that the boundary between our two countries doesn't protect us from dryness advancing northward from the US Southwest.

Think about what you are watching could mean.

What it means is that if warming continues, western North America could become more arid. What it means is that if we don't do something to control the rise of temperature, over time we could very well turn the western interior of our continent into a desert. At present there doesn't seem to be any reason why that desert couldn't extend from the Mexican border to the Beaufort Sea.

Imagine what water will be worth in such a West, and what it will be worth in the rest of the world as a consequence.

Contemplating the threat

In the public imagination almost no one thinks of British Columbia as a dry place. The reason for this is that most of the province's population lives on the coast, where locals complain it seems to rain all the time, at least in winter. Because of their exposure to the open Pacific, the west coast of Vancouver Island and the mountainous north coast of British Columbia are the wettest places in Canada. According to Environment Canada the rainiest place in Canada is Ocean Falls, BC, where some 4386.8 millimetres of rain have been known to fall in a year. That is about 14 feet of rain in 12 months. Precipitation decreases with each mountain range that blocks the inland advance of moisture-laden Pacific clouds. In Hope, BC, where the Cascade Mountains begin, precipitation averages around 2000 millimetres a year. At Revelstoke, where the Selkirk Mountains begin, annual precipitation averages only half that. By the time Pacific winds reach the sun-hot prairies they are able to contribute little moisture. Average precipitation on the Great Plains of Canada is in some places less than 200 millimetres a year, a tenth of what it is on the coast. In drought years, however, it can be much less.

Because of the rain shadow effect of the coast and interior mountains, British Columbia also has its own dry prairies and substantial interior deserts. These arid regions are invariably found in the lee of great mountain ranges that pull inland-bound precipitation out of the air, leaving dry winds to drop into valleys in the lee of the peaks. These semi-arid or steppe climate zones receive between 250 and 500 millimetres, or about 10 to 20 inches, of rainfall a year. The best examples of the steppe climate in British Columbia are the Okanagan Valley and the Cariboo Plateau. There are, however, many places in the interior of British Columbia that are just as dry. Real desert conditions extend, along with the range of the rattlesnakes, rare lizards and cactuses that characterize it, all the way from Osoyoos near the US border northward to Kamloops and beyond, a distance of more than 300 kilometres. Dry conditions also exist in the intermontane Cariboo region, which extends from the Fraser Canyon to the Cariboo Mountains. In many ways British Columbia is like Australia. Despite an abundance of mountain and coastal water, British Columbia has a dry heart. The fear, of course, is that warming temperatures associated with current global climate disruptions could cause this dry heart to expand, with consequences for the entire province and for all of the Canadian West. All it would take to expand British Columbia's dry interior is a deep and prolonged drought, which is exactly what has happened recently in Australia.

Most British Columbians don't think about drought very much. But they should. Of all the natural calamities that have plagued humanity since the birth of civilization, drought has been the most devastating and the most costly. Drought causes more damage and costs the global economy far more than all the impacts of tropical storms, hurricanes, tornadoes, earthquakes, volcanoes, landslides, tsunamis, avalanches, epidemics and famines combined. Only major floods come close to the devastating impacts drought has had on humanity.[2] Drought is also linked to water's diametric and symbolic opposite, fire. The drier it is – and the more pine bark beetle devastation that takes place – the more wildfire occurs.

Droughts, floods and fires are projected to occur more frequently in all climate change scenarios that have been modelled for the government of British Columbia.

Addressing the threat

The government of British Columbia has recently taken a new interest in the province's water resources. One of the reasons for this is that the province recognized it did not have adequate regulation of groundwater resources and that changes in surface water supply were likely, given projected climate change effects particularly on mountain glaciers, snow cover and snowpack.

British Columbia was the first western Canadian province to publicly take climate change seriously. At a time when deniers continued to control the environmental agenda in neighbouring provinces and in the nation's capital, British Columbia decided to introduce a carbon tax aimed at beginning the process at least of ratcheting greenhouse gas emissions down to below 1990 levels. Informed by excellent research conducted at universities throughout the province, the government of the day correctly realized that argument about whether climate change is happening is over. Humanity is altering the planet's atmosphere in ways that are very likely to cause societal disruption. What remains unknown is how much of that disruption we can avoid by changing our habits.

Climate scientists, economists and policy scholars successfully demonstrated to political leaders that economic growth based on high carbon emissions is a self-terminating strategy. The notion that the costs of reducing emissions are greater than the benefits was seen as just plain wrong. Experts put forward to the government that climate change policy could not consist solely of a single investment decision, analogous to building a new bridge. The kinds of changes that British Columbians had to make to their way of life were much more difficult and far-reaching.

As more research findings poured in it became clear that the province should expect greater risks and more severe and rapid climate change effects than had been earlier anticipated. While it might be possible to adapt to a 1°c mean annual temperature change, larger rises in mean temperature would be accompanied with the growing risk of ever more catastrophic effects. Suddenly it became obvious that to argue that it was too late to mitigate the effects of climate change and that we as a society should simply commit to adaptation was a reckless response to the problem.[3] Mechanisms had to be put into place to begin the process of characterizing the "externalities," or the unaccounted for costs to society over time associated with using the atmosphere as a garbage dump for CO_2 and other problematic greenhouse emissions.

It was quickly realized that analysis of climate change effects could not be undertaken independently of the province's water resources management strategies. It did not take much analysis to realize that British Columbia's 19th-century water management policies had been established in an era of much greater predictability of water supply and narrower ranges of variability in extremes of both rainfall and drought than exist today in the 21st century.

In 2008 the Water Stewardship Division of the British Columbia Ministry of the Environment released a new provincial water strategy called Living Water Smart. The key point the strategy makes is that "water defines British Columbia." The plan acknowledges that in the next 25 years the population of the province is likely to grow by somewhere around a million and a half people without any change in the amount of water that will be available in its 291,000 individual watersheds. This, of course, suggests that the same amount of water will have to go a lot further, without compromising nature's needs. The strategy then goes on to create a highly idealistic vision of how agriculture, industry and the province's towns and cities might make the water they have now go further in the future. The hope clearly is that in so doing British Columbians will also be able preserve the natural ecosystem integrity of a province that unabashedly advertises itself as "The Best Place on Earth" to live or visit.

While unbridled hope and confidence in the future are implicit in every aspect of the design of the glossy, beautifully illustrated Living Water Smart publication, you don't even have to read between the lines to recognize that there are some genuine fears in Lotusland about what global change might mean on Canada's wonderful west coast. The government of British Columbia recognizes that changing temperatures and precipitation patterns are already affecting weather, water cycles and ecological makeup and function. In what has to be one of the greatest public understatements in history given that 10 million hectares are affected by pine bark beetle devastation, the government of British Columbia acknowledged that climate change is already impacting the province's forests. It has, however, also affected water levels in lakes and rivers, infrastructure, agriculture, industry and recreation. Because scores of interior and northern communities stand to be economically devastated by these impacts, the government announced it was poised to help affected communities adapt to a changing climate.

The report goes on to acknowledge that risks of flooding, sea level rise and storm surges, particularly up the heavily populated Fraser River Valley, pose new threats for human health, safety and property. Warmer and drier conditions are also expected to compound problems already associated with insect infestations, wildfire threats and increasing drought risk. The report then makes a crucially important observation but does so in such a subtle way that many readers may miss its significance. The report quietly argues that the climate change threat actually presents an opportunity to share ideas and to work with other Canadian provinces to use the restoration of natural ecosystems as a means of moderating and even slowing the effects of climate disruption while at the same time buying time for communities to adapt to the changes we know will present themselves in time as a result of the greenhouse emissions we have already released.

What the "Living Water Smart" report suggests is that by restoring as much natural ecosystem function as possible while simultaneously reducing emissions, the people of British Columbia will be able to protect both their economy and the natural splendour of their province. The report promises that, in association with other western Canadian provinces, the government of British Columbia will do just that.

Eight months after the announcement of this strategy, observers in the water community in western Canada were still waiting for something to happen. There then followed a huge economic downturn and the announcement that the budgets of all provincial government departments, including the Ministry of Environment, were to be cut. The Water Stewardship Division was left without the means to implement the Living Water Smart strategy, proving once again how easy it is for governments to make announcements and how hard it is even in developed countries for the right intentions to be translated into effective action. Even in properly functioning democracies it is often hard to get things done and even harder sometimes to keep them done.

Once again we were beaten by the same old enemy: our deeply engrained Canadian habit of continually delaying action on ecological decline until further growth has satisfied what are perceived to be more urgent economic agendas. Though public attention turns almost obsessively to matters economic, real problems still persist.

Two things did not go away when the funding for the Living Water Smart program dried up. The first was the threat of widespread landscape change in the wake of pine bark beetle devastation in the interior of the province. The second was the ever-present threat of deep and prolonged drought, a problem that has the power to pull all the province's other problems behind it like a runaway horse dragging a fallen rider over the rocks.

AUSTRALIA: A CASE IN POINT

Face to face with aridity

It was in Spain that I first encountered clear evidence that what was happening in central British Columbia, in combination with trends appearing elsewhere in the West, could turn the interior of much of western North America into a desert. I was on a field trip with a group of scientists and water scholars who had been invited to attend the Sixth Biennial Rosenberg International Forum on

Water Policy in Zaragoza, the city hosting the 2008 World's Fair, which had "Water" as its theme.

We had stopped at the spectacular medieval hilltop town of Medinaceli in the mountains of Aragon, where forum participants had an opportunity to talk with one another as they wandered through the stone streets of the old town. Here at the frontier between Christian and Muslim worlds in the Middle Ages, conversation between people representing 20 countries was easy and natural. One of the conversations centred on the kinds of water supply problems that were emerging in Australia. This conversation was part of a continuing dialogue I have been having with Leith Boully, a mother, farmer and natural resource and water management expert from Dirranbandi, Queensland, since 2004. Our common concerns relate to appropriate public policy choices available to leaders in the event that persistent drought becomes permanent, as appears to have happened in the Murray-Darling River basin in southwestern Australia.

What Leith Boully has experienced as a farmer, as a founding member of the Wentworth Group of Concerned Scientists and as chair of the community advisory committee of the Murray-Darling basin Ministerial Council speaks to what happens to communities and economies when droughts don't end and aridity becomes the new norm in a formerly rich agricultural landscape.

Not unlike parts of the interior of North America, much of Australia is arid or semi-arid. Just as in Canada, Australia's rainfall history features several distinctly dry periods of a decade or longer. As happened in Canada, the mid-to-late 1920s and the 1930s were periods of drought over most of Australia, with low rainfall persisting over the eastern states through most of the 1940s. Another drought occurred in the 1960s over central and eastern Australia.[4]

As often happens in Canada during dry periods, not every year during these periods of prolonged drought was dry. The problem was that in most years rainfall was below the long-term average, which compounded the effect of runs of years with recurrent dryness. Australia's drought of record – known as the "Federation drought" – persisted through the late 1890s until 1902. The drought of 1991 to 1995, which affected Queensland, northern New South Wales and parts of central Australia, and the most recent drought that most of Australia has been experiencing for much of the past decade are further examples of this most severe kind of drought event in which one or two very dry years follow several years of generally below-average rainfall.

Despite nearly two decades of lingering drought, evidence suggests that the situation is not about to improve for Australian farmers. As part of the government's ongoing review of national drought policy, the Australian Bureau of Meteorology and the Commonwealth Scientific and Industrial Research Organization were commissioned to evaluate the impact of climate change on the nature and frequency of exceptional climatic events. The assessment examined past and future changes in the intensity and frequency as such events, with a specific focus on the impact of high temperatures, low rainfall and low soil moisture. Their joint report concluded that, compared to the past 100 years, there is an increased risk of severe dryness over the next 20 to 30 years, particularly over southern Australia. The reason: increased drought risk will be exacerbated by increasing temperatures – so that droughts in the future will be hotter. In other words, the dryness normally associated with drought in many parts of Australia is about to become the norm rather than the exception.

Researchers noted, however, that this does not necessarily mean the end of farming in Australia. It does mean, though, that farm families and rural businesses and communities are going to have to adapt to the new conditions, which isn't going to be easy. Some areas of Australia have now been experiencing what have been defined as "exceptional circumstances" for 13 of the past 16 years. In the middle of June, when Leith Boully and her colleague, water and rural policy expert Wendy Craik, departed Australia for the Rosenberg Forum in Spain, a significant portion of the entire Australian continent was once again experiencing persistent drought conditions. In some places temperatures had exceeded 50°C, or nearly 125°F.

The depth of the economic and social upheaval caused by the appearance of permanently persistent drought in Australia demanded changes in almost every institution in the country. There were systemic changes to values as idealistic imperatives such as environmental sustainability were challenged by the urgency of making real-life trade-offs in support of community survival. Australians quickly learned that history also matters, especially with respect to laws, policies, institutions and traditions. Unresolved Aboriginal issues stood out in immediate relief. Litigation soared along with buybacks and sales of land and water rights. There were also interests that took to hoarding and profiteering.

Established notions of jurisdiction soon came under attack. Individual states became unruly in defence of their own self-interest. As the crisis deepened Australians ceased to be moved by rhetoric. As community outrage focused more and more upon the failure of state governments to properly frame and address issues related to the emergency, central power ultimately emerged as a dominant influence on national direction. Despite enormous resistance from interests that previously could not have conceived of such a development, the only way the problem could be managed in the end was to have individual states relinquish some of their powers to the federal government.

Previously fragmented and territorial political jurisdictions are now forced to work together and even amalgamate their efforts and programs in ways that would have been unthinkable in the absence of the emergency. The very foundation of the country's laws had to change in order to accommodate shifts in agricultural practices, jurisdiction, power and decision-making. Both federal and some state governments fell, partly as a consequence of their perceived failure to move quickly enough in the right direction to address the impacts of the drought. Ten years have passed and Australian institutions are still trying to facilitate the kinds of changes that may make adaptation to the new climatic circumstances and water supply regimes possible in the future. Lessons for Canada and for the rest of the world derive from the fact that, as a consequence of climate change, Australia was confronted with an unprecedented period of major upheaval in one of its most important economic sectors, to which the country's governments and major institutions, by virtue of the way they were structured, were unable or slow to respond. These same kinds of issues are now beginning to present themselves in rural communities in British Columbia, where forestry economies have been devastated by the pine bark beetle. Not every community has the capacity to suddenly become a tourism destination. The impact of deep and prolonged drought on these already vulnerable communities could be the last straw.

Learning from Australia's Murray-Darling basin

Wendy Craik is the chief executive of the Murray-Darling Basin Commission. Her paper, submitted to the Rosenberg Forum on behalf of co-author James Cleaver, was entitled "Modern Agriculture under Stress: Lessons from the Murray-Darling." In describing the system, Craik explained that the million square kilometre Murray-Darling River basin covers roughly twice the area of Spain but only 14 per cent of southeastern Australia. The basin's two million residents rely on the combined river system for all their water supplies as do the 1.2 million residents of the city of Adelaide, which is located on the south coast, adjacent to the mouth of the basin. The Murray-Darling, Craik explained, is Australia's "food bowl." The 2 per cent of the Murray-Darling basin that is irrigated accounts for 70 per cent of the value of Australia's irrigated agriculture output.

The Darling River region is very flat. Inflows in this system are unreliably tied to episodic rainfall events that lead to major flooding approximately every decade. In most years, however, most of the flows from the Darling are diminished by transmission losses and evaporation before reaching the Murray. Historically, the only reliable rainfall in the entire Murray-Darling system has occurred in the mountain regions of the Murray River. As is the case in so many watersheds, including those in western Canada, the rest of the system relies heavily on the disproportionate amount of precipitation that falls in upland regions.

So reliable were flows in the Murray-Darling system that they were taken for granted in the economic development of the region. Water rights were granted to 99 per cent of the long-term average annual river flows. When these highly reliable flows ceased, however, southeastern Australia found that while increasing agricultural and economic productivity to the full limits of the water supply made for great short-term prosperity, it also left the region very vulnerable to the grief that drought and climate change have caused repeatedly throughout the entire history of settled human society. Rights had been granted for water that no longer existed.

When the drought began it was possible to make do for awhile, but as it wore on, the very institutions the region depended on for its integrity began to unravel under the weight of precedents that could no longer be honoured and governance structures that were not capable of meeting the demands of conditions far worse than anticipated by emergency drought plans.

A drought of uncommon intensity and duration

The current Australian drought began quite innocently, as so many do, with diminished flows in important major rivers. During the early phase of the drought, which began in 1996, the annual flows of the Murray-Darling system, though reduced, remained within the Murray-Darling Basin Commission's planning minimums, which is to say they were well within the historic variability of the system as accepted at the time. As happens in such circumstances, those with "high reliability" water licences barely noticed the drought, as they had all the water they were entitled to, so that critical livestock, urban and domestic water supplies were assured.

The bulk of early impacts of the drought were felt by irrigators with "lower reliability" water licences. In some cases water allocations to junior licence holders were cut by as much as 54 per cent down from a long-term average reliability of 80 per cent. In the beginning most were able to manage their way through.

It is important to note, however, that one valid customer that did not receive the water it was entitled to, even at the beginning of the drought, was the environment itself. As natural floodplain inundation had not occurred in the Murray Valley since 1993, widespread decline of floodplain ecosystems began at the very outset of the drought. This was to have serious implications later, implications that continue to this day.

Instead of letting up over time as the historical record suggested it would, the drought lingered for ten years. Then it got worse. By 2006 conditions had severely deteriorated throughout the Murray-Darling basin. But even more difficult conditions were still to come. When the austral spring arrived in September of 2006, it became evident that the autumn, winter and spring flows had failed completely. It was as if the hydrological cycle had simply stopped. There was, literally, no water.

The Murray-Darling Basin Commission forecast that water storage behind the Murray River dams would be drawn down to extreme low levels by the end of 2006/07 growing season. Two months later allocations to even the most senior water licence holders were reduced throughout southeastern Australia. Conservation efforts were redoubled; neighbours began reporting one another for water use violations; jealousies over who was allocated water for what purpose led to conflicts; and suicide rates in rural agricultural areas began to rise rapidly.

By the end of the austral summer of 2006/07 total Murray River annual reservoir inflows had dropped to approximately 60 per cent below those recorded during the previous drought of record, which occurred in the austral summer of 1914/15. But since then things have gotten even worse. Storage levels at the beginning of summer 2007/08 were very low, and as a result opening allocations even to senior licence holders fell to zero.

As there was no stored water to offer to licensed water users, all allocations were made entirely dependent upon how much rainfall fell and was stored during the summer season. Just as occurred during the southern Alberta drought of 2000 and 2001, Australian irrigators traded water allocation rights in order to reduce the economic impact of the drought. Preliminary estimates indicate that approximately 30 per cent of all available water has been traded during the extended period of the drought. Prior to 2006, when the drought intensified, "leased" water was traded at a maximum value of approximately A$200 per transaction. During the 2007/08 growing season, however, the price of "leased" water was about A$1,100 per transaction, a price increase of 550 per cent in only two years.

At the time Wendy Craik gave her presentation to the Rosenberg International Forum on Water Policy in June of 2008, annual Murray-Darling reservoir inflows remained in the bottom 5 per cent of recorded years. In the entire 116 years during which instrumental records of streamflow have been kept in southeastern Australia, it had never been this dry.

We do not have to wait for the drought in Australia to come to an end to derive valuable lessons for Canada. Given climate change and other factors, the climate and hydrological variability upon which we have built our western economy is very likely to be far more extreme than what we experienced during our established drought of record, the 1930s. What this suggests is that, in defining both our infrastructure standards and the often invisible institutional arrangements and economic instruments we depend on for our ultimate adaptability to such events, we have likely proceeded from an inadequate baseline. Once again we need to ask ourselves how we would deal with, not six years of moderate drought such as we experienced in the 1930s, but ten years of water scarcity followed by a drought half again more severe than anything North America has ever experienced before. This is exactly what has happened in Australia, and it is extremely useful from a public policy point of view to examine the Australian example with the goal of anticipating what we need to change now before we find ourselves in the midst of a drought that could test our very capacity to live in the places and in the manner we presently do in the Canadian West.

Why has the Australian drought been so severe?

The Murray-Darling Basin Commission has examined very carefully all the factors that have contributed to the severity of the drought presently gripping southeastern Australia. The conclusions the commission has drawn could be seen as nothing less than frightening when viewed in the context of our own growing vulnerability in Canada to the same array of extreme conditions that presently persist in Australia. Five factors are seen to have made the Australian drought worse than those that have occurred in the past.

The first thing the Murray-Darling Commission thinks Australia did wrong was to permit overallocation of existing water resources. The commission noted that the second half of the 20th century was significantly wetter than the first half. Wetter climate conditions in tandem with a 40-year period of dam construction between the 1950s and 1990 allowed Australians to arrive at the accepted wisdom of the day, which held that only a small percentage of new water entitlements would actually be utilized.

With this logic as an underpinning, irrigation and other water use entitlements were allowed to expand so as to permit the appropriation of almost every drop of surface water that flowed in the Murray-Darling system. Unfortunately, expansion of water rights exceeded levels of environmentally sustainable extraction. The Australian example proves that even senior water rights can be meaningless if there is no water.

The overallocation of water rights also had – and continues to have – and huge impact on ecosystem vitality in Australia. As Israeli ecologist Uriel Safriel has illustrated, if we are to survive we must recognize "nature" as equal in importance to people in terms of water allocation. It is impossible at this time to say just how much Australia's drought has weakened the country's overall ecosystem health. There can be no question, however, that a great deal of systemic damage has already been done. Even later caps on water use aimed at preventing further expansion of water diversions were unable to reverse the environmental damage caused by overallocation or to lessen the economic impacts associated with investment in business activities that failed when it was no longer possible to access the water these operations depended on for their survival.

Just like southeastern Australia, we have overallocated our southern Canadian rivers, often with little respect for in-stream flow needs or for the need to maintain other biodiversity-based ecosystem services on which we ultimately depend for the sustainability of our way of life, particularly in the dry parts of the West. We have done exactly what got Australia into trouble during a drought that has lasted longer than the established record. They got caught. We haven't, at least not yet.

The second factor making the current Australian drought worse than preceding ones is the fact that mean temperatures in southeastern Australia had been unusually warm in recent years. According to the Australian Bureau of Meteorology, three of the five hottest years on record in the Murray-Darling basin occurred between 2003 and 2008. The Commonwealth Scientific & Industrial Research Organization (CSIRO) in Australia estimates that each 1°C increase in mean annual temperature in the basin ultimately reduced runoff by 15 per cent.

Wendy Craik observed that the impact of higher temperatures and a drier catchment has been evident since 2007. Even though a La Niña event brought above-average rainfall to most of the Murray catchment between September 2007 and March 2008, total inflows remained very low. This suggests that the aridity generated as a consequence of the drought may in fact be irreversible.

The CSIRO also estimates that the largest impacts of climate change in the region will present themselves in the upland areas of the Murray River basin. The capacity of the Murray River to supply water at levels based on historic averages is now permanently in question.

Canada would do well to heed these Australian trends. Drought combined with the loss of environmental water flows can damage "natural" ecosystems to such an extent they are unable to provide normal adaptability to such extremes. As the capacity of natural systems to moderate the effects of extreme weather events diminishes, temperatures can rise and in so doing increase evaporation rates from the soil surface and subsurface. High temperatures also affect other hydrological patterns.

Though we can only speculate on what the exact effects will be, rising temperatures are expected to increase rainfall during the winter and spring in much of the Canadian West. Summers, however, are expected to be longer and hotter. Just as has been witnessed in Australia, higher temperatures are expected to increase evaporation and reduce soil moisture to such an extent in already arid regions that these factors will more than compensate for the small increase in rainfall that is projected in most climate change models. What we learn from the Australian example is that temperature and soil moisture changes projected by climate change models can be for real. Projections based on climate models suggest the same thing can be expected to happen in Canada. If it is happening there, it could happen here.

The third factor that influenced the intensity of the Australian drought was that rainfall patterns changed. Research clearly indicates that there has been a significant reduction in autumn rainfall over the Murray-Darling basin. Researchers have indicated that the reason for this is the strengthening of a high-pressure "subtropical ridge" over the basin during the summer months. The persistence of this high-pressure ridge, which has been linked to climate change, results in the effective diversion of autumn storm systems to the south of the basin. It is not known how long this weather condition will persist into the future.

We have witnessed similar changes in precipitation patterns and snowpack accumulation in the upland regions of the mountain West. While there is no clear indication of what future changes might occur, snowfall is on average diminishing on the east slopes of the Rocky Mountains and also in parts of central British Columbia. While some years bear greater resemblance to established means, the trend appears to be toward more rain and less snow in the Rockies during winter and toward early peak snowmelt and longer, drier summers. If this pattern continues we should expect consistently lower average flows in some rivers and more tension over water rights and uses.

The fourth factor that made the current drought different from what Australians have experienced in the past is that total Murray River system flow during 2006/07 was approximately 60 per cent less than the previous record minimum. As of July 2006, the reservoir behind Dartmouth Dam, despite a decade of very dry conditions, was filled to approximately 65 per cent of capacity. By June 2007, the reservoir held only 13 per cent of capacity. This was unprecedented in the history of settlement in the basin and it almost completely exhausted the system's main drought storage reservoir. Wendy Craik noted that the exhaustion of this reservoir has resulted in the need to allocate water almost entirely on the basis of real-time inflows. She also made it clear that even if normal rainfall conditions were immediately restored, it will still take years to restore former high water-storage levels behind Dartmouth Dam.

The lesson for us in Canada is that it can take a very long time to recover from severe drought, especially if the drought is of an intensity or duration that exceeds the baseline conditions the drought protection infrastructure was meant to address. The Australian example suggests that we need to revisit the standards to which we build and operate our water-related infrastructure, so that we can be prepared for droughts of much longer duration than those upon which our drought protection strategies have been established.

The fifth trend that makes the current drought in Australia different from any that have preceded it is that it has violated all established drought patterns. Never before in the recorded history of the Murray-Darling basin has one extremely dry year been followed immediately by another just as dry. It just hasn't happened before.

Prior to the back-to-back dry years of 2006/07 and 2007/08, every extremely dry year in the meteorological record of southeastern Australia was followed by significantly wetter years. Of the really dry years in the past, including 1902/03, 1914/15, 1982/83, every one marked the end of a drought period. Australians now know, however, that they can no longer expect things to get better as a matter of course. If it is possible to have two extremely dry years in a row, why not three?

Current climate change impact models for Australia have projected that droughts of the current magnitude could become the norm by 2050 under business-as-usual global emissions scenarios. It is not something Australians want to come to pass.

A drought of the intensity of the one currently baking Australia leaves little room for speculation as to whether or not a warmer world might be more desirable than the one we presently inhabit. The three million people who rely on the Murray-Darling basin for the water they need to live have glimpsed what climate change might mean on their continent in their time. Climate change is not something that is happening somewhere else to someone else. It is happening to them. Many Australians are frightened by what the future might bring in an even warmer world than the one we live in today. Ultimately this will have political implications.

The lesson for Canada is that the past is no longer a guide to the future. What we took for granted about our climate patterns is no longer a reliable indication of what may happen in an era defined by a warmer and therefore more energetic atmosphere. We are already seeing this in Canada with the increase in tornadoes, the rising frequency and intensity of extreme rainfall and snowfall events and in rising nighttime and winter temperatures.

What can we do?

A great deal of future climate change impact can be minimized through proactive planning and adaptation. Long-term adaptation, however, cannot be achieved by simple short-term incremental public policy adjustments to climate change impacts. A fundamental shift in public policy framework is required that establishes water sharing arrangements not just for irrigation and other consumptive water uses but for environmental protection over the broadest range of climate change scenarios over the longest possible time frames.

It is important also to note that had Australia taken a different approach to the importance of natural ecosystem function, the results of the drought may have been different. If you believe not only that "natural," biodiversity-based ecosystems deserve equal access to water but that the prospects of human sustainability will be diminished in direct proportion to our failure to supply water to nature so that it can continue to supply life-support services to us, then you may be unable to accept as reasonable Australia's desperate decision to provide water to irrigation agriculture at any cost to natural ecosystem function. If you accept emerging ecohydrological perspectives with respect to the value of natural ecosystem function, you might not allow a country like Canada to use Australia's response to its recent drought crisis as a basis for defining public policy responses to similar threats in this country.

In the face of ecological collapse, Australia chose to save its irrigation community, if only because they had the greatest immediate political influence on the decision-making process at senior levels of government. If there is a real lesson for Canada it may be that, in the end, saving your irrigation agriculture establishment may not be the best choice if that is the only choice you make. In a perfect storm you need to save the ship in order to save the sailors. Save your farmers at the expense of natural ecosystem health and all you may get is farmers and more drought. Save your natural ecosystems, however – especially the highly productive ones that clean and regulate water and climate – and just maybe they will save you and the farmers too. That said, once a drought reaches a certain level of intensity you may be lucky to save anything at all.

Summary lessons for Canada and the mountain West

1. Pay attention to what is happening in your mountain headwaters

Historically, the only reliable rainfall in the entire Murray-Darling system has occurred in the mountain regions of the Murray River. As is the case in so many watersheds, including those in western Canada, the rest of the system relies heavily on the disproportionate amount of precipitation that falls in upland regions. We need to know what is happening to snowpack, snow cover and glacial recession in our high mountain headwaters before changes take place that affect water supply security.

2. New conditions are emerging that will make drought more severe in western North America

The drought in southeastern Australia was unlike any before it largely because of overallocation of water rights in the past 50 years. The impacts associated with overallocation were exacerbated by a measurable rise of atmospheric temperatures, changes in rainfall patterns, record low inflows and an historically unprecedented number of record dry years one after another. There are concerns that these conditions will persist or even become the norm under more extreme climate change scenarios.

What is presently happening in Australia offers insight into the kinds of difficulties western North America has faced with droughts in the past and will inevitably have to address in the future with the more frequent, prolonged droughts that are projected.

3. The immediate past is no longer an adequate guide to the future

What happened in Australia suggests that we have likely defined both our infrastructure standards and the often invisible institutional arrangements and economic instruments upon which we depend for our ultimate adaptability to prolonged drought on an inadequate baseline. We need to ask ourselves how we would deal with, not six years of moderate drought such as we experienced in the 1930s, but ten years of water scarcity followed by a drought that was half again more severe than anything our prairie civilization has ever experienced before.

4. Water markets can alleviate some of the economic hardship of drought, and conservation can help, but neither is a panacea

Just as occurred in the southern Alberta drought of 2000 and 2001, Australian irrigators successfully traded water allocation rights in order to reduce the economic impact of lost production. In addition to encouraging water markets, governments at all levels contributed to public policy that permitted the carrying over of allocation privileges from one season to the next, altered operating rules for dams and related water storage systems, changed emergency measures parameters and involved everyone in the basin in strictly enforced water conservation programs. Many of these programs have now become the norm rather than the exception. But while all of these efforts combined did allow adequate water sharing to meet human needs, they ignored or failed to address nature's need for equitable access to water supply.

5. Expect sustainability-threatening permanent ecosystem damage if water is not also supplied adequately to nature

While southeast Australia has survived the drought, it did not happen without long-term, even permanent, damage to natural ecosystems. The dedication of almost all water resources to human purposes intensified the effect of the drought on natural systems, which may, in part, have exacerbated the intensity and contributed to the extended duration of dry conditions that caused the drought to persist. Damage to aquatic and riparian ecosystems in the basin may be permanent, which will reduce natural adaptive capacity in the face of future droughts, thereby threatening long-term sustainability.

Given the recognized adaptive value of natural ecosystem function, western Canada may not wish to emulate Australia's public policy response to its recent drought crisis in the event of a similar threat. But given that Alberta in particular has already overallocated much of its water resources, we may not have any choice but to respond in a manner similar to the way Australia did, which would result in similar broader ecosystem damage and a consequent diminishment of the broader ecosystem health upon which our long-term sustainability ultimately depends.

6. It takes a long time to recover from extended drought

The impacts of prolonged drought persist long after rains return. Even if normal precipitation patterns are restored, it will take years for storage levels in basin reservoirs to return to levels that will permit reliable water supply during dry years. In the absence of adequate storage the region will remain vulnerable to further drought. Even after precipitation patterns return to normal, if indeed they do, damage to broader ecosystem function will continue if all water resources remain committed to human purposes and not enough water is made available to nature.

Ecological circumstances may never be the same again after a prolonged drought. Inappropriate response to drought can put a region on the slippery slope that leads toward ecosystem decline and gradual desertification.

7. Simply doing more of the same will not allow for adaptability to long-term drought

Overallocation of water resources to human purposes is a serious mistake that can make entire societies and the natural systems that sustain them vulnerable to persistent water scarcity. As Australia discovered, a fundamental shift in public policy is required that establishes water sharing arrangements not just for irrigation and other consumptive uses but for environmental protection over the broadest range of climate change scenarios over the longest possible time frames. Without such protection, broader adaptability to drought conditions cannot be maintained.

GETTING PAST THE TALK TO TAKE SOME ACTION

It is hoped that British Columbia and other vulnerable Canadian provinces will keep these lessons in mind as they plan for what may well be a hotter and often drier future. If we want to avoid turning the interior of the continent into a desert, we need to watch carefully to see how the vast regions devastated by pine bark beetle infestation recover in terms of the effects of invasive species and changes in the kinds of vegetative complexes that emerge as a result of higher temperatures and longer summers. We need to understand how extensive damage to the northern boreal brought about by expanding oil sands development will influence future aridity in northern Alberta and how that might, in combination with pine bark beetle effects, define future ecosystem dynamics in the boreal.

We need to understand the potential effects of polar warming trends, their influence on the further drying of polar deserts, their influence on evaporation rates of northern lakes and the potential hydrological influences of water suddenly mobilized as a result of permafrost melt. We also need to project how rapidly the aridity of the Great Plains will advance northward to meet these other influences as temperatures continue to rise in the central part of the continent. We have to realize that although nature might not turn against us, what we are turning nature into might. This suggests that we also need to reduce our carbon dioxide and other greenhouse gas emissions so that we do not increase the threat of further aridity in the West.

Presently our public institutions are not up for such multi-jurisdictional analysis and public policy action. On the Canadian prairies climatic conditions are already at a threshold at which rising temperatures could create aridity as quickly as they did in Australia and in so doing could push our agricultural sector beyond its current capacity to adapt, with devastating impacts on our regional environment and economy. Our institutional arrangements with respect to water resources management in Canada are presently as territorial and jurisdictionally fragmented as Australia's were at the outset of the change in climatic circumstances that devastated that country's agriculture.

We may wish to advance reform of our institutional arrangements so as to enhance our adaptability to climate change effects before unforeseen events make our society vulnerable to the same social and economic catastrophe that befell Australia. One option is to create a regional drought preparedness plan that links jurisdictions, not just on the prairies but in all the western provinces and northern territories that draw their water from rivers that originate in the Rocky Mountains. A complementary option might be to move toward an overarching, pan-Canadian framework for sustainable management of our water resources on a watershed basis.

Viewed in the context of the good it might bring, climate change effects may in fact present an important, historic opportunity in Canada to redraw jurisdictional lines around watersheds. By being proactive in anticipating climate-related impacts on water quantity and quality, we may at least be able to consider the option of returning to the point in our history at which we drew artificial lines of jurisdiction on a map to create Canada as we know it today, and in so doing restore the watershed as the fundamental geographical and hydrological unit in the country.

Leith Boully had the last word in our conversation about the drought problem in Australia. In the direct, no-nonsense language that only an Australian mother could summon, she protested that in terms of the state of contemporary public policy with respect to water, "We have got to get past discussions of motherhood and get down to changing the nappie." If we North Americans want to avoid turning the interior of our continent into a desert, there are quite a few nappies that need changing here too. And soon.

CHAPTER TWO

Diminishing Flows

A GOURMET RECIPE FOR UPLAND WATER

Ingredients

24,406 square kilometres of superior-quality mountain landscapes, "superior quality" meaning that these landscapes should
contain no less than:

4 national parks

3 provincial parks

13 national historic sites

No fewer than 27 mountain
ranges plus 669 prominent peaks

600 species of plants

277 species of birds

69 species of mammals

13 species of carnivores

To those ingredients, add:

7 cubic kilometres of rain

21 cubic kilometres of snow

10,000 appreciative mountaineers

1 clear idea of a desirable future

Preparation

Use sunlight to preheat a medium-sized planet to an average surface temperature of 14°C.

Disturb the surface of the planet to create mountains. Choose a place where the mountains are particularly beautifully formed that you would like to designate as a World Heritage Site.

Separate these resulting ranges by altitude into three biogeographical regions, with the valleys at the lowest altitude, the steep, forested walls of the valleys next and then the highest alpine regions at the top. Stir in plants and animals, concentrating them in the valley floors. Be careful not to add too many people.

Alternately sprinkle 7 cubic kilometres of rain and 21 cubic kilometres of snow over the desired mountain area.

Permit the rain to stream from the mountaintops into the valleys. Do not let too many chefs contaminate the broth. Ensure the vegetation is healthy so that it can help filter the water to keep it clear.

Allow the snow that falls to build up to the point where it begins to turn into ice under its own great weight. Allow this ice also to flow into the valleys.

Bake for four months at a time at 30°c and freeze for eight months at a time at -40°c. Continue alternate freezing and thawing for 10,000 years while allowing continuous flow.

Serving tips

Provided the ingredients are not in any way compromised, this recipe will yield a World Heritage Site that possesses 12 major icefields, 384 glaciers, 44 continuously flowing rivers and 164 named tributaries. It will also create 295 lakes. Judiciously served, this recipe should be adequate to supply water for the entire West. Properly executed, this recipe will continue to generate trillions of litres of safe, delicious, cold and refreshing mountain water every year for eternity.

Naturally refreshing mountain water is best served ice cold at room temperature. Where uncontaminated by humans, fresh mountain water can be enjoyed as easy as cupping one's hands and scooping this delicious nectar from a mountain stream. Natural mountain water pairs nicely with exercise and is the ultimate complement to any kind of food. It can be served as part of any alpine adventure or celebration.

It should be noted that millions living downstream swear by these ingredients and this delicious natural treat.

ENSURING WATER SECURITY IN THE MOUNTAIN WEST [5]

The link between economics and ecohydrology

For a hundred years following Confederation, Canada's population was too small and the country's economic activity too limited to create issues of water quality or availability anywhere except on the dry interior plains where drought had already been a persistent problem for thousands of years. In the span of barely a single lifetime, that has changed.

In the beginning the water policy that emerged organically in each of the developing provinces and territories during Canada's first century was perfectly adequate to meet the needs of water users. Over the past 50 years, however, water needs have grown dramatically in much of the heavily populated southern part of the country. Rapidly growing demands on water supplies, particularly in the last 20 years, have begun to test water resources management policies and procedures that were designed for an earlier and less dynamic era of Canadian history.

As Chris Spence and his colleagues have written, for much of the 20th century, the focus of water management was on where and when water was available rather than on the understanding of the processes that created the observed patterns.[6] As water resources have in many places become scarce, however, water managers are no longer satisfied with reports of mere abundance or state. While everyone working in the water management field has long known that complex changes in landscape and climate variability have an impact on water, it is now widely recognized that a much better understanding of biogeophysical processes that generate water is required. We are for the first time beginning to see important links between ecohydrological processes and our nation's ultimate economic well-being.

There are now concerns that unless our national and provincial policies and practices can respond more quickly and effectively to emerging realizations of how our water resources are generated, the needs of a growing number of water users may not be fully or even adequately met. Without action the fear is that, despite our relative water abundance, Canada's economic and social future may be constrained in many regions by water scarcity.

As many Albertans know, this is already a concern on the eastern slopes of the Rocky Mountains, where resource-based prosperity has generated rapid and spectacular population growth in one of the driest areas of the country. Development in this area is of an order and has occurred at a pace that has begun to influence water supplies and quality in the entire region, including parts of adjacent Saskatchewan. Water supply pressures that used to exist only in Alberta's dry south are advancing outward in tandem with expanding interest in resource development. Given the extent of these development pressures, it will not be long before water supply issues that at one time existed only on the Great Plains will begin to appear in river basins to the north and to the east.

In Alberta, perhaps more immediately than anywhere else in Canada, the potential exists for future prosperity to be limited by water availability and quality. To prevent this from happening, we need to know the current and future needs of all water users. We also need to better understand how much water we have – above and below ground – and how much will be available to us in the changed climate we anticipate will exist in the future. We will then have the information we need to adjust our water allocation strategies accordingly so as to meet the needs of users.

Who currently are western Canada's main water users?

There are a number of well-known traditional water users in the Canadian West. A few new ones are also emerging, and one that has been around for a long time is making new demands on old claims. The main traditional water users in the West are hydro-power utilities, agriculture, municipalities, industry and conventional oil and gas exploration, and tourism and recreation. Emerging users include expanding oil sands and related developments such as petroleum upgrading and nuclear energy generation. The long-time user that is making new demands on old claims is nature itself.

Hydro-power generation

Hydro-power generation is important to the West. While we far too often take it for granted, reliable electricity supply has been the foundation of the ongoing development of the region over the past century, and its reliability remains a central contributor to our prosperity. Rational development of hydro-power capacity is completely dependent on a sound knowledge of how much water is reliably available from year to year over the long term and a practical understanding of when that water can be employed in meeting the electrical power needs of an ever-growing population. The spectre of climate change presents a considerable challenge and a potential threat to reliable hydro-power generation everywhere in Canada. In future, major dams may be important, not just because of their hydro-power generation potential but for the important role they play in the multipurpose management of water supply.

Historically the operation of large storage reservoirs has been a hindrance to the perpetuation of aquatic diversity and healthy riparian zones. Recently, however, hydro-power generators have demonstrated that they do in fact have the capacity to do more to restore aquatic ecosystem health and local fisheries vitality as well as to support flood and drought mitigation by expanding storage and modulating downstream flow fluctuations. In this context, increased storage can be used to simultaneously improve water quality and increase water supply. The case for increased water management potential, however, needs to be supported with good science. As increased storage will likely be necessary, at least in some places, to respond to greater variability in the timing and extent of precipitation, hydro-power generators need to be able to better predict how much water may be available in any given season.

To be successful in managing future energy and water demands, hydro-power generators will also need to know more about ecohydrological dynamics. In the case of an east-slope river such as the Bow, which flows through Calgary, this means building a clearer understanding of the hydrological effects of pine bark beetle devastation, especially as they relate to headwaters regions. It also means better understanding of the hydrological effects of wildfire and prescribed burns; the potential impacts of drought; and long-term climate change impacts on snowpack, glaciers, wetlands and groundwater as they relate to water availability and quality. Only better and more comprehensive monitoring of our water resources can provide hydro-power operators with the information they need to plan with confidence for the future and to have their contributions to integrated river basin management recognized.

Agricultural water use

Canadian agriculture is important to world food security, and as is the case everywhere else in the world where irrigation is practised, agriculture is the biggest water user in Alberta and the other western provinces. As we come to realize the importance of water's role in the stabilization of natural and agricultural ecosystems, we begin to see the ways in which our population density may be altering the very systems upon which we depend to sustain food production at levels that will be needed in the future.

As mentioned in the introduction, we are beginning to observe that rapidly expanding cities have begun to compete with agriculture for both land and water on a global basis. Agriculture in turn has begun to compete with nature for land and water. We are increasingly concerned that we cannot meet both agricultural and urban needs while at the same time providing enough water to ensure the perpetuation of natural ecosystem function.

Canadian agriculture also plays a role in energy security but only with the contribution of water resources. Water is not only used by plant transpiration of soil water to grow the intensive crops and trees for biofuels but it is directly used in the processing of ethanol at a ratio of up to 10 litres of water per litre of ethanol. The water for ethanol processing plants must be reliable and plentiful to meet the efficiencies of scale required for these plants to be economic and carbon emission efficient. This means either a major surface water supply such as the large rivers draining the Rocky Mountains or a sustainable groundwater supply. Current limitations in surface water supplies are already restricting our ability to process biofuels in southern Alberta. Development of biofuels infrastructure must take into account full consideration of whether there is sufficient water both for crops and for processing. This requires improved prediction of water supplies flowing from the mountains to the dry prairies where this processing and crop production will occur.

The needs of agricultural users matter not just to us but to the rest of the world. Billions of dollars a year ride on providing the quality of information farmers need to determine whether there will be enough water when it is needed to grow the desired crops. Not unlike the hydro-power generation sector, agriculture needs to constantly update its understanding of the potential impacts of drought by improving its knowledge of possible long-term climate change impacts on snowpack and rainfall as they relate to water availability and quality. Only better and more comprehensive monitoring of our water resources can provide the agriculture sector with the information it needs to plan more effectively for the future.

The water needs of the oil and gas industry

Though not a large consumer of water compared to agriculture, the oil and gas industry in western Canada continues to be a major water user whose needs cannot be ignored now or in the future. Because of their experience with the subsurface of the West, the conventional oil and gas industry knows a great deal about water resources. While discovery of conventional sources of oil and natural gas have likely peaked in western Canada, water remains important in recovery and refining and will continue to be so until present reserves have been exhausted. Non-conventional oil and gas recovery, however, will require even greater volumes of water in the future. Coalbed methane capture throughout the West and bitumen mining and upgrading associated with oil sands development in vast areas of northern Alberta and Saskatchewan will make increasing demands on available water resources.

The oil sands and related economic sectors in Alberta are also important water users. Billions have been invested into this sector, which has become an important revenue source not just for the province but for the region and the country. Oil sands development has also become a geopolitical as well as economic force continentally and globally. Water availability, however, may be a limiting factor in future development. This is also true of considerations of nuclear power as an alternative to the large amounts of natural gas required in steam-assisted gravity drainage and for various upgrading processes currently used in oil sands projects.

To ensure that users in the non-conventional oil and gas sector such as coalbed methane and oil sands mining have adequate water supplies, much more ultimately needs to be known about the current state and projected future of both surface and groundwater resources in all the watersheds originating in the Rocky Mountains. This knowledge can only be garnered and applied through a more comprehensive water resource prediction system based on a sufficient network of hydrological and climate observations and with interpretation of the results so that industry can apply them in its operations and infrastructure design.

Municipal water use

Though cities such as Calgary have large senior water licences that guarantee adequate water supply under current conditions for decades to come, not every community on the eastern slopes of the Rockies is satisfied it has enough water for the future. Because of growing populations and greater demand, short-term water supply concerns have already been identified in the Bow River basin.

The closing of the South Saskatchewan River basin to new water licences in 2006 means that that those communities with licences for withdrawal from the Bow River and its tributaries will have to find other means of securing water once they reach the limit of their existing licences. Options may include transferring licences or obtaining treated or raw water from licence-holders that have excess capacity.

This means that any new developments in areas surrounding the city of Calgary, such as the County of Wheatland and the municipal districts of Rocky View, Foothills and Big Horn that do not hold a water licence, will require licence transfers or external water supply. These estimates do not take into account the significant role that strictly applied water conservation programs can play in making water go further in each of these communities. Conservation programming has already been initiated in most or all of these jurisdictions. New mechanisms for coming to terms with the sharing of water resources within existing licensing frameworks will also help these communities manage future growth and development within the confines of growing scarcity. *None of these current projections, however, have taken climate change impacts on water supply into account.*

An example is taken from the rapidly growing rural acreage

belt in the rural municipality of Corman Park, surrounding Saskatoon, Saskatchewan. Rural subdivisions in this municipality relied on groundwater until the drought of 1999–2003 caused widespread water well failure in 2002/03. Now there is an expensive and widespread program to pipe South Saskatchewan River water to all rural homes in the southern half of the municipality. This is only possible because there are no restrictions on water use in place in Saskatchewan at this time. Such a switch from groundwater to surface water supplies in response to drought or climate change is not possible in much of Alberta, due to much higher water use.

As they represent the largest populations and most concentrated political influence, municipalities are perhaps the highest-profile water users in the region. Because of their capacity to influence water allocation and use in surrounding areas, municipalities need an ongoing understanding of the potential impacts of drought and long-term climate change on snowpack and snow cover as they relate to water availability and quality. Without this urgently needed information, even the wealthiest cities will not be able to forecast water shortages or predict what climate change might do to the availability of the water resources upon which their sustainability ultimate depends.

Tourism and recreation: water as an attraction in its own right

The tourism and recreation sector is also a significant water user, though in a very different way than agriculture or industry. In fact, water itself may well be our most important tourism attraction. People come from all over the world to see our glaciers, marvel at our rivers, lakes and waterfalls and ski on our snow. Though these resources exist everywhere in the West, the bulk of the most popular of these attractions are in the uplands of our major watersheds.

In these upland areas there have already been climate change impacts on vegetation and wildlife and more are expected, especially at higher altitudes. For the last century, the alpine tundra zone has been defined as those places having a mean annual temperature between 8°C and 9.5°C in the warmest month of the year. In the last 20 years, however, rising temperatures have raised these averages to above 10°C in large areas of the alpine tundra climate zone in North America.[7]

By this measure it has been determined that 73 per cent of the alpine tundra in the western United States can no longer be climatically classified as such and that this change has occurred in only 20 years. It is anticipated that, in time, vegetation will respond to this climate change such that these current areas of tundra will become treed or covered with shrubs. This is already happening in the Canadian Arctic and it is not unreasonable to anticipate that rising temperatures will have a similar effect over time in our mountains, where temperatures near treeline in winter have already risen 3–4°C since the 1960s.

The projected temperature increase of between 1°C and 6°C will change the nature and character of our western mountain region. Mountain vegetation zones are expected to shift upward by approximately 500 to 600 metres or a range of about 1600 to 2000 feet, the equivalent of one vegetative zone in any given mountainous region. A study commissioned by Parks Canada predicted that many of our most treasured national parks and reserves may no longer be within the biogeographical regions they were created to represent. Currently we have no structures in place to help us manage such a development.

The foundation of the entire global protected places program, of which our mountain national and provincial parks are an important part, is that these representative areas will remain biogeographically stable and that natural water and energy cycles can be maintained through local park management. The "Alberta Climate Change Vulnerability Assessment" argues that global climate change impacts may already be invalidating these assumptions. If this is the case, then the maintenance of global biodiversity will require us to aim to protect what will effectively become "a moving target of ecological representativeness." Protecting existing landscapes will require that disturbances be managed. New stresses will need to be controlled and habitat modifications will likely be necessary to reconfigure protected areas so they can survive emerging climate conditions. Whole ecological systems are already advancing northward. Mountain ecosystems are moving upward. Invasive species are already appearing right before our very eyes. Current ecological communities are disaggregating and reassembling into unpredictable new combinations. The mountain West will be a different place by 2050. Biodiversity managers will have to figure out how to become "creation ecologists" as they learn to adapt to change. To be successful at such formidable challenges these managers will need to know what is happening to water and energy cycling and associated water resources in the regions they are responsible for.

We already know that even before global warming has finished reducing the length and depth of our glaciers it will already be after our mountain snowpacks, wetlands and groundwater, with huge potential impact on everyone who lives downstream. Changes in snowpack, however, are just the beginning of changes that are likely to converge upon us over time. In anticipating these changes, the past may not be a reliable guide to the future.

There are many uncertainties. For example, we know very little about the role that permafrost plays in the larger geomorphological context, even in the relatively extensively studied Alps, never mind the Rockies, the Columbia Mountains or the Coast Ranges. Because of the work of scientists like Gordon Young, Brian Luckman, Scott Munro, Mike Demuth, Shawn Marshall, John Pomeroy and others, we have a foundation for understanding what is happening to water in our mountains, but even they would be the first to say that we don't know enough.

The Canadian Rockies have experienced a 1.5°C increase in mean annual temperatures over the last 100 years.[8] During that time, increases in winter temperatures have been more than twice as large as increases in spring and summer temperatures. This has resulted in loss of at least 25 per cent of the glacial cover area in the Rockies. It has also begun to affect the temperature and biotic composition of glacial lakes.

Most of the evidence relating to changes in glacier dynamics in the Canadian Rockies comes not from the Columbia Icefield as one might expect but from research conducted over the past 40 years at the Peyto Glacier, in the upper reaches of the North Saskatchewan basin, in Banff National Park. While the Peyto currently covers about 12 square kilometres, it has lost 70 per cent of its volume in the last 100 years, and the duration of snow cover in the Rockies has shortened by more than a month since the early 1970s.

Even non-glacial mountain watersheds are changing. Marmot Creek in the Kananaskis has suffered a 30 per cent decline in its peak streamflow and summer streamflow since the 1960s, associated with a 3–4°C rise in winter temperatures. Yearly precipitation is not declining, but what was once snowfall is now falling as rain due to the warmer winters. Overall, the South Saskatchewan River basin has suffered a decline of about 15 per cent over the last century in its yearly natural flows, but human consumption of water has made the real decline much larger, about 40 per cent on average and much more in dry years. It does not flow at the same time or with the same consistency it used to, when larger glaciers provided supplemental ice melt in drought summers.

But it is not just mountain landscapes that are changing. Human activity will change with the climate. Warmer temperatures are expected to increase the length of the summer season for a broad range of activities. Taking advantage of these opportunities, however, will demand effective collaborative mechanisms that will help avoid conflict over water use and allocation. More care than ever will have to be taken to protect and conserve water. Activities such as golf and downhill skiing can also demand a lot of water. Snowmaking for downhill skiing also demands intensive water use in midwinter when streamflow is at a minimum. It may no longer be possible to take these activities for granted.

To appreciate the potential impact climate warming can have on tourism activities in a cold climate, tourism interests in the Bow River basin would do well to look at what is happening in other mountain regions around the world. Nowhere is climate impact better understood than in Europe, where it is now predicted that Germany, Austria and Italy will not have reliable, permanent winter snow within a decade.

Already, ski areas below 1700 m in altitude are threatened by the shorter winters and fast spring melt associated with high mean annual temperatures. A good example is the Rhône River basin, which is similar enough to the Saskatchewan River basin to be of value as a comparison of potential climate impacts. Climate impact trends in the Rhône basin are not static. As these trends continue to accelerate through time, the cumulative impacts on water will be dramatic. Snow depths in lower-altitude valleys may be reduced by as much as 50 per cent annually. In the upper Rhône basin the snow line is projected to ascend by roughly 150 m for every 1°C increase in mean temperature. The 4°C temperature increase forecast for the region would reduce average winter snow volume in the Swiss Alps by half.

Warmer winters have already begun to affect ski resorts in the Alps in a number of ways, each of which should be of interest to ski resort operators in Canada. There is consistently less snow at low altitudes. Snowfalls are melting faster, reducing the number of ski days. The viability of many ski areas – as defined by a snow cover of at least 30 cm over a period of at least 100 days – is projected to be greatly reduced. It is now projected that a modest 2°C warming will reduce the reliability of Swiss ski resorts from 85 per cent in the late 20th century to 63 per cent by mid-century or earlier, particularly at low altitudes.

Snow cover in the Alps has already become more and more uncertain at lower altitudes, as it has in Canada. In 2002,

85 per cent of the 162 ski resorts in the French region of the Rhône basin were able to extend the ski season by producing artificial snow. They have done so on 15 per cent of their terrain, between 1500 and 2000 m. The altitude at which snowmaking has become necessary, however, continues to rise. The Europeans have also discovered that snowmaking can be detrimental to local water resources.

The tourism and recreation sector is a bona fide water user. It is important to our economy that this sector have the water it needs, now and in the future. In order to adapt to climate change, managers of our national and provincial park landscapes and water-based tourism attractions will need the very best information they can get on the potential impacts of extended regional drought and of long-term climate change on snowpack and snow cover as they relate to water availability and quality. As is the case with our region's other economic sectors, only better and more comprehensive monitoring of our water resources can provide tourism and recreation with the information it needs to plan optimistically for the future.

Nature as a water user in and of itself

Legislators and public policy scholars around the world are reacting to groundbreaking research that indicates that natural ecosystems may be far more important to global economic security than many may have appreciated. The ecohydrological principles at the core of this insight are breathtakingly simple: nature has survival value to people, and much of that survival value is defined by the fact that nature is our only provider of water. In order to provide water and other critical benefits to people, however, nature needs water, too. We need water to prime the pump, so to speak, and the hydrological cycle is a very large pump. It follows, then, that if we want nature to continue delivering valuable ecosystem services for free, we must, in the context of water resources management, regard nature as a legitimate water customer in its own right.

In a 2005 US National Academy of Sciences report entitled "Valuing Ecosystem Services," the chair of the committee producing the report, Dr. Geoffrey Heal of Columbia University, noted the importance of integrating the disciplines of ecology and economics so as to advance the developing new field of ecosystem service valuation. Heal pointed out that this is not yet an established field in that ecologists have only very recently begun to think in terms of ecosystem services and their determinants, while for their part economists have only begun to incorporate the factors affecting ecosystem services into their valuations of these services. The report went on to suggest that if as a society we are to understand properly the value of our natural capital, then this field must be developed further.

Ecosystems provide a number of marketable goods – fish and timber being obvious examples. But as we have begun to understand in Alberta, most benefits of biodiversity are external to present economic models and have not yet been priced in a market. Examples of ecosystem services that depend on healthy biodiversity include biological water filtration, detoxification and breakdown of wastes, nutrient conversions, maintenance of soil cover, pollination, suppression of pests and diseases, and perpetuation of healthy wildlife populations and fish stocks. As well as less tangible values such as personal fulfillment and visual appreciation of the environment, ecosystem services also include aesthetic qualities that add significantly to tourism, to the attractiveness of immigration and to human health. Most of the functions and advantages of biodiversity that are realized at longer time scales are strongly dependent on weather and climate and thus are difficult to replace with alternatives.

Despite growing recognition of the importance of ecosystem functions and services, these are often taken for granted and overlooked in environmental decision-making. Some ecosystem goods and services cannot be valued, either because they are not quantifiable or because available methods are not appropriate or reliable.

Failure to include some measure of the value of ecosystem services in cost/benefit calculations, however, will implicitly assign them a value of zero. But despite these limitations, we are gradually acquiring a sense of the economic value of biodiversity, especially as it relates to aquatic ecosystems.

Biologically diverse ecosystems are generally more sustainable and resilient when challenged, for example by a change in climate or increase in variability. Diverse ecosystems are more likely to successfully adapt to changing climate. Diverse biodiversity-based ecosystems also appear to be the foundation of our planet's greater life-support capacity. We are increasingly reminded that natural and aquatic ecosystems do not exist just to supply and purify water for human use. Natural systems perform many other functions as well, and when natural ecosystems diminish or disappear, these functions have to be reproduced or enhanced elsewhere if our planetary life-support system is to continue functioning in the manner we have come to rely on.

If ecohydrological research tells us anything, it is that we are not reproducing or enhancing ecosystem function in places outside our influence to make up for the widespread global environment decline we are causing. All over the world, complex natural systems are being simplified in order to concentrate specific benefits in human hands. We may wish to avoid doing that here. But this point should be understood in context. What evolving ecohydrological perspectives put into relief is not that we should stop relying on engineering solutions. We can't go back now; if anything, we need solid engineering solutions more than ever. But we do need to improve our understanding, not just of fundamental ecohydrological function but of the expanded services our natural, agricultural and urban ecosystems might be able to provide in the future, and we need to engineer toward realization of that potential. But here's the kicker: we then have to reserve enough water through our management mechanisms to make sure these ecosystems have the water they need to perform these functions under current circumstances and in the altered circumstances we may have to live in as a consequence of higher mean global temperatures and changing precipitation.

But in order to provide nature with the water it needs for perpetuating planetary life support function, we need to know exactly what those support functions are and how much water they need to sustain themselves at adequate levels of performance. We need enhanced monitoring and better research to find that out.

The political process as water information user

If we had better and more complete data, we could not only do more for all of our region's immediate and emerging water users but also serve broader needs related to larger policy issues. The newly formed Western Watershed Stewardship Council is a case in point. The premiers of Canada's western provinces and territories are water data users of the highest order. We need to know what tools we need to have and what supporting data we need to supply to meet the premiers' public policy development interests and needs.

We need to be able to provide information from reliable predictive models that will help our leaders anticipate and address concerns related to the stress that drought might put on already existing interprovincial prairie waters apportionment compacts and water users in the Alberta headwaters regions. We need to consider how water delivery from our mountains to the Arctic is exacerbating global change in the North. We also need to be able to supply the high quality, reliable information that negotiators will need in order to properly frame the changes in hydrology that have already occurred and those that will have taken place by the time the Columbia River Treaty comes up for reconsideration in 2014.

The very highest quality hydrological information is also required to lay down the foundation for compacts that need to be developed between British Columbia, Alberta and Saskatchewan related to downstream flows and water quality in rivers in the Northwest Territories. The very best observational data and predictive modelling capacity will also be required to appropriately serve Canadian political interests in our continuing discussions over increasingly scarce continental water resources with our US neighbours.

There is no question that our ability to predict water can be better. At the moment, unfortunately, we are at or near the limits of our own current predictive modelling capacity. Our observational networks were developed before our current suite of predictive tools developed. Without creating a pragmatic, integrated program of better observations to run our weather and hydrology models, we cannot provide the level of predictability water users and political leaders want. Quite simply, if we want better forecasts and better models, we need more accurate and more comprehensive data, and at least some of that data must come from places we do not at this time adequately monitor, which is to say the upper elevations of our western mountain ranges.

The high benefit-to-cost advantage of hydrometric monitoring

We do not need new facilities nor is it necessary to create any additional organizations to do what we need to do to ensure we know enough to protect water security in the mountain West. But we do need to bring existing and additional data together with our hydrometeorological understanding and hydrological modelling expertise in new ways to create useful information for water management. ·

A relatively small investment in the creation of an improved prediction and observation network will bring substantial benefit to all water users. This can be done at considerable value to the taxpayer. In 2003, consultants for the British Columbia Ministry of Sustainable Resource Development produced a report called

"Water Quality Monitoring in British Columbia: A Business Review of the BC Hydrometric Programs." The report concluded that the cost/benefit ratio for typical hydrometric monitoring networks was very high. In British Columbia alone the benefits were measured at $80-million, while total costs were between $4-million and $5-million, indicating a benefit-to-cost ratio of close to 20 to 1. The report went on to note that one of the reasons the ratio of benefit to cost was so high was that even a limited amount of hydrometric data was extremely valuable.

It is now well understood that too little information can be costly in terms of the decisions we make about the management of our water resources. More than that, however, it is increasingly being realized that too little information that doesn't tell us where water is and when can be even more costly.

We need to bring meteorological data together so that it can contribute to better regional climate and weather prediction, coupled with hydrological prediction, as a subset of hemispheric and global efforts to characterize climate change effects and impacts. Through an interchange of tools and processes, we can bring hydrological data together at the level of linked basin subsets and provide the kind of interpretation of that data that will make it valuable to users. In so doing, we can use better observation and prediction to improve water security everywhere in the West – and that is what good science is supposed to do.

We should build this kind of scientific capacity now, before climate change effects are upon us that will limit our choices and our capacity to adapt. It is a small price to pay to ensure that western Canada's recipe for generating clean water in its upland regions continues to serve millions of people every year.

CHAPTER THREE

The Dust Bowl Then and Now: Drought and Climate Lessons Learned and Not Learned on the Great Plains

In the public imagination, the drought of record for North America is the drought that marked the 1930s as one of the most desperate times in the history of the Great Plains. As time passes there are fewer among us who actually experienced that drought and who are able to give first-hand testimony to its impacts on landscape and culture. There are, however, excellent historical records that allow us to compare our current circumstances with what happened then.

In examining what the global water crisis might mean to Canada, it may be useful to revisit the catastrophe of the 1930s to determine what we actually learned from it about our relationship to the land and to see how much our practices have actually changed over time in response to deep and persistent drought. It might then be instructive to consider how we might get it right in the face of the potentially longer and even more intense droughts that are projected to challenge us in the future.

Part 1: The Catastrophe

Authorities on world food production have ranked the North American Dust Bowl of the 1930s as one of the three greatest ecological disasters in human history. The list is impressive. It is generally held that the greatest human-caused ecological disaster since the beginning of recorded time was the deforestation of China's uplands. The second was the later destruction of the vegetation of the Mediterranean region by livestock. The Dust Bowl that emerged as a result of the ecological destruction of the Great Plains of North America is held to be of a similar order of magnitude.

The relevance of the Dust Bowl in our time was first brought to life for me through family stories. Later it came to life in two very significant books, one written from an American perspective, the other by a Canadian.

Dust Bowl: The Southern Plains in the 1930s was written by Donald Worster, a professor of US history at the University of Kansas.[9] The Canadian whose perspectives on the Dust Bowl have affected me greatly is University of Calgary history professor David C. Jones. His 1987 book, *Empire of Dust*, remains, in my estimation, one of the most influential works of history published in western Canada in my time.[10]

While I have borrowed from both authors in this effort to transpose the lessons of the Dust Bowl into our own time, it is from Worster that I have borrowed most heavily. While both historians have derived the universal from the particular in their analysis of the Dust Bowl, it is Worster who enabled me to see most clearly how the crisis on the North American plains in the 1930s might play itself out again on the larger stage that climate change is creating as it superimposes itself on the impacts we have already had on the dry interior of our continent.

Defining drought in the context of the Dust Bowl

Drought, as expert Donald Wilhite explains, differs from other natural hazards in a number of interesting ways. First, since the effects of drought often accumulate slowly over often considerable periods of time and may linger for many years after the drought has formally ended with the return of normal rainfall, the onset and end points of drought are often difficult to pinpoint. For this reason, drought is often referred to as a creeping phenomenon. It is sometimes difficult to know you are in one. One day there is rain which is followed by a long period of fine weather. It is hard to know how long a drought will last or how much impact it will have. Any spell of fine weather could be the start. The first day without rain contributes as much to the drought as the last. For this reason there appear to be as many different definitions of drought as there are places where drought has occurred.

For the purposes of examining what we learned and didn't learn from the North American Dust Bowl, we will use Donald Worster's definition of drought. In his estimation, drought can be defined as a precipitation deficiency of 15 per cent or more over the course of a year or more. Under this definition, the Dust Bowl drought lasted six years, from 1930 to 1936, in 20 us states and three Canadian provinces.

It must be noted, however, that the Great Plains had already been through severe drought in the decade preceding the 1930s. As David Jones points out, most of the serious economic damage had already been done long before the Great Depression. Even in the worst of the Dust Bowl years, the situation in Canada never became as bad as it was in 1926, when there were 10,400 vacant or abandoned farms on the Canadian prairies, comprising some 2,337,715 acres. Even in 1936, in the depths of the Depression, there were 1,102 fewer farm abandonments in Alberta than there had been ten years earlier. In an area that extended roughly from Lethbridge east through Saskatchewan and from the Red Deer

River south to the Montana border – an area known as the Palliser Triangle – there were four times as many farm failures in 1926 as there were in 1936.

What made the drought of the 1930s so remarkable was its intensity, extent and duration. Temperatures on the Great Plains during the 1930s sometimes reached 118°F, or 48°C. By the time the drought ended, some 4,500 people had died from excessive heat. But the biggest problem was there was no water. During some growing seasons the drought was so severe that there was no soil moisture down to a metre in depth over parts of the Great Plains. Water had to be shipped into the West by converted tank cars and oil pipelines. With water scarcity came other problems. Clouds of grasshoppers ate what little remained of many farmers' wheat and corn. Grasshopper plagues also ate farmers' fenceposts, even the washing hanging on their clotheslines. As the drought persisted its impacts accumulated. The financial cost of the drought in the United States alone amounted in 1934 to half the money the government had spent on the First World War. By 1936 farm losses in the US had reached $25-million a day and more than two million farmers were on relief.

Droughts are common on the prairies, but no one was prepared for this or for the weather phenomenon that emerged after the heat had dried out the millions of acres of plowed plains. The dust storms that came in the wake of the drought were of such violence that they made drought a secondary problem. As Donald Worster points out, these storms were so destructive that they left the region reeling in confusion and fear. They were of such a magnitude that they made people feel completely helpless. It is not exaggerating to say that the dust storms utterly humbled an entire generation living on the Great Plains.

Worster reports that in the United States alone in 1932 there were 14 major dust storms. In 1933 there were 38; in 1934, 22; in 1935, 40; in 1936, 68; in 1937, 72; in 1938, 61; in 1939, 30; and in 1940, only 17. In 1942 the rains at last returned.

During the Depression, February heat waves often announced the beginning of the dust storm season. These storms were often accompanied by winds that reached 100 km/h. Each storm seemed to leave its own mark. Depending upon where the dust came from, the dirt left behind might be brown, black, yellow, ashy grey or even red. Survivors of the storms told Donald Worster that each colour of dust had its own remarkable aroma, ranging from a sharp, peppery smell that burned the nostrils, to a heavy greasiness that could induce nausea.

Another measure of dust storm severity was the number of hours each year during which such storms caused havoc on the plains. These storms would sometimes blow for 11 hours without interruption. Worster reports that some regions of the southern plains suffered through these storms for more than 900 hours, or nearly 38 entire days in a single year. During the Dust Bowl some 408 tons of soil were lost from the average prairie acre. Some 10 million acres lost the upper five inches of topsoil; another 13.5 million acres lost the top two and a half inches. By 1938 the Great Plains were losing 850 million tons of topsoil a year to erosion.[11] That dirt was winnowed and blown in every direction. Dirt deposited in bake pans during the largest storms yielded estimates that indicated that 4.7 tons of dust was falling out of the sky on each affected acre. The drought that began as an environmental disaster became an economic catastrophe. Then it became a public health threat. Worster reports that the death rate from acute respiratory infections in 45 counties in western Kansas, where the dust storms were the most intense, rose from a statewide average of 70 per 100,000 residents to 99 per 100,000, an increase of 41 per cent. Infant mortality in these counties also rose, by 29 per cent.

People stayed inside or at least tried to. When they ventured outdoors they wore bandanas over their mouths. Once outside they stumbled in almost complete darkness, banging into telephone poles, fences and buildings invisible in the gloom. During the storms electric lights burned continuously, cars left tracks in the dust-covered streets, and schools and offices stayed closed. Trains were sometimes derailed by shifting dunes of blowing top-soil. In farmhouses picture wires gave way to the excessive weight of dust on the frames. Livestock suffocated; fish, even in streams that continued to flow, died. Jackrabbits, birds and field mice expired in droves. By 1937, the dust storms were lasting from spring right into fall.

The first steps in recognizing and addressing the Dust Bowl problem

Once the magnitude of the disaster began to be realized, the first step the federal government in the United States took was to entice people off the rolling dunes of the worst-damaged regions of the plains so that a stabilization effort could begin. It was gradually accepted that it was better land use practice to buy up problem areas and remove the people rather than try to regulate use and rehabilitate land still being cultivated. On the positive side this resulted in the creation of more protected areas, reserves and national parks, which in turn resulted in later societal as well as environmental benefits.

But there were limits to how much land could be taken perma-nently out of production. While it would have been a great deal cheaper and faster to stop the damaging plowing in other areas and let nature restore the plains rather than spending millions trying to repair the damage while it was still being done, something had to be done to keep people on the land. Many farmers from that era recall an urgent need to achieve permanence in their lives, a desire to stay put rather than go on roaming around in quest for some-thing better. Recovery in human terms, therefore, came to involve not merely restoring the vegetation, but also giving people a chance to hold on. Greater financial security was obviously a major part of that chance, but it was only part. Recovery also required that a more secure, lasting social order be created which would come from a larger commitment to place and neighbourhood – but given the Dust Bowl circumstances, the development of such an order was not going to be easy. For those who remained on the plains, mobility was greatly reduced, which meant that the speculators and outside interests didn't stay, only the stickers. When the trouble came it was the people who were profiting from afar – the non-resident operators who comprised one third of farmers – who fell out first. These people were major causes of the damage that led to the Dust Bowl in the first place, because few of them were interested in the land as a home for themselves or their children. They were interested in the Great Plains only as a means of making more money. The land, however, was not a factory. A transient, exploitative relationship to the land couldn't be sustained if people expected to find a settled place on earth.

The second step was the creation of an economic relief structure. As Donald Worster explains, the term "relief" was meant to be a positive word that suggested the "succouring and comforting" of those overwhelmed by powerful outside forces. It was meant to suggest support for those who found themselves on the battle line against drought. Individualism and an intense pride in themselves and their achievements were fundamental elements of established prairie culture. Pride alone required that applying for relief be a last resort that could only be taken in the most circumspect manner. In accepting relief there was to be no confession of failure. Everyone understood that work was clearly preferable to the dole and that relief was meant to be temporary only. Despite this, those who accepted relief became marked people. As Worster notes, the names of those receiving relief were often published in local newspapers, ostensibly for the edification of those in their community who supported them. While relief was absolutely necessary in the short term, its long-term benefits were mixed.

Back in the 1890s, when little outside assistance existed, the Great Plains settler had to learn to either adapt to nature or leave.

As Donald Worster points out, the generation that came to plow in the 1920s and eat their dirt in the 1930s did not experience much of that earlier ecological disciplining.

Instead they found themselves in a far more humane age in which society was reluctant to see poor western farmers suffer so grievously for the sins committed by the larger agricultural community. Under relief programming, however, the farmer could emerge from his difficulties without having been forced to ask what he and his neighbours had done wrong. Large-scale relief was an unprecedented development, forming a watershed of sorts in the history of the Great Plains. But in the end it did nothing to produce a turning point in basic economic values. Worster offers that, in fact, it may even have worked against such a change.

Great Plains restoration

Once it was realized that the Dust Bowl was in fact caused by ecological breakdown and land misuse, an extensive long-term program of soil conservation came into existence. In December of 1936, advisers from the US Bureau of Reclamation, the Works Progress Administration and the National Resources Committee put a 194-page report before President Franklin D. Roosevelt that proposed a new model for regional land use planning that would also serve as a blueprint for restoring environmental stability on the Great Plains. "The Future of the Great Plains," as the report was called, made a number of recommendations about the restoration of the Great Plains that are just as relevant today as they were in 1936. They may, in fact, be more relevant in that they apply not just to the Great Plains but to the management of land and resources on the entire continent, where a changing global climate is now being superimposed over a broader range of human impacts.

Land destruction, the report argued, was basically the result of "attitudes of mind" which had to be changed if the Great Plains were to be restored to any semblance of their former ecological vitality and agricultural productivity. The heart of the problem was the expansionist, free-enterprise culture that had emerged on the Great Plains in the absence of any kind of regional public oversight. The free-enterprise culture that enveloped the Great Plains leading up to the Dust Bowl was seen to have subscribed to seven ultimately destructive self-deceptions, which can be summarized as follows:

- the domination-of-nature ethic, which reduced the land to nothing more than a raw material to take advantage of and exploit for private ends
- the corollary view that natural resources were inexhaustible, a self-deception preventing environmental adaptation and restraint
- the notion that what is good for the individual is good for everybody
- the idea that an owner may do whatever he likes with his property
- the notion that markets will grow indefinitely, and
- that the factory farm is generally desirable, which is what led to the cumulative problem that resulted in the Dust Bowl in the first place, namely
- irresponsible non-resident ownership, speculative commercialism and land-abusing tenancy among less-successful operators

Whether the shift away from these deeply embedded ideals had to occur first in the attitudes themselves or in the institutions in which they were entwined was not spelled out, and have yet to be spelled out to this day. What really mattered in the midst of the Great Plains emergency – if you followed the report's causal reasoning – was that there had to be far-reaching changes made in the Dust Bowl economy. These changes included:

- an end to factory farming
- tight controls over agricultural investment, profit-making and land ownership
- the establishment of a permanent and enduring great plains culture

The most amazing limitation of the report, however, was that the destructive attitudes it enumerated were implausibly explained as "humid land" notions that had been carried too far west. The Great Plains committee accepted that notions of conquering the land, industrial farming and aggressive self-interest that appeared to work well enough in the East were unsuited to the drier prairie environment.

The committee – perhaps out of timidity – then went on to base its recommendations on geographical distinctions and fundamental institutional adjustments to climate rather than on forms of co-operative settlement and environmental realism that might have resulted in a paradigm shift in our attitudes about how we might live sustainably and enduringly on the Great Plains.

Among the institutional changes they recommended were:

- larger farm units
- purchase of submarginal land
- co-operative grazing associations and soil conservation districts
- farm loans conditional upon approved land practices
- county zoning to protect the most erodible lands
- consolidation of local governments into more efficient units
- property tax relief in drought years
- conservation training in school curricula
- the creation of a permanent dust bowl agency to promote these policies

Having destroyed the ecological order of the Great Plains, the only choice left was to either restore the old order or create a new one of humans' own making. As it was impossible – and in many ways seen as undesirable – to restore the presettlement climate order, the only practical option was to create a different ecological climax equilibrium based on what humans demanded from the Great Plains. This required the remaking of the Great Plains around human needs and desires, which could only be accomplished through the creation of a new steady state that would only persist if humans managed it themselves forever. This, however, still meant preserving as much of the original ecosystem as a basis of adaptability.

Outside of research areas, the land, unavoidably, would be put to intensive agricultural use. But there were to be constraints:

- On the looser soils, use would be strictly limited to grazing, with the grasses to be maintained or to be restored where they had been plowed under.
- On tighter lands, the monoculture of wheat would not be permitted. Creating a man-made climax ecosystem required following nature's way, which was to work toward sustaining as much variety as possible in an area. Complexity of plant life was the best guarantee of stability.
- Each farm, in order to function as a well-balanced, organic unit, ought to be species diversified; it ought to support a carefully integrated assemblage of crops and animals, just as the grasslands had done.
- Millions of acres of growing nothing but wheat, however, was, for all its profitability and ease of management, an invitation to disaster – to insect and disease outbreaks, soil depletion and wind erosion. It was economically shortsighted to place so much reliance on a single crop, and it was ecologically unworkable.

These recommendations resulted immediately in improved agricultural practices. Terracing attempted to do what native grasses once did far more efficiently in that it acted to make run-off move back and forth across a field "until it got tired and quit." Contour furrows would put 25 per cent more rain and snow into the soil. In these efforts there was a need "to reassure the suspicious and police the mavericks" to ensure the new approaches were actually put into practice.[12] To this end, separate agricultural districts were set up with five-year mandates, the same kind of districts that might in our time promote and manage local climate change offset projects. These districts required 75 per cent local support to qualify for federal subsidies. These groups did not press for land reform but for limited agronomic improvement, which unfortunately meant that a narrow view of the land was retained.

Stunningly there was considerable local resistance to some of the proposed new practices. There was surprising resistance, for example, to the idea of planting shelterbelts, even though it was well known that the presence of trees manipulated the climate, stopped the winds, let more precipitation be absorbed and more slowly released, and saved the soil. Everybody knew a row of trees around a house would cut wind velocity and cool the air in summer. It was found that winds of less than 20 miles an hour were reduced by more than half over distances from four to eight times the height of the trees. With belts growing a mile apart – or even better yet a half a mile apart – there was far less evaporation. There was also improved refuge for winter-weary livestock and the added bonus of birdsong from spring until mid-summer. Expand the row around the farm and across the plains and the dust would cease to blow, offering crops a better chance of maturing.

Though the practice of planting shelterbelts had already proven enormously successful in similar circumstances in Ukraine, Great Plains critics raged against the plan, claiming it was as ridiculous as the idea of spraying banana oil on the fields to stop the dust from blowing. Others claimed that only ignorant Easterners could come up with such an expensive plan to plants trees in a semi-arid climate. Still others thought shelterbelts would be of limited geographical value.

Though they were expensive investments, shelterbelts worked. Trees did get planted, some 220 million of them on 30,000 farms in the US alone. Many of these shelterbelts survive to this day, each still bringing the benefits promised in the 1930s. Unfortunately, very few of these shelterbelts were actually planted during the Dust Bowl.

In the late 1930s the agronomists, like the ecologists, were highly optimistic about the power of educated reason to rule over tradition and habit on the Great Plains. They were even more confident than the scientists of their ability to work on the farm gate level with producers. They believed that conservation and business could pull together in the same harness, and for a time it appeared they might. But, as Donald Worster observed, the agronomists soon discovered that Great Plains farmers needed blinkers to keep them in the conservation furrow. At the first sight of better profits elsewhere, the commercial farmer was all for pulling away from conservation objectives and was soon "snorting and straining, and dragging the agronomist after him." By the late 1930s the farmer was already veering off, wildly ignoring the advice of professional agronomists and charting his way back toward old commercial and industrial ideologies. When the rains returned and the Second World War created a broader market for agricultural production, commercial farming stampeded back to its old ways, proving that the old established economic culture could still pull stronger than any conservation ideal. As if "yoked to a runaway, the field of scientific agronomy was dragged jerking and in panic" toward a future no one foresaw or desired.

While recommendations made by ecologists and conservationists did result in changes in agricultural practices in both the US and Canada, no fundamental reform of attitudes would result from these proposed solutions. The people of the plains were simply unable to make any fundamental changes to the system. Government programs perhaps unwittingly favoured those whose all-out production practices caused the Dust Bowl. Relief and conservation programming addressed the immediate needs of many farmers and their families, but it did not address the problems that created the Dust Bowl in the first place. In the end the principal outcome of government support programs was to continue propping up an agricultural economy that had proved itself to be socially and ecologically erosive. Many have argued that this is exactly what we continue to do in our time in the context of what we know about the climate change threat to the culture that exists today on the Great Plains.

The problem was that the soil conservation districts did not have the backbone to stand up to the money pressure of Big Ag, which sought to perpetuate the continued plow-up of the Great Plains. Most people don't remember this, but the conditions of the 1930s returned to the Great Plains from 1952 to 1957 with even more damaging effects. The big difference was that this Dust Bowl didn't happen in the middle of a Depression.

The renewed post-war order

When the rains returned, conservation advancements such as terraces were suddenly inconvenient to construct, shelterbelts in many places were seen to take up too much space, wetlands were seen as a nuisance and soil conservation practices were deemed too restrictive. After the Second World War, agriculture returned to its old ways. The Dust Bowl scientists and agronomists were horrified. "We haven't stemmed the tide," said Howard Finnell. "We are heading into the same conditions that gave us the old Dust Bowl. The next Dust Bowl will be bigger and better . . ."

The kinds of practices conservationists proposed in the wake of the Dust Bowl were anathema to large-scale corporate agricultural interests, if simply because an abiding awareness of limits would constrain the kind of economic expansion that can only come about under a system that promotes limitless growth. Aided by the obvious urgencies and exigencies that emerged from the Second World War, business farming defeated any hope that an abiding sense of limits as proposed by the conservation-based countermovement to defend the Great Plains environment would define the next stage in the region's development.

After the Second World War, expanding production rather than facing limits remained the major function of our economy and of the agri-monoculture that was created on the Great Plains. The post-war generation committed itself to expanding production and engineering our way out of emerging problems rather than acknowledging and facing limits. As a result, we did not solve the problems that created the Dust Bowl. Agricultural engineering merely band-aided them, allowing production to continue to grow and gradually elevating the Great Plains to a new and higher level of vulnerability once billions of dollars had been spent in partial implementation of the recommendations of "The Future of the Great Plains" report. The same problems that emerged on the prairies in the 1930s are still with us today, but on a much larger scale. We do not yet realize the extent of that scale, but we will as our climate changes.

Part 2: What Has Changed, and What Hasn't

In *Dust Bowl: The Southern Plains in the 1930s*, Donald Worster poses some interesting questions. Why is it that it is on the Great Plains, where the grass has always struggled to hold the land against powerful winds and recurrent drought, that the self-seeking agricultural entrepreneurialism of the 1930s so stubbornly persists? Why is it that here, where we need to summon all of our humanity's co-operative and cautiously self-effacing qualities to live successfully, we find it most difficult to nourish and express those qualities? Why, Worster asks, was it easier to dismiss the grass as unproductive, unprofitable and unnecessary, and to force the land to grow wheat instead?

By virtue of the values they had been taught, Great Plains farmers were justified in what they did. In their minds they were contributors to settlement of the plains, community well-being, national growth and general prosperity. But as it fell out, the culture they had brought to the plains – just like the culture that had brought them there – was ecologically unsustainable because it could not and would not adapt to the real conditions of the Great Plains. That, at least, was the message Worster saw written in the dust.

The lesson we might learn from the Dust Bowl is that we must at all cost avoid creating an ecologically erosive and adaptively unresponsive culture. That certainly may be the message written in our warming temperatures, our melting snowpack and the growing power of contemporary storms.

The question then becomes this: what specific lessons can we learn from the Dust Bowl so that we do not repeat in our time the mistakes that were made then? As it turns out, there is much that happened then that we can learn from today.

Denial

If there is one thing that stood out throughout the hardships of the Dust Bowl, it was the tenacity of optimism and optimism's imperviousness to all warnings. Over the course of six years, however, blowing dirt gradually eroded the most cherished assumptions of middle-class farmers and merchants about the inevitability of progress.

Up until the 1930s, the outpouring of colonization from Europe had been viewed from a contemporary historical perspective as the gradual establishment and expansion of empires and the bringing of "civilization" and "progress" to less-fortunate peoples.

Suddenly a new ecological perspective presented itself that made the outpouring of people and practices from Europe suddenly appear more like a wave of destruction advancing across the world.

No one wanted to believe this to be true. As a consequence, many felt that the effects of the Dust Bowl had to somehow be minimized, discounted, evaded or ignored. This habit remains one of the greatest cultural obstacles to the sustainability of the human presence on Earth. When confronted with our mistakes we often respond by shouting down nature's message with a defence of the old assumptions – the very assumptions that got us into trouble. Many on the plains, including businessmen in the small towns, bitterly resented their growing "Dust Bowl" reputation, which had begun to affect property values, bank credit and business prospects in their region.

Some communities and districts went so far as to form "truth squads" whose work it was to get the facts straight to the rest of nation. Locals who did not conform to their optimism and embrace their boosterism – or who saw different messages in the blowing dust – were in for trouble. They either had to speak very carefully to truth squad vigilantes or were forced to join them. It was also a time of great religious revival and of active and vocal fundamentalism that supported local optimism. By 1939, however, ready optimism was no more effective against the wind than censorship. In that year, dust storms were covering as much as 100,000 acres at a time and enough dirt was blowing around in the prairie sky to cover five million acres one foot deep. But, in the end, even a calamity of this magnitude did not elicit change at a fundamental level in the economy or culture of the Great Plains.

In the midst of the Dust Bowl several states and provinces passed soil conservation laws and tested them successfully in the courts, but when the national emergency passed, public conscience declined. The laws were repealed and exploitation of the land was continued. As one pundit exclaimed, "The Dust Bowl is dead. Long live the Dust Bowl!"

Even major disasters may not result in changes in societal attitudes or direction

It did appear, at least at first, that a major change in cultural values might be possible. In 1936 California newspapers carried stories about how the dust storms on the Great Plains might herald a new form of national planning. But optimists did not take all of the extra-regional factors into account: the hucksters, investors, grain purchasers, commodities futures marketers, machinery salesmen who formed the tangled web of opportunity and exploitation that had created the Dust Bowl. In the end it was conceded that no conservation program, however ambitious, and no new land use policy, local or federal, could ultimately succeed where the dominant societal values support the "autonomous, competitive struggle for progress" and the "bigger is better" mentality that was the underpinning of North American culture in the 1930s and remains the dominant cultural mindset today.

By the end of the 1930s the people of the plains found themselves still unable to accept their place in nature on its own terms, to regard its limits without apology and to shape their culture by nature's imperatives and not by capitalistic and consumer-culture drives established elsewhere. As Donald Worster observed, "Their eyes were still on the far horizon, their feet not planted firmly on the ground."

The survivors of the Dust Bowl stuck together, arguing the plains were the better for the absence of those who were driven out. In a sense theirs was an idealism that masked failed environmental adaptation and a failed sense of place. Once the rains returned, those who stayed set out to repeat the very mistakes that led to the Dust Bowl. Six years of Dust Bowl life was apparently not enough to cause a change in the fundamental societal values that favoured the endless pursuit of increased wealth over the health of Great Plains ecosystems. If the Dust Bowl tells us anything about what we learn from our ecological mistakes, it is that we forget adversity the moment it is over and that the only way we are going to make fundamental changes in the underlying values of our society is if the impacts of our mistakes don't let up and we can't engineer or subsidize our way out of them.

If we can derive anything positive from this it may be that the current convergence of population growth, ecosystem decline, water scarcity, habitat loss, species extinction, the destruction of marine fisheries, growing food scarcity and food security concerns superimposed over climate change might just do the trick.

Calculating economic costs

Our greatest climate change fears with respect to potential damage to our economy are summarized by Donald Worster's story of one Oklahoma county during the Dust Bowl. In a single year, one farm implement dealer in Boise City sold 65 new tractors to local sodbusters. With this new equipment and access to new rail lines, the county temporarily became a wheat empire. From 1926 to 1930, area rainfall exceeded 19 inches a year, two inches more than average, which encouraged agricultural expansion into what had previously been marginal areas. By 1931 the number of acres in wheat had doubled, production rose to 21 bushels per acre and some 6 million bushels of wheat was harvested. In 1932, however, total precipitation fell to 12 inches and in 1934 to less than nine. From 1931 to 1936 the yearly average was only 11 inches and wheat production fell to less than a bushel an acre, not enough in most seasons to provide seed for next year's crop. Of the 250,000 acres of winter wheat planted in the fall of 1936, not one head of grain matured in the entire county the following year.

As Donald Worster points out, the entire environmental experience of the agricultural West was telescoped into a single generation. In less than a lifetime the Great Plains had gone from wild prairie range where never was heard a discouragin' word, to the Santa Fe railway hauling bounteous harvests of grain to Chicago, right back to an empty shack on the empty plains where the dust has drifted as high as the eaves.

Though the collapse was essentially agricultural, everyone from school teachers to implement dealers, railway workers to dentists, depended upon the farmer and his crops. When the farmer was in trouble, so was everyone who depended on him for their livelihood. By the time the Dust Bowl came to an end, nearly four million people in Canada and the US became environmental refugees. In the dust they left behind were more than 10,000 abandoned homes and more than 10 million abandoned acres of farmland.

The situation was no different in Canada. David Jones reports that in all census divisions in Saskatchewan the population of the Great Plains region in that province peaked in 1931. In that year, the population of the southern part of the province was 159,382. By 1936 this region had lost 14,743 people. Alberta was not as hard hit in the 1930s, only because its population had already been hammered during the drought of the 1920s. The population of the three dry-belt census divisions in Alberta had peaked in 1921 at 81,787. By 1926 the region had already lost 16,798 of these people. Only in the most northerly portion of Alberta's prairie region would conditions in the 1930s be worse than in the decade before. In the region roughly between Hanna and the Red Deer River there were more than 3,700 farm abandonments in 1936 alone, two and a half times more than in the worst-hit census division in all of Saskatchewan.[13]

The population in many parts of the Great Plains never returned to what it was before the Dust Bowl.

The fundamental change we seem unable to make

It would be easy to dismiss our experience on the North American plains as merely another case of human misjudgment, greed, innate aggression or stupidity. The historian, though persuaded by such arguments to be realistic about human behaviour, cannot be ready to let the explanation rest there; it is, in the first place, too comprehensive – what explains all may explain nothing. It is also an excessively pessimistic way of thinking about the human relationship to the rest of nature, which is often harmonious. The farmers in North America in the 1930s were as intelligent as farmers anywhere else in the world. They were by no means the first to exceed the limits of their environment. But the reason they did so must be explained not by simple "human nature" but rather by the peculiar culture that shaped their values and actions. It is our culture that defines our innate qualities and determines our choices. It was our culture that created the Dust Bowl just as it is because of our culture that our climate is changing.

Looking back, it can be seen that at least two cultural traits worked in tandem to bring about the Dust Bowl. The first was the belief that we are autonomous in nature. We believed then, and still believe today, that we are sovereign creatures, independent of the constraints that hobble other species – not controlled by nature as they are, but in control of nature. As evidenced by North American First Nations, this has not been the dominant cultural trait throughout all of history. There has perhaps been no more important change in human culture in the history of our species than the one that took us from a traditional sense of intimate dependence on the ecological community to our modern confidence in total free will and human autonomy.

The second cultural trait that got us into trouble on the Great Plains in the Dust Bowl years – and one that is still getting us into trouble today – is our relentless obsession with economic growth. Newspaper advertisements published widely on the southern plains in 1930 clearly articulate this dangerous cultural insistence.

THERE IS NO STANDING STILL, the advertisement trumpeted. WE MUST MOVE FORWARD – OR, WE

MOVE BACKWARD. A town cannot be bigger until it is better, and it cannot be better until it is bigger. Let us remember that it is natural and normal for a community to grow – unless there is something wrong, something lacking.[14]

The same logic is applied today, not just to communities but to every aspect of our economy. It is not too much to say that our entire industrial world was made possible by these two changes in human perspective.

Exotic proposals for addressing the problem without solving it

Just as in today's climate change debate, a great number of hare-brained proposals were put forward to halt the dust storms. For many, the solution was to cover the Great Plains over. A Chicago papermaker proposed a tough, waterproof paper that would cover acres at a time. An asphalt emulsion spread over millions of acres was also proposed, as was wire netting. Someone proposed to cover the Great Plains with cement with holes in it for planting seeds. Another proposed moving rock from the western mountains to stabilize the prairie soil. It was also proposed that junked cars be sent from population centres in the east and that they be used to anchor the blowing soil. Leaves from eastern forests were proposed as mulch that would bind humus to the soil. Building wind deflectors was also proposed. These deflectors would be made of cement slabs or board fences 250 feet in height which would serve to direct the winds away from the plains. Evil outsiders were also implicated in the problem. Some writers argued that German agents were behind the disaster; others suspected alien radio waves. Some blamed it on pollution from local oil and gas refineries. No one wanted to talk about agricultural practices.

It is remarkable how similar these notions are to the proposals being put forward in this generation to address the climate change issue without having to change our collective habits. Similar to the 1930s idea of somehow covering the prairies to prevent them from blowing away, it has been proposed that we somehow capture all of the world's errant CO_2 emissions and pump them to the bottom of the ocean where very high pressures will keep them in liquid form stuck to the ocean floor forever. The problem with this idea is that the oceans are already turning acidic from absorbing too much CO_2 and adding more means risking that some time in the future our oceans will be too acidic to support current marine ecosystems.

Similar to the idea of bringing leaves from the East to cover the plains is the contemporary notion of dumping iron filings into the southern oceans as a way of extracting CO_2 from the atmosphere. The problem is that even if you were somehow able to fertilize the required millions of square kilometres of ocean with the requisite amount of iron, you might only be able to remove 30 per cent of humanity's annual CO_2 emissions. The introduced iron would also affect ocean chemistry and ecology. Another proposal recommends extracting carbon dioxide from the atmosphere and then making it into carbonate rocks. This is the same process nature uses to create marine sediments. Related to this is the idea of passing CO_2-laden air over an extraction agent like quicklime to form calcium carbonate, also known as limestone. The idea is to install such plants in the ten major CO_2-emitting countries, which include both the United States and Canada. Unfortunately, there are some 3.2 billion people living in these countries, which would require a quicklime processing plant of about 3200 square kilometres in area. While thousands of smaller reactors could be created and distributed throughout the world, the problem is that we can't keep up with our CO_2 production even today and we don't quite know what we'd do with all the additional limestone we would create.

Similar to the Dust Bowl notion of constructing deflectors made of cement slabs or board fences 250 feet high to direct the winds away from the plains is the contemporary idea of launching millions of mirrors into space to deflect the sun's rays away from the Earth so as to reduce the amount of radiation reaching the surface. Another really good contemporary idea is to use rockets to inject millions of tonnes of sulphur into the stratosphere on a regular basis so as to deflect an amount of radiation sufficient to cool the Earth to the desired temperature. The former of these proposals is expensive beyond imagination. The latter would create a horrendous acid rain problem. Like the proposals put forward to address the Dust Bowl problem in the 1930s, none of these proposals gets to the fundamental cause of the problem – the excessive emission of greenhouse gases.

We are addressing contemporary problems in the same way we addressed the problems created by the Dust Bowl. We refused to look the problem in the eye and we are no closer to doing so now. Where does the blame reside for the problems we are creating for ourselves?

It was very difficult for farmers and ranchers in the 1930s to admit that what they had learned and had always been told was right was actually responsible for their predicament. It was natural for them to be defensive. They felt – as the petroleum industry feels today – that they were being unfairly singled out for blame and criticism by many outsiders, when it was they who had to face the dust and struggle hard to save the farms that produced much of the nation's food. And they were right, at least to the extent that they were largely unwitting agents caught in a larger economic culture and were dependent on its demands and rewards. They in fact represented the values of that culture, which included uncritical faith in Providence and devotion to self-aggrandizement. The ultimate meaning of the dust storms that occurred in the 1930s was that North America as a whole, not just the Great Plains, was badly out of balance with its natural environment.

It was understood also that the Great Plains could not get out of the trap it created for itself without outside government help. Just like the climate change threat today, the Dust Bowl was a national problem requiring national answers. What the people of the Great Plains needed was hope, but hope of a higher order than had existed in the past. What was needed was a mature hope that did not gloss over failure, deny responsibility or stand in the way of fundamental change. What was needed then – just as now – was a disciplined optimism, tempered with restraint and a realistic attitude toward the land and what could be expected from it.

What was in essence required then was nothing less than a complete reform of commercial farming. As we see today, that never happened. There is surprisingly little difference between then and now. The fundamental North American economic ethic remains the same today as it was in 1930.

Environmental refugees then and now

Regardless of where they were actually from, everyone who left an American farm became an "Okie." In the eyes of those who were not wiped out by buying stocks on margin in the 1920s, these refugees from the dust were inferior people who were ridiculed for their failures. America refused to see in the disaster the failure of its own economic promise. When John Steinbeck published *Grapes of Wrath*, the Dust Bowl states banned it. But as Donald Worster has pointed out, even censorship wouldn't make the dust go away. The storms just hung there in the air, persistent and black, symbolizing to all the effects of soil erosion and improper management of the land.

The dust said that the symbiosis between people and land that had held the plains together for thousands of years had disintegrated. The moment that the relationship between people and the land is no longer symbiotic, is the moment the slide toward collapse begins. The Dust Bowl was a symbol of the bankrupt relationship between people and the land and of ecological decay caused by short-sighted economic self-interest. When North Americans were forced to look into the mirror of their own economic idealism, what they saw reflected in the dust was the realization that the uncontrolled economic monster they had created would grow and grow until it had consumed everything and made all into a desert. More painful yet was the realization that when the monster stops growing, it dies, taking almost every living thing on the desert it created with it. It was a mirror no one wanted to look into then. Or now.

Bitter and disillusioned Dust Bowl conservationists like Howard Finnell later articulated the reasons why agricultural conservation failed on the Great Plains. Neither the federal land use planners nor the ecologists made a lasting impression on the region. Clearly the region would not have come back as quickly as it did, without their help, and farmers did learn a few things from these advisers that made them better agriculturalists, but the advisers' impact was partial at best. Nothing the planners or ecologists did encouraged Great Plains farmers to think of the land as something more than a commodity – a "resource" for their enrichments. They offered farmers a technological panacea for ecological destructiveness, when the root issue was an absence of vision of what we want the West to be like at its future and ultimate best. They fixed the short-term landscape problem without addressing the root of the damage that had been done. Technology was seen as the answer when it was only a partial solution. Science put the emphysema into temporary remission but the patient only briefly quit smoking.

In response to the Dust Bowl disaster we moved briefly toward sustainability but then turned back. We got partway but then turned around. But the problem has not gone away, and it won't until we face it.

Appropriating and commodifying environmental values

Through solid science and applied agronomic technique the Dust Bowl dunes were in many cases turned back into productive soil. It was a triumph of practice over the need for institutional and societal reform. Improved business practice won out – and still wins out today – over the need to change fundamental ethics. But unfortunately, the Dust Bowl was not the end of drought. The dunes created during the 1930s were sometimes stabilized and restored within three years, but in the droughts of the 1950s they appeared again where they hadn't existed before.

While Big Ag attacked some of the broader recommendations of Dust Bowl era conservationists, they could not deny the efficacy of improved agronomic practices. It was soon accepted that conservation agronomy was good business. In other words, conservation measures became a business in their own right. An operator who used the best technical advice available would get the best returns from the land, not in a single boom year, perhaps, but over several years of thoughtful management. The Dust Bowl was seen as proof that technique was lacking: remedy incompetent farming, and the agricultural factory that was the Great Plains would be saved, rationalized and made operational again. The fundamental principles did not change. Greater output meant greater profitability. It was as simple as that. The aims that had fuelled the tractors in the great plow-up would be the reward as before, but not the risk of destroying the landed capital. The notion of conservation was torqued into a new shape. For the post-war agronomist, conservation would mean a renewed commitment to making the land pay off.

Conservation was redefined in corporate parlance as an investment in:

- maintaining productive potential
- decreasing productivity deterioration
- enhancing productivity potential

Even the editor of *Business Week* could call himself a conservationist by this definition, for, as he indicated, "every progressive industrial leader could see the wisdom in this 'scientific agriculture' and support its efforts to put the Great Plains back to work, earn a better dividend and produce more efficiently."

Every aspect of environmentalism today – from landscape to climate change – has been hijacked from its original purpose and appropriated through exactly this same strategy. Define any problem in economic terms and the market will solve it. We have seen in our time that any environmental problem, from the desertification of the Great Plains to rapid warming of our planet's atmosphere, can be absorbed profitably into the global economy, where it will contribute to our prosperity rather than diminish it. But creating a booming market for partial solutions in localized circumstances does not solve the larger problem we are creating for ourselves.

We presently continue to create agro-monocultures on such a scale that there is hardly any question that, with each level of advance, we are just setting ourselves up again for an ever more destructive Dust Bowl eventuality.

Why are our major institutions unable to effect lasting change?

While the Great Plains Committee that was set up to address the Dust Bowl problem was aware that new engineering technology, new agronomic practices and new tax laws would prove inadequate over time without basic changes in attitudes and the function of major institutions, it was not prepared to go far enough to meet its own announced ends.

The members of this blue-ribbon committee were problem-solvers, not broad thinkers. They didn't have time to be the latter. They generated the kinds of recommendations that emerge in a crisis. They did what you have to do when you are in trouble. Faced with a national emergency they had to act to solve the problem in the immediate term. They had neither the mandate nor the political support to go further. And for all its concern about the suffering and devastation caused by the Dust Bowl, neither Americans nor Canadians were ready to hear about or support the need for more fundamental reform. As Donald Worster put it, the gospel of More was still the universal religion. For most of the people in North America in the 1930s, the Great Depression and the Dust Bowl brought only a momentary disenchantment with their maximizing creed, and that soon gave way to a determination to see their old creed revived as soon as possible.

The dust was hardly settled when it became clear that the thrust of the ecological ideas put forward as a solution to the Dust Bowl were decidedly threatening to the laissez faire, business-based systems of corporate agricultural interests. It was not long before Big Ag mounted its countercharge. By the 1950s industry had begun a sustained attack on the science and conservation programs put forward by Dust Bowl scientists, conservationists and agronomists. They attacked first on the grounds that the scientific theories of ecological equilibrium and climax made the grasslands too idealized a world and suggested that European settlement practices had been characterized as being far more disruptive than they had really been.

In an astounding preview of what would happen two generations later in the climate change debate, professional deniers argued that the dust storms of the 1930s had not in fact been as severe as many thought and that certainly they did not have the lasting impact on the Great Plains that many conservationists had indicated. It was put forward that the distorted views of conservationists were in fact leftist attempts to put unacceptable limits on human exploitation of nature and to diminish human dominion over the Earth. The attackers did everything possible to paint conservationists as unprogressive socialists who lacked faith in an American form of ingenuity that would always find the resources needed to advance future economic expansion. Just as in today's climate change debate, the attack grew more personal and vicious as time passed. Every age appears to have its share of well-paid

professional deniers. Big Ag let it be known through every possible means that conservationist recommendations would reduce
the Great Plains to a regimented welfare state in which the individual landowner would no longer be given the liberty, or the
encouragement, to maximize his profit. "Scientism, along with
statism," one critic wrote, "have become major social myths that
threaten freedom."

The main institutions responsible for resolving the problems
created by the Dust Bowl were an easy target for such criticism.
Land use planners in one government department who favoured
conservation and who felt that the Great Plains had more productive capacity than was good for the land and that the public ought
to restrain the agricultural economy were opposed by agencies
dedicated to helping local farmers manage their soils for greater
productivity. Tensions grew between those who maintained that
large sections of the Great Plains should be put back into natural
grasses and those who vociferously opposed making any land off-
limits to the plow and who put their trust in better farming tech-
niques as the best solution to the Dust Bowl problem. In the end,
however, it was the gospel of More than won out.

Such attacks prompted questions that have not been answered
to this day. In nature there is no such thing as unlimited
growth. Our human economic drive, which has at its foundation
an obsession with unlimited financial and material increase, is at
diametric odds with the natural system in which it is embedded.
The Dust Bowl example also invites the question of where our
major institutions – fragmented in their function and purpose as
they have proved to be – are ever going to be able to address this
problem.

We can no longer keep up with the problems we are creating
for ourselves. Our best science and technological innovation are
mocked and overshadowed by relentless population and economic
growth. At the moment, our governments do not appear capable
of, or even interested in, addressing the large-scale problems that

are emerging as a consequence of our numbers and our material needs and desires.

Perhaps the most important lesson we can learn today from the Dust Bowl is that we failed to learn anything from the Dust Bowl. Fundamentally nothing has changed. Ecological values and conservation practices are still only accepted in North America where and insofar as they help business achieve its expansionist aims. If that is not failure, then success has a dusty taste to it.

Clive Ponting, in his *A Green History of the World*, got it right, after undertaking a similar examination of the human failing to understand our place in the natural order except in the context of how that order might be exploited:

> From one perspective this invention of new techniques and more complicated production processes and the utilization of more resources can be viewed as *progress* – the increasing ability of human societies to control and modify the environment to meet their needs through sheer ingenuity and a capacity to respond to challenges and to engage in problem solving. From an ecological perspective, the process appears as a succession of more complex and environmentally damaging ways of meeting the same basic human needs.

Part 3: Getting It Right This Time

We have only been practising agriculture on this continent for a few centuries. Along the Nile and the Yangtze, farmers have been planting fields for 4,000 years. Their soils are as rich today as they were 4,000 years ago. That kind of soil management, however, takes the kind of work we are no longer prepared to do. We want to make a lot of money quickly, but the land doesn't always co-operate.

Industrial farming has robbed the Great Plains of its original identity and compromised local relationship to place. Increasingly absent is the sense of living in the presence of nature or working with and being a part of an organic order that is complex, mysterious and alive. The agri-monoculture we have created on the Great Plains is by and large as sterile and uninteresting as a shopping mall parking lot. Almost every acre is rigidly managed for maximum output. Under this regimen, soil has been divested of its life-giving qualities and has become a simple medium in which food is grown. A few wild creatures are still allowed to live here as long as they stay out of sight. It is an environment that has been created out of alienation and that leads right back to it. It has become a landscape most want to drive through quickly on their way to more ecologically substantive places.

Can any genuine, fulfilling culture take root, flourish and endure in such a setting? Will there be a community here not only 40 years from now but 40 centuries from now? Or will it have become of graveyard of industrial farming?

With the Dust Bowl, we had a chance to reconcile ecology with our economy, but we did not have the courage to choose between these two incompatibles. The market has got us. Our economy has become our ecology. Evidently, something more than science was needed then – and is needed now – to effect the fundamental shift in human values that will make sustainability possible on the Great Plains and on this continent.

Finding our way back to place

Early in the European settlement of the Great Plains, communities were absorbed slowly into the landscape, creating just the kind of relationship to place that might allow us to endure here, but with the advent of mechanization, this changed dramatically. Prairie communities no longer paced themselves to self-generated, self-contained rhythms of local place. Instead, they began to vibrate to the rhythms of disruptive urban material excitements and economic interests that had little to do with local sense of place. This resulted – as it still does today – in a loss of connection with the inside through a focus on the outside.

But as Donald Worster has pointed out, human adaptation to nature is never simply a matter of technological application and practical inventiveness. If that were so, then the most highly technological societies in the world today would have the least impact on their physical environments. In fact, the opposite is true: it is our most highly technological societies that appear to have the least respect for natural limits and that practice the least environmental restraint.

Until we change this fundamental circumstance, we are not going to achieve the sustainability we so desire. Until the public knows why we must constantly invest in more and more expensive technologies to do what nature used to do for us for free, we will never be able to catch up to the problems we are creating for ourselves with respect to ecological collapse, water supply and quality and climate change.

We are seeing increasingly in our time, however, that technology and development cannot improve a place in the absence of a deeply felt local sense of the natural order. The most enduring communities are those in which the identity of the self and the character of the community became indistinguishable from the nature of the land and the fabric of life that supports the uniqueness of place. This can only emerge locally where this is at once an understanding of what makes a landscape function the way it does and a feeling of belonging to and sharing in its uniqueness. As Worster put it, sense of place is a special adaptiveness that emerges when the individual reflects the community and the community reflects the landscape in which it is embedded, and out of these interdependencies there emerges a unique and local cultural ecology.

Throughout history humans have now and then upset the ecological order, sometimes because we have had to in order to make a new home for ourselves, sometimes because we did not know that we were doing so. To avoid further abuse of the Great Plains we need what Wallace Stegner described as a willingness to look at what is rather than what fantasy, hope or private interest says there should be.[15] We need to take a hard look at what makes the Great Plains what they are.

For all its variability, the Great Plains was one of the most remarkable landscape features in North America. Covering some 1.4 million square miles, roughly 3.6 million square kilometres, the prairies were not just the fabled home of the buffalo. While perhaps as many as 60 million buffalo ranged across this eternity of grass, the bison-based ecosystem may also have supported as many as nine million antelope, three million deer, two million elk, two million bighorn sheep, half a million bears and perhaps 400,000 wolves. It is said that one prairie dog town covered 25,000 square miles, some 65,000 square kilometres, and had a population of 400 million individuals. In dry periods a two-acre population of grasshoppers could eat as much as a buffalo could. But European settlement and the economic expansionism that arrived in its wake changed all that. Barely 1 per cent of the natural prairie still remains. Landscape changes that were once measured in epochs are now measured in lifetimes and even mere decades. Only diminished remnants of this Great Plains abundance still exist in small wildlife populations that cling to the foothill and mountain margins of this once great ecosystem.

In their original natural state the North American prairies were composed of hundreds of species of grass. This vast, living, inland sea of grass produced almost no runoff because of the absorptive nature of the sod.

Today, just as then, the key to the ultimate sustainability of the Great Plains both as an ecosystem and as an economic region may be to put sizable parts of it back into native grasses and to protect the mountain headwaters of the rivers that provide the little water that is available to the region.

The key to recovering from the Dust Bowl was to increase water uptake and storage at the subsoil level. In this function, natural grasses were perfect sponges, taking up and retaining runoff 30 times more effectively than wheat. The same native grasses also possess the capacity to store huge volumes of carbon, so much so, in fact, that some healthy rough fescue grasslands are thought to sequester as much carbon as a forest.

Wes Jackson has envisioned an agriculture based on evolutionary biology and ecology which he has called "a polyculture of perennials." In Jackson's view the prairie should serve as a model to be imitated rather than an enemy to be destroyed. In its natural state a prairie can include dozens or even hundreds of plant species, some well adapted to drought, others fertilizing the soil by fixing nitrogen, others emitting chemical protection from voracious insects. Mostly, these plants are perennials that last for years before offspring take their place. Where the conventional farmer buys a single variety of seed every year, plows and plants on an annual cycle, and expends much human labour and fossil fuel in order to raise a crop, nature follows a different strategy. Agriculturalists, according to Jackson, would do well to learn from those natural processes and to imitate the prairie.

Scientists need to identify which native plants have the highest protein yield, then help those plants improve with selective breeding, then learn to grow them together to mimic the prairie, then figure out how to harvest these kinds of new crops and turn them into foodstuffs. Another strategy is to perennialize major food crops like wheat and sorghum. Jackson and company have gone back to a time when these plants were wild grasses and are trying to recover the natural resilience that has been bred out of them over the centuries.

Restoring prairie watersheds

While restoring natural ecosystem resilience is important, we cannot create sustainable prairie agriculture without improving the way we manage our water resources. In the context of our current situation with respect to water supply and quality on the Great Plains, we might do well to look to the lesson of the Danube and what Europe discovered about itself and its future by examining its most important river.

Flowing through 18 nations, the Danube is world's most international watercourse. Representatives from the Danube River Commission explain that the river's water is the engine that drives industrial and agricultural prosperity in all the jurisdictions through which it flows.

Members of the Danube River Commission recognize that water also provides, free of charge, valuable services related to the absorption of the wastes that are by-products of European prosperity.

As the European Union could never afford to provide all these services itself, it is working to ensure the health of the Black Sea and its wetlands, for it is into the Black Sea that everything that somehow finds its way into the Danube ultimately comes to reside.

If the Saskatchewan River is our Danube – and Lake Winnipeg our Black Sea – the lake is an indicator of how well we are managing the water that flows through the centre of the continent. The state of Lake Winnipeg is a reflection of the condition of the tributaries that contribute to it.

In 2008 Ducks Unlimited Canada completed the first phase of a project to determine the impacts of wetland loss and associated drainage activity in the Broughtons Creek watershed, located north of Brandon in southwestern Manitoba. The water of Broughtons Creek ultimately flows into Lake Winnipeg. The area was selected as a study watershed because the land use and wetland loss trends are representative of other agricultural watersheds across the Prairie Pothole Region of Canada. Results from the first phase determined that wetland loss since 1968 in the Broughtons Creek watershed has resulted in:

- a 30 per cent increase in stream flow
- a 31 per cent increase in nitrogen and phosphorus load from the watershed
- a 41 per cent increase in sediment loading

- an estimated 28 per cent decrease in annual waterfowl production
- net annual extra release of about the same amount of CO_2 as in the exhaust of almost 23,200 cars

What this report suggests is that agriculture as it is presently being practised in the Broughtons Creek area of Manitoba is not only non-sustainable, it is self-terminating. What is happening in Broughtons Creek is one of the reasons why algal blooms of 8,000 square kilometres are now regular features in Lake Winnipeg in late summer.

In the case of Lake Winnipeg, it is held in many international circles that, at this moment at least, we have the potential to create a freshwater catastrophe of continental proportions. This is not what we want Lake Winnipeg to say about how we manage fresh water on the Great Plains.

As bad as what is happening in Lake Winnipeg may be, however, it is nothing compared to the damage caused by short-sighted agricultural practices in the interior of North America on the Gulf of Mexico, where a large area of coastal waters experience seasonally low levels of dissolved oxygen, a condition known as hypoxia. Excess discharges of nutrients – especially nitrogen and phosphorus – cause nutrient overenrichment along the Gulf coast and stimulate the development of huge algae blooms similar to those that appear each summer in Lake Winnipeg. The nitrogen and phosphorus nutrient discharges that create this dead zone come from many different sources and many different watersheds within the basin.

There is absolutely no reason for this to happen anywhere in Canada. But the first thing we have to realize is that safe, clean water in southern Canada is no longer a slam dunk.

We can address these problems by getting back to basics. We have to reaffirm our connection to place and listen to what water is telling us about where and how we presently live and how we might want to live in the future. Ultimately, we are going to have to decide what kind of West we want in the future and then start creating it.

Bridging the gulf between promise and practice

In 1954 Howard Finnell concluded that it is not more laws, nor incentive programs, nor more scientific information that we need. It is the will to conserve. Now, just as then, it is the failure of the will to conserve that is missing.

There are a great many people on the plains who understand that land, water and climate are reflections of one another. By managing one, we are in effect managing the others. We also know that intact ecosystems slow and moderate the impacts of climate change. We know that different types of landscapes and ecosystems retain, purify and release water at different rates. We know that, for this reason alone, we need to take land use impacts seriously. Though we sometimes pretend otherwise, we also know which land use impacts to avoid.

We know the value of ecological services. Some of us have learned that technology will never be more than a partial solution until we make the public understand why we need to invest more and more into expensive technological applications that perform functions that nature used to perform on our behalf for free. We also know that engineering alone will not save us. To make even the best engineering work in a perfect storm we have to demand changes in our collective habits. The destruction of the aquatic ecosystem health of our rivers and streams through poorly considered land use policy is the landscape equivalent of wiping out the immunological capacity of your own blood stream.

When we destroy terrestrial and aquatic ecosystem health, we wipe out the self-purifying capacity of natural systems, the very capacity upon which we rely to supply us with the air we breathe and the water we need for drinking, for life and for everything we do and make. In the absence of ecosystem health all we have are engineering solutions that are the equivalent of putting all of nature and all of humanity on dialysis.

Unless we all know why it is impossible to slow our global destruction of natural ecosystem health and understand where this destruction and our over-reliance on technology is taking us, we will never be able to keep up with the difficulties we are creating for ourselves in terms of water security, ecosystem integrity or climatic stability.

Only by building a better bridge between science and public understanding that leads to public policy action can we break out of this vicious circle. We need to find the language, create the images and imagine the solutions that will allow us to break out of the cycle that threatens the sustainability of our society by threatening the health of our landscapes and water sources. The people who live on the Great Plains care about where they live. Together we can make true sustainability possible. And we can do it with humour. We can do it with style and we can do it with grace. But we have to do it.

CHAPTER FOUR

Corralling the Water Hole

The myth of limitless abundance is so deeply entrenched in the psyche of Canadians that we have trouble imagining waking up one day and having to face the water scarcity problems others in the world have been forced to confront for generations. Because we feel we are someone special and will somehow always be exempt from water scarcity concerns, we turn a blind eye to problems common elsewhere when they show up at our door. The fact remains, however, that we are no different than anyone else. As our populations grow we will put increasing pressure on our water resources. In dry parts of the country this is already happening. The problems that have so commonly presented themselves elsewhere are beginning to appear here, only we refuse to see them as such.

In examining what others have done in situations similar to those emerging here in Canada, California is a good place to look for examples, both good and bad. We can learn from the Middle East. We can also learn a great deal from the European experience and especially from Spain.

Part 1: Water and Urban Power in an Era of Climate Change

What is the value of water?

After an evening of visiting World's Fair pavilions that celebrated the relationship of water to local culture in each of the host countries, I arrived back at the Hotel Meliá in Zaragoza, Spain, with three small, trilingual books I had bought at the World's Fair Bookstore. Each volume in this series was an essay relating to the importance of water to our modern way of life. The one I chose to examine first was written by an activist named Susan George on the subject of water and sustainable development. George's essay made it clear that she was highly sympathetic to the work and views of Canadian water rights activist Maude Barlow. Like Barlow, George is deeply troubled by how quickly water is being commodified in the world marketplace, and she is very articulate in outlining her concerns. By the time I finished reading the essay I wondered if Maude Barlow should be quoting Susan George instead of the other way around.

George's essay is about market forces that in her opinion are diminishing public control over water resources so quietly and with such pervasive intent that the average person would not know what had been done to their inherent right to water until long after that right had been extinguished through gradual, incremental appropriation of those rights by nearly invisible market transactions. She makes her point simply by outlining why water is such a perfect market product. Abundant resources, George points out, can be almost valueless. Water, however, is suddenly becoming rare and scarce. As economists have been proclaiming for two centuries, the scarcer a good, the higher its price becomes. As we know, water really is becoming scarcer with each passing day. Ergo, given that the rationing of scarce resources is what the market does best, it should not be a surprise to anyone that water is being commodified by market forces.

Water has other qualities as well. For one thing, it is indispensable. As George points out, nothing can live without water. Moreover, the supply of water cannot be increased, which assures its continued and growing scarcity.

Another quality of water that lends it great market appeal is the fact that there are no substitutes for it. No other marketable product possesses the same characteristics. No one is going to invent anything that is somehow going to cheaply replace water. That being so, the market for water is permanently assured.

Because of these qualities, and because human populations and economies are growing, the demand for water will increase regularly, even exponentially, as water becomes scarcer. As demand continues to rise, so will price. Because water is central to life, people will in the end pay whatever the market demands for it, and consumers will be forced to set aside an increasing proportion of their income to assure survival. This, asserts Susan George, is what the invisible hand of the market wants to happen to water. But it can only happen if control over water resides in private hands. In order to prevent water from being commodified into the perfect market product to be made available to "consumers," George argues that people should be very cautious of market appropriation of this life-giving, life-supporting common good.

Though their two views are complementary, Susan George approaches the importance of water for life from a slightly different human rights perspective than Maude Barlow. George wants to make sure water is identified and treated as a common good so that it cannot be appropriated by market forces. She wants to get at this problem before it threatens the right each person on Earth is held to have to the basic resources that make life possible and meaningful.

What is noteworthy about Susan George's perspective is that declaring water a universal public good does not necessarily mean water has to be or even should be free. George maintains that the price of water should be differentiated according to use. She maintains also that pricing should be determined politically and not purely by economic forces of supply and demand. George further argues that precisely because water is a perfect market product in any capitalistic system, water capture, treatment and distribution must remain under democratic control that includes "robust and enforceable" price-setting mechanisms.

While George's economic and political views are unpopular in some North American circles, she makes an incontestable point in her evaluation of the importance of not losing public control of water to entrenched private interests. George contends that in the end water must be considered a universal public good under public control. By public control she means not only government oversight but public involvement in decision-making related to the management of water resources characterized by active, popular, democratic citizen participation.

There is the appearance of this kind of oversight and public participation in Canada, but there is also growing concern over the power of vested interests to control the water agenda. Some fear, for example, that in Alberta, where I live, these interests are putting a corral around the provincial water hole. While many working in the water resource community would dismiss such a claim out of hand, what happened in California suggests there may be enough truth to that claim to warrant giving it consideration.

The first-in-time, first-in-right prior appropriation water doctrine, or how to put a corral around your water

In the early years of European settlement in California, there was little legislation to guide the development of water resources, particularly in terms of urban expansion. Federal and state interests were dominated at the time by concerns related to flood control, drainage, the improvement of inland navigation and reclamation of wetlands. These were principally issues of abundance rather than scarcity. More problematically, the practice of water law in California, after the first state legislature adopted English common law in 1850, rested upon riparian principles derived from that law, which wasn't well suited to dealing with problems of aridity. Under the English common law riparian doctrine, the primary right to the use of water in a stream belonged to whose land bordered on those waters. The right to use of water in the English system was not appurtenant to the land, but was part and parcel of it and could not be transferred independently of ownership of the land.

By denying the transferability of water rights, the English riparian doctrine vested in the owners of lands adjacent to natural watercourses in California an advantage that others, whose lands did not adjoin natural streams, could not enjoy. Landowners without direct access to water could take water from elsewhere, but these appropriative rights were always subordinate to the riparian doctrine. Those reliant upon an appropriative right ran the ongoing risk of have their investments invalidated at any moment by an assertion of the superior rights of a riparian owner. Another problem was that the rights of the riparian owner remained superior and inviolate regardless of whether that owner made any use of the water to which he or she was entitled.

English riparian rights also held that a riparian's legal right was coequal with other riparian rights owners along a given stream, which put the rights regime at considerable odds with what was happening at the time in the California goldfields, where access to water meant immediate access to wealth. In the goldfields a different kind of law emerged, based on an appropriation doctrine that was accepted into legal practice and endorsed by the California Supreme Court in 1855. This doctrine decreed that the prime water right belonged to the first person using the flow of the stream for as long as its use was deemed to be beneficial. The prior appropriation right did not require that the user own the land bordering a watercourse. It also permitted diversion of water from streams and rivers and the use of that water consumptively for mining, irrigation or other reasonable purposes even if that use resulted in reduced stream flows. In addition – and perhaps most importantly – the prior appropriation right was deemed personal property, which meant that the right could be sold without selling the land.

A landmark court decision in 1886 left California with new state water legislation consisting of elements of both riparian and prior appropriation systems. The court affirmed that the English riparian principle that had been adopted by the California legislature in 1850 inhered in the case of all public lands when those lands were passed into private hands. The law also decreed that an appropriator could possess a superior right to a riparian if he had begun utilizing water before acquiring his property. In other words, both systems continued to exist side by side, with the timing of use being the criterion for resolving conflicts over who got water first.

It was soon seen that by tying water use directly to ownership of the lands immediately adjacent to the supply, the English riparian doctrine would only allow the state's development to follow the natural courses of rivers and streams. It was quickly observed that communities located along major rivers in the interior of the state possessed a legal and natural advantage favouring ongoing development that California's two biggest cities – Los Angeles and San Francisco – did not enjoy. San Francisco overcame this disadvantage by obtaining a federal grant that allowed the city permanent access to a water supply lying within the public domain in the Hetch-Hetchy Canyon in the Sierra Mountains adjacent to what is now Yosemite National Park. Los Angeles overcame the limits of the English riparian doctrine by quietly buying up land in the Owens Valley and appropriating the valley's water resources for downstream use in the city. Both approaches resulted in considerable conflict over the effects of urban growth on surrounding regions and on the supply of water that would remain available to outlying regions after the state's two biggest cities got what they wanted.

As water scholar Norris Hundley has noted, the development of this hybrid system of water rights meant that California, from its inception as a state, had adopted two contradictory systems of water law that reflected conflicting economic interests and environmental realities.[16] In terms of water policy, California is still wrestling with those deeply ingrained contradictions in law and precedent to this day.

As it was already an institution in most western US states, the prior appropriation doctrine was immediately adopted by irrigators who came to the Canadian West after the first transcontinental railway was completed in 1885. The "first in time, first in right" doctrine decrees that senior licence holders in southern Alberta have first right to all the water they want, even in a drought, and for whatever agricultural purposes they desire, even if it means denying junior licence holders, including other farmers and municipalities, the drinking water they need for survival. Huge licences were granted to early irrigation districts long before anyone in government could begin to imagine the explosive growth that would occur a century later in the Canadian West. The City of Calgary also got one of those big early licences.

Now, according to many observers, the irrigation community and the City of Calgary want to corral the province's public water resources solely in their own interests. They want to keep their huge, historic, often unused, water allocations even if it means that other parts of province will be forced as a result to accept limits on economic and social development brought about by water scarcity. The City of Calgary and the larger irrigation districts also want the right to sell for profit the water that has been granted to them out of the public domain. In some ways it is California all over again in terms of cities competing with agriculture for water.

In another sense, what is happening in southern Alberta symbolizes a serious global situation in which cities and agriculture are beginning to compete with one another and with nature for increasingly scarce and precious water resources. Though few are prepared to admit it publicly, there is a gunfight brewing around the water corral. Both situations deserve consideration. We will look first at how cities argue their way into control of regional water resources. Then we will explore how agriculture has corralled 70 per cent of southern Alberta's water supply for its own use and why it refuses to give up a drop of that supply without compensation.

Troubling comparisons: Los Angeles and Calgary

Both Los Angeles and Calgary rely on what would naturally be very limited water supplies. Los Angeles, however, was a hundred years ahead of Calgary in realizing this. In 1900 Los Angeles was already having trouble providing enough water to accommodate rapid growth. By 1902 the city already understood the value of water metering, something the City of Calgary was only just beginning to appreciate 110 years later. The new Los Angeles metering system that accompanied the decision to take public control of the water system cut per capita water consumption by one-third in only two years. But that was still not enough. LA just kept on growing, right up to the limits of every water conservation innovation. Driven relentlessly by the growth imperative, Los Angeles simply kept pushing the limits of its water supply until costly and impractical options became a necessity.

The desire for more water for the city led, as it so often does, to competing and then conflicting public interests. The directors of the city's Department of Water & Power, chaired by the legendary William Mulholland,[17] quietly began looking to other regions of California to find additional sources of supply. Though the United States Reclamation Service had already identified the water-abundant Owens Valley as an ideal area for further irrigation development, Mulholland and his colleagues had other plans. In 1903 the City of Los Angeles affirmed that the desire to realize further growth expectations was a reasonable rationale for appropriation of water supplies in the Owens Valley by way of a 235-mile-long canal that would bring water "ample for all the needs of the City and its suburbs for all time to come."[18] Observers since have commented on how little it actually took politically to get a large, expensive proposition like the Owens Valley aqueduct to succeed.

The Owens Valley example demonstrates that in controversies over the supply of water to thirsty cities, public institutions and agencies can end up undermining the very purposes they were created for. Much subterfuge was employed in separating the people of the Owens Valley from their water rights. Bitter jurisdictional jealousies between federal departments emerged and were exploited by both sides in what had become open war. It soon became evident that the irrigation lobby wasn't above hardball politics, either. Strong positions and bitter rhetoric became the foundation of the industry's public relations and national image.

The City of Los Angeles demonstrated how an urban area can create its own water crisis and then bully its way out of it. In 1905, the year Alberta became a province, Los Angeles was forced to annex the San Fernando Valley so as to increase the city's asset valuation enough to be able to legally float a bond issue large enough to pay for the completion of the aqueduct. As it didn't as yet actually require the Owens Valley water when it arrived, the City moved to immediate full use by irrigators in surrounding rural districts as a means of bringing their municipalities under urban control. Little thought was given to anything but growth.

In an engineering report published in 1911, it was estimated that upon completion the Owens Valley aqueduct would provide the city with eight times as much water as it could immediately consume, and four times as much as it would need once all the lands within its limits were fully developed. It was estimated that the resulting surplus, even at full buildout of the city, would be enough to irrigate 135,000 acres of land each year. A policy was established that water would not be supplied to those areas outside the city, however, unless there was a "reasonable assurance" of ultimate annexation. After an opposition referendum failed, Los Angeles – in a stunning sleight of political hand – was able to expand, five times, by making annexation a condition of water service.

As the Owens Valley shrank and Los Angeles grew, so grew the bitterness over the appropriation. To counter growing outrage in the rest of California, the City of Los Angeles mounted a public relations campaign that claimed that the theft of their water was actually going to improve the lives of the residents of the Owens Valley. In the end, LA got its water and the Owens Valley became an arid plain. This did not come about without a cost, however. Los Angeles was widely seen as "simply a huge corporation . . . [whose] citizens are stockholders and [whose] purpose is not to promote the well-being of the community and to conserve the interests of the people as a whole."[19]

The story of LA's thirst does not end there, of course. By 1920 the city discovered that, all the optimistic water supply projections aside, population projection made water needs more than double the anticipated amount. Much was also made of the fact that the system would be particularly vulnerable to the sudden appearance of drought as the population continued to increase. Once again Los Angeles went looking toward the mountains for additional sources of supply.

By 1921 the City was becoming embroiled in yet another bitter controversy, this time over its plan utilize the Mono Lake basin for power generation. This could not legally be accomplished, however, without the agreement of local irrigators who would be affected by construction of a dam and reservoir, which led to vicious arguments pitting irrigation water use inefficiencies against the efficiency of power production. When the City began buying up land and water rights to get rid of the irrigators, things got nasty. In the midst of all this unhappiness, the unthinkable happened. There were five years of drought. By 1923 water supply to the City of Los Angeles fell to 56 per cent of normal flows and stayed that way. By 1926 Los Angeles had started jettisoning annexation plans, stopped watering alfalfa crops and expanded its reservoir storage capacity. It then began to eye the distant Colorado River as an additional source of supply. The argument was made to the federal government that without more water, the City of Los Angeles would decline.

The efficiency of irrigation was once again called into question. Then the City decided to pump both groundwater and surface water out of the Owens Valley, threatening what was left of the valley's agriculture in support of further urban growth. In the end, however, the remaining ranchers in the Owens Valley could not prevent their groundwater from being taken from them, because President Theodore Roosevelt, 20 years earlier, had decreed that the greater public good would be served by Los Angeles having their water.

An argument was put forward that Los Angeles should just pay the upstream towns and locals for their losses and take the water instead of atomizing communities and taking water piece-meal, but the City didn't think it needed to compensate a dying valley. The City simply dismissed Owens Valley antagonism and mocked local opposition. The drought, however, persisted and groundwater levels, even in the Owens Valley, began to drop. It wasn't long before the cost of pumping the water was greater than the value of the uses to which it could be put, even in Los Angeles.

Just before Teddy Roosevelt left office he gave a final communication to Congress in which he expressed grave concerns about the impacts of big corporations, national labour unions and growing urban centres on the American way of life. "Every new social relation," he wrote, "begets a new kind of wrongdoing – of sin to use an old-fashioned word – and many years always elapse before society is able to turn this sin into a crime which can be effectively punished."[20] He might have been speaking specifically about Los Angeles.

After the drought of the mid-1920s had passed, a movement emerged to prevent other cities in California and in the rest of the United States from doing what Los Angeles had done. The Owens Valley example put into relief the tension between public and private water and power interests as well as the need to reform the state's outmoded water laws. It has taken more than 80 years for legislation in California to catch up with the water resources management activities of Los Angeles and to finally constrain the city's strident self-interest.

The similarities between Calgary and Los Angeles are of precautionary value. In many ways Calgary is where Los Angeles was in the 1920s in terms of its relative development. Instead of having an expensive and bitterly contested aqueduct from the Owens Valley, however, it has a huge senior water licence that gives it priority access to far more water than it deserves or needs. The Los Angeles example warns that having more water than you can use at the expense of surrounding areas invariably causes problems and leads to challenges and conflict. Control over such a volume of water is the result of a combination of historical accident and a water policy created in the 19th century that will not address the 21st-century problems Alberta has begun to face.

In Los Angeles and in Calgary we are at last confronting the limits of how much water we have, and this threatens the status quo in profound ways. At the moment, the panic politics that so characterized much of the water resources management history of the City of Los Angeles doesn't play well in Calgary. Calgary's waterworks, by Canadian standards, are well run. But this does not mean that there aren't political concerns about the city's agenda with respect to using its huge water licence as a hammer to solidify regional power.

According to a technical study on water and wastewater servicing in the Calgary region undertaken by the Calgary Regional Partnership in 2007, under existing use regimes, the communities of High River and Strathmore will exceed the limits of water use prescribed under current licences in 2012. The town of Turner Valley will reach its licence limit in 2016, Black Diamond in 2020, Cochrane in 2022, Nanton in 2025 and Canmore in 2028. The report noted that the community of Redwood Meadows, near Bragg Creek, reached the limits of its water licence allocation in 2006.

Serious questions are being asked in rural communities surrounding Calgary about just how it is that Calgary should have such a huge water licence when water is already becoming scarce in surrounding areas. Concerns are being expressed about the City's obvious plan to use its large licence as a means of pressuring water-scarce rural communities in the direction of annexation as a condition of providing supplementary water supplies. It many ways it is Los Angeles all over again, except that the Owens Valley aqueduct Calgary possesses is only an imaginary one. Calgary's abundance of water is only real on paper. It is nothing more than a licence.

How long Calgary can convince its neighbours that its huge supply is anything more than imaginary remains to be seen. Some communities are already arguing they are not prepared to play Calgary's water and power game. As was the case with the state government as Los Angeles bullied its way into possession of all the water it needed, the Alberta provincial government is, at the time of this writing at least, staying out of the fray. In the competition between public interests, economic growth often wins.

As LA discovered, however, winning a regional water war can be a hollow victory if it involves a fundamental shift in the relationship between a city and its surroundings. Over time, the City of Los Angeles was forced to change its approach to how it assured water supply to its four million citizens. In May of 2008, Mayor Antonio Villaraigosa announced a new strategy creating sustainable sources of water supply for the city. The plan involved a multi-pronged approach that includes investment in state-of-the-art technology; a combination of rebates and water conservation incentives; the installation of smart sprinklers, efficient washers and urinals; and long-term measures such as the expansion of water recycling and investment in cleaning up the local groundwater supply. The premise of this plan was that the City of Los Angeles will meet all new water demands – which were estimated to be about 100,000 acre-feet a year – through a combination of water conservation and recycling. Mayor Villaraigosa projected that by 2019 half of all the demand for additional water supplies will be met by a six-fold increase in recycled water supplies and that by 2030 the other half of the demand will be met through ramped-up conservation efforts.[21]

Many highly credible critics have argued that Calgary could live almost indefinitely within the small portion of its bloated water licence it currently uses if it did more to encourage its citizens and businesses to conserve. Though the city's water department is working hard to curtail per capita water use, Calgary remains adamant that it does not want to give up any of its water. It has built a corral around its water hole and will do whatever is legally possible to defend it. So too has southern Alberta's other big water user – the irrigation community. The irrigation districts don't rely on a corral to keep others from threatening their water rights. They keep their water in reservoirs and canals where it can be carefully watched. And watch it they do.

Questioning tired assumptions and old laws: prior appropriation and agriculture's right to water

Though many irrigators will argue that they own the water they use, irrigation water is still just paper water to the extent that it is a public resource to which farmers and ranchers have been granted access through a legally binding licensing process. This process was based on the 19th-century legal doctrine of first in time, first in right, or FITFIR as it is known in the water resources community. The running joke now is whether FITFIR is still "fit fer" the 21st century.

Irrigators are right to complain that urbanites do not understand how their food is grown or where it comes from. Nor does the average city slicker appreciate why agriculture requires a lot of water. There is a good reason why this is so. It all has to do with the process of photosynthesis. The water vapour pressure gradient between the interior of a leaf and the atmosphere is such that for every molecule of CO_2 taken up in photosynthesis, between 50 and 100 molecules of H_2O are lost. Thus the use of large amounts of water by crops is dictated by the evaporative demand of the environment and is tightly associated with biomass production and yield. This is why the production of food requires large volumes of water, as indicated by the well-known fact that 70 per cent of all the water diverted by our civilization is used in agriculture.

Irrigators in Alberta also get upset when their contribution to the development of the agricultural promise of the southern part of the province is not recognized. They have a point here too. Without the enhanced productivity brought about by irrigation technology, southern Alberta would not be nearly as prosperous as it is. Cities like Lethbridge and Medicine Hat would not exist and there would be no universities, colleges and shopping malls there. All that would exist would be dryland plains.

The myth of the good farmer and the role of agriculture in the development of the West is so deeply ingrained in the Alberta psyche that to publicly question anything to do with this economic sector is held to be an affront bordering on high treason. But when compared to what is going on in this same sector elsewhere in the world, one has to question some of the directions in which we are going, especially when we appear to be heading blindly into terrain determined to be dangerous by those who have preceded us into it though longer agricultural association with the landscapes in which they live.

The first lesson we might derive from international examples is that public policy in Canada would be wise to move toward supplying adequate water to nature as well as to people before overallocation for human purposes makes it difficult to do so. Another perspective that emerges from international examples is that it is very difficult for those claiming to be leaders in the management of water resources when allocation of some of the rivers upon which they depend has reached 118 per cent of the water that is typically available. It is also hard to claim leadership when, even after decades of trying, no agreement has been reached on what constitutes the minimum amount of water nature requires to sustain in-stream flow needs

While it will hardly endear me to the irrigation communities of either Alberta or Saskatchewan for saying so, the agricultural sector could be seen as one of the country's least sustainable water users if their use is examined in the context of the long-term health of the river systems in which irrigation agriculture is so intensely practised. While irrigation farming is far more efficient in terms of production per unit area than dryland farming, I question how this form of agriculture can be said to be sustainable in the long term when the accounting includes the demands this type of farming makes on surrounding biodiversity-based ecosystem function – which humans ultimately depend upon every bit as much as they depend on their food supply. I question whether the southern Alberta irrigation community should be claiming to be leaders globally when, because of the extent of their water withdrawals, irrigation appears to responsible for an average decline of some 30 per cent in the flows of the South Saskatchewan River over the period since flows have been measured in this system.

Can the irrigation community make the claim that it is managing southern Alberta's rivers in a superior manner when 50 per cent of the wetlands in the basin in which they practise this form of intensive agriculture have been drained and when 31 or 33 reaches of the South Saskatchewan River are listed as moderately to heavily impacted or degraded because of nutrient and pesticide loading that are the direct impacts of non-sustainable agricultural practices? Can the irrigation community truly be a superior steward of our western Canadian water resources when the entire water management system in southern Alberta is tied first and foremost to agricultural production that defines aquatic ecosystem health in terms of how much biodiversity exists in and around its storage reservoirs rather than in the streams and rivers from which it diverts for its own purposes 70 per cent of licensed allocation? Should the irrigation community be pronouncing itself a world leader in water management when scientists are pointing to the fact that the health of the entire South Saskatchewan River is in persistent long-term decline and will remain so until agricultural practices with respect to the management of water improve significantly?

In Alberta the irrigation community has aggressively acted to prevent questions such as these from being asked with any seriousness by stressing its own efforts to increase water productivity as measured by such standards as "crop per drop" and "cash per drop," which reinforce the notion of responsible farm families practising the highest level of land stewardship. But productivity is not the issue here; we're talking about environmental impacts. While it would almost be unpatriotic to suggest that agriculture isn't committed to the highest standards of stewardship, the fact remains that prairie irrigators measure their success by self-serving productivity standards that do not adequately account for the impacts this water-intensive form of agriculture has on the production of goods and services of equal long-term value that are no longer functioning for want of water or because too much of the water that is returned to nature after being used by agriculture is of poor quality or has been contaminated to such an extent that it can no longer contribute in the way it once did to enhancing aquatic or terrestrial ecosystem vitality. You can arrive at unsustainable agriculture and agree to live with it as such, but this should be a decision you make rather than a condition you simply accept.

Whenever such issues are brought up in any kind of forum the automatic public relations response of the irrigation community is to loudly protest that any criticism of agriculture is an attack on the history, heritage and economic foundation of the Canadian West. The irrigation community's public relations strategy is to dismiss the first hint of criticism by claiming that anyone who would question irrigation agriculture practices is "just another ungrateful urban dope who doesn't know or appreciate where their food comes from."

At present the irrigation community will not countenance outside claims that water for agriculture is not being managed in anything but the most progressive way. In the context of traditional "water resource development" ideology they have a point. Unfortunately, the focus of traditional "water resource development" has been proved to be non-sustainable in the global context. At the moment at least, the irrigation community in southern Alberta appears unwilling to accept that. Instead they are standing fiercely by legal interpretations of an outmoded and what many perceive as an unfair first-in-time, first-in-right licensing system that grants them all the water they want first, even in a drought, and permits them to use that water for any purpose they desire, even if it means legally denying towns and cities around them the drinking water they need for survival. No one doubts that in the great tradition of the frontier West, at least some of them will bring out their guns the moment the equity, practicality and sustainability of those antiquated water rights are challenged.

Such responses do much to ensure that important questions don't get asked – and that the true value of agriculture to our future may never be realized or understood until it is too late to achieve that potential because of our failure to address the need to improve agricultural practices.

The questions that are not presently being asked are crucial to our future. What happens if our agricultural practices are in fact compromising and degrading our system's overall capacity to supply a broader range of biodiversity-based ecosystem services that are just as important to our sustainability as a society over time as food production is? What if it is true that we have to share more water with nature if we are going to be able to ensure other forms of ecosystem services delivery which we depend on for our well-being? If we really do need more water for nature – and clear evidence exists widely elsewhere in the world to suggest we do – how are we going to get the irrigation community and neighbouring cities to give that water up?

We have to go elsewhere to find out how these questions have been answered in situations similar to ours. For purposes of comparison we will go to two places that have relied for a very long time on irrigation and where efforts have been made over centuries to address some of the problems agriculture now faces in Canada. We will go first to the water-scarce Middle East and then to Spain.

PART 2: HERDING SOME SACRED COWS

Shawki Barghouti: Corral irrigation, not water

Shawki Barghouti knows a great deal about irrigation agriculture. As director general of the International Centre for Biosaline Agriculture and a member of the Arab Water Academy in the United Arab Emirates, Dr. Barghouti is considered a world expert on productivity challenges facing agricultural development. He is very concerned about the global food and water crisis.

In a paper entitled "Water Productivity: Challenges Facing Agricultural Development"[22] presented to the 2008 Rosenberg

International Forum on Water Policy in his absence, Dr. Barghouti observed that a slowing of yield growth in Asia was due to a reduction in investment in infrastructure and research, a shift toward more profitable crops, the reaching of productivity limits made possible by application of fertilizers and pesticides, resource and environmental limitations, and constraints imposed on further agricultural productivity by ineffective or inappropriate public policy.

He went on to point out that less-regulated trading regimes and declining water supplies in many regions of the world could make grain imports more attractive than local production. He pointed out that, on the other hand, upward trends in grain prices could have the opposite effect. Public investment in agriculture, even in water-scarce areas, could grow as the pressure to provide affordable wheat and rice to millions of poor households in places like South and East Asia increases. Dr. Barghouti also noted that subsidies aimed at diverting more crops to biofuel production could also have a significant impact on attitudes toward the need to achieve greater national food supply security worldwide.

Dr. Barghouti went on to confirm what Uriel Safriel, Pete Loucks, Malin Falkenmark and Margaret Catley-Carlson said about the growing threat beginning to be posed by unsustainable agricultural practices in terms of their impact on the global natural resource base. Barghouti then pointed to the fact that approximately 16 per cent of agricultural soils currently are degraded, with significant impacts on food production, rural incomes and national economies. He noted that the potential for expanding the extent of global cultivated land is nearly exhausted, demanding that available water resources be used more efficiently, especially given that global fish stocks are also in decline. After claiming that agriculture was the planet's greatest user and abuser of our natural resource base, Barghouti underscored his point that agriculture has reached the limits of available natural resources, by illustrating declining per capita water availability worldwide.

Barghouti's central point is that measuring the productivity of the water sector in relation only to its short-term contribution to economic growth and national food security is different from measuring water productivity in real terms at the field level. We may increase water productivity at the field level through improvement of on-farm water management, better crop husbandry and advances in irrigation technology, but these measures are meaningless if they do not take into account the adverse impacts these approaches may have on water quality or the degradation of aquatic ecosystems. This is of considerable importance, not just in the Middle East but in Canada as well.

Barghouti is concerned that when we talk about water conservation in agriculture we may be deluding ourselves. Barghouti does not believe we are talking about actual water conservation in agriculture if water freed up through conservation measures is not contributed directly to the provision of environmental services. In other words, freeing up water through improved efficiency and then simply committing it to further agricultural expansion is not water conservation, because even though it may contribute in the short term to economic growth or national food security, it continues to rob biodiversity-based ecosystem functions of the water needed to supply services that will ultimately prove to be every bit as valuable and important to people as food production.

Barghouti notes that we are already at the limits of water availability in many parts of the world. He also observes that we are heading for declines in food production in many places. For this reason, many countries are exploring non-conventional sources of water. These include deep water aquifers, which can only be exploited at high pumping and transportation costs, and investment in seawater desalination. Barghouti mirrored the views of many others in suggesting that pressure to reallocate water among various users is likely to intensify worldwide in the next decade. He then pointed out that since agriculture is the main user of scarce water resources, pressure is mounting in places like the United States, the Middle East, North Africa and South Asia to reconsider how much water should justifiably go to agriculture.

Around the world, formal justification of water allocation has increasingly been pressed to include expanded consideration of the needs of increasing urban populations and new industries. In addition it is gradually being accepted that more water globally has to be allocated to address serious impacts on ecosystem service provision caused by short-sighted investments in previous years in water management regimes that ignored the need to allocate water for environmental protection. Barghouti then committed what would be a grievous heresy in southern Alberta. He observed that an important question is being asked more and more frequently around the world, and then he asked it: Does agriculture do enough for the economy and are its impacts on surrounding environments neutral enough to justify agriculture's disproportionate water allocation?

The fact that the intensive forms of agriculture we have been practising in Canada are not practically or environmentally sustainable has escaped broader public notice in Canada for generations. Now that water has become scarce on the Canadian prairies, however, agricultural water use will not escape the attention of a growing urban population. Our society is no longer in thrall to the myth of the family farm and farmers committed from birth to the best thing for the preservation of the land at all costs. In the public imagination, agriculture is on the way to being viewed as just one more industry, with its ultimate motives and impacts no less suspect than those of the oil patch. While the agriculture industry's confidence in its own public relations remains high, it will be increasingly difficult for agriculture to prevent long-established myths from coming under closer scrutiny once public attention is focused on the growing global and national environmental impacts that are being caused by non-sustainable agricultural practices.

The public is unlikely to know whom to believe or what public policy direction should be followed when it becomes clear that agricultural allocations are robbing nature of the water it needs to do things for us and for the world that may ultimately be as important in the long term as agricultural production is in the short term. At the moment it appears likely that, initially at least, agricultural will not stand for any suggestion that it lacks sustainability. But on the other hand, neither will it, as an industry, be willing to grant more water for nature when there are so many people who rely on agriculture for their livelihood and so many people who need to be fed.

There are a great many people who believe the marketplace will take care of this problem. Returning to Shawki Barghouti, we are offered a glimpse of how market forces have already begun to dramatically influence attitudes toward common pool resources. In his paper, Dr. Barghouti cited a recent study conducted by the Asian Development Bank that estimated that the average price charged to urban customers by water utilities in 38 large Asian cities rose 88 per cent in the four years between 1993 and 1997. While it would be interesting to know what has happened since, Barghouti's point is very clear: water supply in urban areas in many parts of the world is becoming more expensive to assure. The reasons for this include higher costs to develop more distant sources; more complex and therefore more expensive source development; greater need for higher-cost treatment facilities; and the lack of flexibility of other users of low-cost water. In mentioning the lack of flexibility of other users of low-cost water, Barghouti was talking about irrigation farmers.

This general lack of flexibility within the global irrigation agriculture community with respect to the sharing of low-cost water with cities should be of interest to policy-makers in Alberta, especially given that the province's two major cities may be facing challenges – in the one case, how much water they are entitled to, and in the other, how much will be available for future growth and development. As in much of Asia, Alberta too has an irrigation constituency. And this constituency has not only strong views about the primacy of agriculture, but powerful political connections it is quite willing to call upon the moment challenges to historical water rights emerge. One wonders, however, what would happen if the unit cost of water in Alberta's cities were to double or triple because of the need to expand supplies, as has happened in increasingly water-scarce parts of Asia. Could irrigators continue to assert their claims with the same effect in the court of public opinion as they have in the past? Maybe. Maybe not.

Barghouti cites a World Bank Evaluation Group Study in 2006 which, in combination with studies by the UN's Food & Agriculture Organization and others, provides interesting insight into irrigation investment. The report reviewed irrigation investment between 1994 and 2004 and found that the average cost of irrigating one hectare of land during the period 1967 to 2003 was about US$5,021, ranging from $6,590 for new construction to $2,882 for rehabilitation. Not surprisingly, the study also noted there were significant diseconomies of scale as projects got smaller. In sub-Saharan Africa, where farms are small, the cost of new irrigation developments rose to between $6,500 and $8,500 per hectare. Barghouti noted that in Africa the cost/benefit of irrigated crops, especially low-value coarse grains such as sorghum and millet and even corn, would not justify costly investment in irrigation in today's real markets. The cost/benefit of irrigation investment might, of course, completely change with the current trend toward rising food prices. But even as that happens the rising value of water for purposes other than agriculture will continue to call into question whether such large allocations to growers can be justified economically.

A recent review by the World Bank concluded that the price change for municipal water supply was, on average, about 35 per cent of the actual cost of supply, and that charges for water in many irrigation districts were even lower. The impacts of cheap water supply to irrigation, Dr. Barghouti pointed out, could no longer be ignored. Irrigation productivity rose dramatically over the past 40 years as a result of the Green Revolution. But even if we disregard the environmental impacts caused by that revolution, we are no closer to achieving global food security than we were 40 years ago, because every time we come close to filling the food production gap, population growth and ecosystem decline associated with water diversions to human purposes set us back again. Barghouti pointed to analyses that suggest that another 29 per cent increase in irrigation area will be needed by 2025 to meet the United Nations Millennium Goals for hunger reduction. Meanwhile, the environmental community, which is concerned about larger ecosystem function, would like to see irrigation decrease by 8 per cent during the same period to reduce damage to natural ecosystem productivity.

These observations lead to a number of questions we should be asking ourselves in Canada and especially Alberta. What would the doubling of the unit cost of water do to agriculture on the Canadian prairies? What crops would you grow if the cost of water were to double?

After the initial smoke cleared, the agricultural community on the Canadian prairies would likely react to these questions with a great deal of soul-searching over the ultimate value of the uses water is presently allocated for. As Shawki Barghouti points out, humans on average eat some 70 times more water than we drink. Food production is important not only in the context of nutrition but also in the context of hydration.

The grim fact remains that we may be facing widespread global famine even before we deal with the challenge of allocating more water from agriculture to nature. As Dr. Barghouti pointed out, the challenge to agricultural productivity is no more starkly evident than in the fact that the world's aggregate land area available for food production was 0.44 hectares per person in 1961 and is projected to decline to 0.15 ha per person by 2050, a two-thirds reduction. Per capita food production per hectare must increase commensurately if we are to avoid mass famine among the rapidly growing populations of the developing world.

We are already putting a great deal of faith globally in an already stressed and demonstrably non-sustainable agriculture. Add the requirement of having to free up water for nature and what you end up with is a toss-up between equally undesirable alternatives. Either you do everything you can to produce enough food to feed our teeming populations and risk bringing down the "natural" productivity that provides the stability and resilience upon which we depend for our long-term survival; or we give water to nature at the risk of condemning hundreds of millions of people to death by starvation.

Shawki Barghouti would argue that we have a few more cards to play before we are faced with such a terrible choice. In the Middle East the new paradigm for increasing water productivity revolves around the capacity to use water of marginal quality for food production. Barghouti puts forward that in most countries drinking water supplies in cities and towns account for only 10 per cent to 15 per cent of all water consumption. In contrast to agriculture, where consumptive losses in the form of evapotrans-piration and losses to non-recoverable sinks average around 50 per cent at the field level, municipalities generally only consume 10 to 20 per cent of their water. This, Barghouti suggests, means that 80 to 90 per cent of municipal wastewater either becomes a disposal problem or is available for reuse, nominally for agriculture.

At present only about 2 per cent of current water use, in the Middle East at least, comes from treated wastewater, while some 50 per cent of municipal water is released untreated. Barghouti believes that municipal wastewater could become an important water resource in the Gulf State region if economically efficient and environmentally safe ways are found to reuse it. But this of course is not without its own problems. While the notion of water reuse has been touted so widely for so long that it is beginning to sound like conventional wisdom, it may not be wise at all, especially given the growing global problem that has emerged around food quality assurance. Concerns have also been widely expressed over the potential impacts of wastewater contaminants on soil structure and water infiltration, as well as on salinity and groundwater quality.

Dr. Barghouti's Zaragoza paper concluded with observations on the importance of decentralizing the management of water down to the basin and community level, a subject that proved near and dear to the hearts of leaders in Spain, who were in the throes of a decades-long reformation of their nation's water and agricultural policies.

Part 3: Water Teachings from Europe

Iberian suite: A very long road toward change

We tend to look to California and Australia as the places we should emulate in the development of water policy with respect to agriculture in western Canada. I have discovered, however, that what is presently happening in Spain is perhaps even more instructive for Canadians than what is happening in either California or Australia.

In Spain – as in many other parts of the world – tensions are rising over how water should be managed to ensure there is enough available to produce food, meet growing urban needs and ensure that adequate supplies of high enough quality water are available to perpetuate essential natural ecosystem function. These growing tensions have led to dramatically increased public pressure to find ways to free up water currently perceived to be used for low-productivity purposes by the agricultural sector so it can be used in other functions, including ecosystem protection, without at the same time severely damaging food production capacity and rural livelihoods.

Since such tensions are likely to become universal as human populations grow and water scarcity becomes a greater problem worldwide, public policy lessons Spain can offer may be of great value to nations and regions that presently face or will soon face similar public policy choices. What Spain teaches others is that it is possible to downscale the global principles of sustainable water and agricultural policy to address regional water management practices. As the Spanish example indicates, you may not get what you want at first, but with persistence it can be done.

Introduction: No rain in Spain

Long before participants from around the world departed for the 2008 Rosenberg Forum, each understood that there was probably no better place to hold high-level discussions about the relationship between water quantity and quality and food production than in Spain. In addition to possessing a large agricultural sector, Spain is a water-scarce country that has been experiencing for decades the kinds of water shortages that are only now beginning to appear in parts of Canada. As it happened, at the time of the forum Spain was also facing a particularly acute water shortage as a result of recent drought. A little over a month before the forum opened, the *New York Times* ran an article by Lisa Abend on the problems that were confronting the city of Barcelona, which at the time was facing the worst drought in a century.

According to the *Times* report, Barcelona was so short of water that it had been forced to charter ten tanker ships for a period of six months to deliver 92 million cubic metres[23] of water a month from other parts of Spain and from France to augment the city's drinking-water supply. This drastic measure was not going to be cheap. The bill for the six-month supply was expected to be in the order of us$68-million, or about $12.36 for each of the 5.5 million men, women and children that currently rely on Barcelona's water supply.

This would have been an interesting case study even if Rosenberg VI were not being held in Spain. Where water has generally been considered a free good to be reliably provided in perpetuity by nature, the people of the Province of Catalonia could no longer take water supply for granted. An invisible threshold had been crossed and there was no easy way back. Population growth, increasing withdrawals for agriculture and industry, and climate change were pushing the region's hydrology toward disequilibrium, resulting in more frequent drought and persistent water shortages. Spring rainfall in the region had been only 40 per cent of the long-term average. Reservoirs in Spain were averaging only 30 per cent full at the outset of what many expected to be a very hot summer. The reservoirs that make life possible in the crowded city of Barcelona were only 20 per cent full, making action by the government necessary to prevent full-scale emergency.

Unfortunately, however, Barcelona was not the only place facing water scarcity. Almost everyone else in the region was experiencing the same conditions. The tankers supplying Barcelona were bringing their precious cargoes from the French port of Marseille and from Tarragona and Andalusia in Spain. Farmers in those regions vigorously protested the transfers on the grounds that they simply didn't have the water to give. Farmers in the Ter area north of Barcelona had been prohibited from irrigating, so that the water they would normally use to grow crops could be diverted to the city. As a result, the Government of Spain had to compensate irrigators for the water and the crop income they had had to forgo in the interests of the City of Barcelona, adding further to the cost of supply.

This problem was not likely to go away any time soon. It is expected that climate change will likely exacerbate many of the problems that already exist in the Mediterranean region, including desertification, water scarcity and limits to food production.[24] This suggests we can expect increasing tensions over who gets water for what purpose and how much specific economic sectors will be compensated for forgoing use in periods of persistent scarcity. Water managers and policy scholars are already thinking beyond immediate tensions in southern Spain to consider what it might mean to Europe as a whole if such scarcity becomes the norm over the long term in the Mediterranean.

In 2008 farmers in Spain were compensated for not growing food so that there would be enough water for people in neighbouring cities to drink. As a consequence, food production dropped because there was not enough water for both plants and people. All evidence suggests, however, that the crisis will not stop there. This may just be the first of an eternity of increasingly thirsty Mediterranean summers. At the same time as water is becoming increasingly scarce, the populations of Spain's major cities are expected to continue to grow, creating the prospect of even more tension over water supply.

The City of Barcelona aimed to address this problem by diverting water from the Ebro, Spain's largest river. The plan has been the object of bitter political opposition, however, as adjacent regions circled their wagons in defence of their own agricultural economies and municipal interests. Underlying the debate was the clear realization that the regions with enough water will have a future, while those without will not. These realities have been defining development and limiting human settlement in the dry regions of the world for centuries, but this was the first time water scarcity on this scale had appeared on what appears to be a permanent basis in Europe. As Lisa Abend concluded in her *New York Times* article, this new level of vulnerability to water supply disruption puts into relief how much more money and political energy will have to be invested in the management of water resources in the future, not just in Spain but around the world.

If there is a lesson for Canada in this, it may be that we should

take neither water demand nor hydrological stationarity for granted. We should recognize that serious problems of water supply can
develop, even in the absence of drought, if population pressures
on limited water resources are exacerbated by climate change.
Population growth in southern Ontario will put pressure on local
water resources just as surely as it has in Spain. Global warming
could just as easily and suddenly reduce the amount of water
available on the prairies as it has in the Mediterranean region. At
a certain point, cities and agriculture can find themselves competing for limited water resources.

The Spanish example demonstrates that all of these problems
can come together quite unexpectedly within a very short period
of time. Regions that have not prepared for the sudden emergence
of such problems, or that do not have the institutions in place that
can react promptly to emergencies, will be particularly vulnerable.
Another lesson we learn from this is that institutions created in
earlier periods of history may not be prepared for the nature or
magnitude of the kinds of problems that could emerge. Drought
preparedness plans developed 20 years ago on the Canadian
prairies will not be adequate to deal with the much larger populations and greater economic activity that presently exist in the
region. Nor are attitudes and approaches that have served well
in the past guaranteed to be adequate if drought becomes a more
common and persistent feature of a warmer and more unstable
climate.

If we can learn anything from Spain it may be that we should
expect a great deal of tension between big cities and the irrigation
agriculture community if such circumstances come to be. We
might also anticipate that the cost of emergency measures could
be very high indeed – high enough, in fact, to alter the very structure of the economy around the dramatically increased value of
a resource previously held to be so common as to have almost
no value.

Spanish water and Spanish farmers: Some history

According to Dr. Alberto Garrido, of the Universidad Politécnica de Madrid, irrigation in Spain has been evolving for more than 12 centuries. Over the course of development in the past century, irrigation agriculture expansion was founded on supply-side policies that relied on the construction of large-scale publicly funded water infrastructure such as dams, reservoirs and water distribution networks. Surface water was delivered at subsidized costs, and irrigators were granted extensive water allocation concessions that in effect transferred water rights from public ownership into private hands.

In the past 50 years, however, Spain has witnessed a great number of innovations and improvements in irrigation agriculture productivity. Because of effective irrigation management during the last half century, there has been a population explosion in arid lands in Spain that would otherwise not support many people. Breakthroughs in well drilling and pumping technologies also allowed for a quiet explosion in groundwater utilization. All of these developments were encouraged through favourable domestic agricultural policies.

Following Spain's entry into the European Union in 1986, EU Common Agricultural Policy programs based on production-related subsidies further encouraged irrigation expansion. This led to positive development, particularly in economic and socially stagnated parts of Spain. Irrigation became the main driver of prosperity and helped address many of the country's endemic drought problems. Unfortunately, the focus on irrigation development also led to excessive groundwater mining and over-exploitation of the La Mancha Aquifer and subsequent degradation of important wetlands. As the situation worsened, unlicensed expanded annual water withdrawals greatly exceeded the aquifer's natural recharge rate. By 1991 the aquifer was in serious trouble.

With the aim of reversing this potentially devastating ecological damage, two new policy structures were put in place. The local Guadiana River basin authority adopted a strict water abstraction plan that imposed quotas on withdrawals which reduced entitled water volumes to irrigators by almost half. Farmers strongly opposed the restrictions. Social unrest grew until the river basin authority found itself incapable of enforcing the policy or of controlling the actions of the irrigators.

In 1993 a parallel EU Common Agricultural Policy directive emerged as a result of broader EU agricultural reform. This new program's objective was to recover the damaged Guadiana wetlands by way of compensation to irrigators that voluntarily joined the effort to maintain the thriving agricultural economy of the region. Hard pressed by a five-year drought, an overwhelming majority of the region's farmers participated in the program. Though the program was extended for five years, its high cost and low effectiveness led to its modification in 2003 when for the first time water use limitations were tied to both EU water management targets and the national Spanish Water Plan.

In the meantime, Spain committed to its own very aggressive national irrigation improvement program. Since then, modern irrigation technologies as well as better conveyance and management systems right from the reservoir to the farm gate have played a significant role in improving irrigation efficiency. At present, 35 per cent of irrigated territories in Spain still employ traditional gravity irrigation. These areas are in the relatively water abundant regions of Castilla y León and Aragón. Modern pressurized systems cover 65 per cent of the total irrigated surface of Spain. Water scarcity and the resulting need for increased precision in water application have led to the expansion of drip irrigation for high-value olive, vineyard and fruit crops, especially in the dry southern regions of the country. Some 42 per cent of the 65 per cent of irrigated farmland served by pressurized systems is under drip irrigation. This means that 27 per cent of all of the irrigated

land in Spain is presently employing highly efficient drip irrigation technology.

Coming to terms with the need to balance the environmental impacts of agriculture with economic realities has not been
easy, in Spain or anywhere else for that matter. Because of its
Mediterranean climate, Spain's water problems are particularly
acute. This is a view shared by Dr. Consuelo Varela-Ortega, also
of the Universidad Politécnica de Madrid, who explained in her
presentation that irrigated agriculture in Spain now occupies
a mere 15 per cent of all farmland but accounts for almost two-
thirds of the nation's agricultural production value and more than
80 per cent of all farm exports. Productivity of irrigated crops, as
measured by net margin per hectare on a national basis, is about
4.5 times greater than that of rain-fed crops. The value of production can be nine times higher in irrigation farming and is as much
as 20 times higher in some southern regions. This productivity,
however, does not come without costs. As in parts of Canada, irrigation agriculture in Spain consumes more than two-thirds of the
entire country's water resources. It has reshaped the Spanish landscape, which has caused considerable damage to river systems,
aquatic ecosystems and to biodiversity.

Increased environmental damage, unacceptably high water
losses in conveyance systems and increasing competition for
water resources from other sectors and from growing urban
areas made it necessary to launch an expensive nationwide irrigation modernization program in 2003. But despite huge investments in improved irrigation efficiency, Spain still does not have
any more water to spare. Moreover, actual total farm productivity has not increased. While rapid evolution of new policies have
resulted in changes in the crop types some growers now cultivate,
farmers have proven themselves unwilling to give back the water
they save so it can be used for other purposes. Water savings go
to more food production, not to nature. According to Dr. Garrido,
the non-agricultural academic community and the media have

ignored both reforms and progress toward greater agricultural efficiency at lower environmental cost and focused unfairly on the failure of the sector to deliver up water savings. As a consequence, the Spanish public sees the irrigation community in an unprogressive and negative light. With some reason, perhaps, as we shall see. But no one has given up on a better future. The Spanish lesson tells us a great deal about how persistent public policy will have to be to balance the need to grow food with the urgency of sustaining vital ecosystem function.

From the top: The European Union Common Agricultural Policy

There are two main public policy bodies that directly and indirectly affect water consumption in Spain and in other EU states. The first of these is the European Union's Common Agricultural Policy, or CAP. Through this program, initiated in the 1980s, irrigation expansion and increased water use were encouraged through higher production subsidies that were granted for irrigated crops. This plan has clear benefits for farmers but it stimulated overuse of irrigation water and undesirable impacts on aquatic and other ecosystems. As a consequence, CAP programs are progressively including new environmental regulations that support natural ecosystem protection.

The European Union Common Agricultural Policy reform of 2003, which is currently in force in all EU countries, no longer ties subsidies to farm-level agricultural productivity. Single farm payment subsidies are instead tied to a mandatory "cross compliance" scheme by which all farmers are required to comply with specific environmental and other regulations to qualify for receiving subsidies for specific crops. These regulations relate to soil-conservation tillage practices, use of fertilizers and chemicals and protection of flora and fauna. The CAP reforms also demand more efficient water management measures to protect watercourses and climate change adaptation considerations.

Recent studies have argued that while these environmentally focused programs have contributed to better enforcement of ecosystem protection regulations throughout the EU, farmers in Spain are having difficulty meeting environmental requirements. It has also been found that enforcement, control and follow-up of the many measures demanded by EU regulations entail burdensome costs for the regional administrations responsible for the implementation of these programs.

The 2005 iteration of the CAP seeks to promote nothing less than a multifunctional, environmentally oriented, sustainable agriculture. The foundation for this proposed new sustainability is the dual objective of increased agricultural production and water resources conservation on irrigated lands. The main thrust of this new policy shift is away from intensively irrigated crops such as maize and legumes toward low water consumption crops such as winter cereals. As of 2008, maize had lost its comparative advantage, as farmers producing it no long benefited from the higher yield-based subsidies that were part of previous EU Common Agricultural Policy. Low-water-demand crops such as winter cereals now enjoy an equivalent subsidy under the new CAP rules. As a result, land cropped for maize dropped by 22 per cent while the area under cultivation for winter cereals increased by 13 per cent. At the same time, there was a parallel increase in the amount of irrigated land under olives and vineyards. The expansion of these crops demonstrated that higher profits could be obtained by specialized farming that took full advantage of modern drip irrigation and market opportunities to reduce demands on water resources. In actual fact, however, reductions in water use were small if they occurred at all.

The extent to which crop changes in Spain actually translated into a reduction in the area of irrigated lands and water use remains unclear. What is clear is that the water savings brought about through change in Common Agricultural Policy subsidies were not returned to nature or to river basin authorities for allocation to other users. Instead, the water savings were invested in increases in the area of irrigated lands that could be cultivated in high-value olives, vineyard and other products. In other words, actual water savings didn't materialize, because water meant to be conserved through subsidies paid to farmers is simply being used to grow more crops. In the eyes of many observers, Spanish farmers managed to get their cake and eat it, too.

Despite the imposition of more environmental considerations, the principal goals of the EU Common Agricultural Program remain at odds with another European Union policy directive that seeks to measurably improve water quality in river basins in member states.

This policy structure, which is the second major public policy structure that influences Spanish water use, is the European Union Water Framework Directive, or WFD. Among other things, the WFD employs water demand instruments and water pricing schemes to attain full cost recovery for all water services. If fully implemented, the WFD will have enormous impacts on irrigation agriculture in Spain and elsewhere. It could even inspire changes in the way we do things in Canada.

The European Union Water Framework Directive

Possibly the single most important environmental legislation created since the inception of the European Union, the Water Framework Directive was enacted in 2000 with the goal of full member state implementation by 2012. The WFD is part of a wider public policy framework that has inspired the creation of the EU Sustainable Development Strategy, which aims to promote a sustainable link between economic growth and the protection of natural ecosystem function and productivity.

The key objective of the Water Framework Directive is to achieve good ecological status of all water bodies in the European Union by 2010 and to promote sustainable water use over the long term.

To these ends, the EU established that each member state should carry out for all its river basins the following research:

- analysis of each basin's characteristics
- a review of the current and projected impacts of all human activities on the status of surface and on groundwater
- a thorough economic analysis of water use

These requirements resulted in the completion of massive studies for each country in the European Union. Though some regional governments in Spain – including Catalonia – opted to exempt the farming sector from higher water tariffs demanded by the EU Water Framework Directive, every part of the country was subject to a thorough re-examination of the state of its water resources. This resulted in a complete overhaul of the inherited criteria by which all water monitoring was conducted and how data were recorded, interpreted and shared – something that desperately needed to be done in Spain and but also needs to be done in Canada if we are to aspire to more holistic management our of water resources.

The EU Water Framework Directive calls for more efficient use of water resources. To achieve this, the framework calls for the application of economic instruments such as higher water tariffs to recover the costs of water services, including environmental, as well as resource costs in accordance with the "polluter pays" principle. The WFD also demands that water pricing policies must recognize the specific climatic and geographical circumstances and be respectful of the social, economic and environmental impacts of each EU region. In Spain it is not yet clear how principles of cost recovery will finally be applied.

It is widely held that in some parts of Spain at least, water consumption is not expected to decrease sharply when the cost of water increases to full cost recovery levels, because of inelastic demand related to already existing water scarcity due to climate conditions. It has been calculated by Consuelo Varela-Ortega and others that if the WFD is applied to the full cost recovery of water in Spain, farm incomes will be reduced twofold in most of the river basins in which irrigation utilizes surface water without supplemental groundwater availability. Economic and social devastation in these areas will lead to irrigation abandonment and social conflict. Some places will be hit particularly hard. According to Dr. Varela-Ortega, the full implementation of the EU Water Framework Directive will have especially devastating social and economic impacts on irrigation farms in Spain's less fertile inland regions. In other words, it will be farms on marginal lands that will be economically hurt.

Full implementation of the WFD will also impact irrigators who enjoy the benefit of groundwater use. Groundwater irrigators already incur the full costs of irrigation operations. If, for example, irrigators utilizing the Western La Mancha Aquifer were in fact required to recover environmental costs related to maintaining aquifer sustainability, tariffs would have to increase to the €0.54 per cubic metre of withdrawal calculated to be necessary to stimulate the 30 per cent reduction in withdrawals presently required to enable recharge of the aquifer. This would reduce farm incomes in this area by 20 per cent unless farmers were able to change their crop types.

This is not how others see it. The EU argues that social, environmental and economic impacts can be reduced to tolerable levels if farmers on marginal agricultural lands invest in modern irrigation technologies and cultivate market-oriented, high-value-added crops such as vegetables and vineyard products. It has also been put forward that if farmers adjust their cropping mix to reduce water consumption, it will be possible to attain aquifer recharge targets that comply with Water Framework Directive requirements at tolerable social cost. Efforts are being made to move in exactly this direction, but there remains a great deal of tension and doubt surrounding the achievability of these goals.

A microcosm of the world, the European Union experiences internal tension over the tradeoffs that need to be made between the water quality and ecosystem integrity demands of the WFD and the agricultural productivity and economic well-being expectations to which the Common Agricultural Policy aspires. The main battleground of these conflicting policies is the dry Mediterranean region of southern Spain. In Spain the European Union policy frameworks are not only at odds with one another to some extent, they are also at odds with Spanish national legislation that assures water services to all users in all the country's river basins.

Spain's National Irrigation Rehabilitation Project

In 2000 the Spanish government embarked on a massive irrigation rehabilitation project that sought to modernize all of the irrigated regions in the country, which at the time still relied mostly on 19th-century irrigation technology. The cornerstone of this modernization of existing irrigation technology is the goal of achieving total national average annual savings of 1,300 million cubic metres of water. Presently covering 1.4 million hectares, or about 40 per cent of all of Spain's irrigated lands, the plan aims to guarantee water demand to irrigators while at the same time reducing the impact of climate variability, mitigating drought effects, increasing farms' competitiveness and crop diversification, encouraging expansion of irrigation-related industries and services, expanding employment opportunities and promoting population stability. Complementary ecological measures include better soil use and the reduction of contamination of rivers from agro-chemical residues.

About 80 per cent of the €6-billion budget was committed to modernization of existing networks. The average investment for modernization projects covered by the four public agencies responsible for funding the National Irrigation Plan ranged

between €4,000 and €5,000 per hectare, a high figure by international standards but not unreasonable given the degree of sophis-
tication of the new pressurized and computer-managed systems.

About 50 per cent of the €6-billion budget was financed by
public funds. The other 50 per cent of the project's cost is paid for
by EU funds and by the irrigators who benefit from the program.
The EU funds finance about 24 per cent of the cost in low-income
areas and 17 per cent in other areas. Irrigators pay the rest but
were permitted low-interest loans of up to 50 years to minimize
the hardship. But even with irrigators paying only 26 per cent to
33 per cent of the costs of modernization, it is a big load for an
industry to carry. Though loans were of long duration, increasing capitalization in agriculture has dramatically increased farm
debt. Outstanding farm debt increased from €15.8-billion in 2004
to €21-billion in 2006, making outstanding debt the equivalent of
the entire agricultural sector's net income.

All 1.4 million hectares of the targeted irrigated areas in Spain
were replanned and completely refurbished from scratch between
2000 and 2008. Alberto Garrido notes that this expensive but
urgently needed irrigation renewal program enjoyed bipartisan
political support and continued uninterrupted through the terms
of two different national governments. The program was, in fact,
reenergized through the new "Priory Plan," which invested an
additional €2.4-billion in improvements to an additional 868,000
hectares between 2007 and 2009. Garrido further notes that since
this national irrigation revitalization program began in 2000, it
has met 100 per cent of its objectives. This claim, however, seems
somewhat at odds with the fact that the irrigation revitalization
plan has yet to release water from agriculture to other purposes.

According to Garrido, evidence to support the beneficial
effects of innovative irrigation management and improvements in
technology is overwhelming. Water savings of 30 to 40 per cent –
without yield reduction – have been reported, resulting from better management of application schedules. Technology shifts at

both farm and district levels have demonstrated that effective water conservation makes solid economic sense. Control of key factors such as soil moisture has been found to contribute significantly to reduced water consumption. It has also been discovered that the most efficient irrigation schedule may not be the one that yields maximum production. The change in irrigation technologies is most evident where farmers are growing typical Mediterranean crops such as wine grapes and olives. By 2005 drip technologies well adapted to these particular crops became the dominant form of irrigation in the country. Some 1.3 million hectares of Spain is now efficiently irrigated by drip technology, which is more land than is under irrigation in all of Canada.

If this were the end of the story, there would be no tension between agriculture and other water interests in Spain. Unfortunately, not all of Spain's water use is committed to high-value crops. While modernization has made Spanish irrigation more efficient, most of the water used still goes mainly for low-productivity farming. A comparison of water use, crop productivity and gross value added shows that two-thirds of all water used in agriculture in Spain is utilized for crops that generate value of less than €0.40 per cubic metre of water used to grow them. In other words, two-thirds of all the water employed in Spanish irrigation produces only 16 per cent of the gross value added through that use.

Thus we discover that only 4 per cent of Spain's agricultural water allocation is used for high-productivity crops, which are defined as those that generate €1 to €3 or more of value for each cubic metre of water applied in production. But high water use committed to the production of low-value crops is only the beginning of the problem that is emerging in Spain. The real problem is that even though billions were spent in improving irrigation technology at the farm level, irrigators will not give any of their water savings back so that they can be used for other purposes.

In spite of all efforts to improve the efficiency of irrigation technology and the long-standing socio-economic benefits that accrued to irrigation farmers and rural communities, it is now questionable whether Spain's National Irrigation Program will achieve its water savings goals. The main reason for this is that in 80 per cent of all systems, water continues to be priced not by volume of use as it was meant to be under current reforms, but at a low unit price tied to the surface area under irrigation. In other words there is not yet any incentive for farmers to use less water. In fact, reduction of conveyance losses has increased on-farm use of existing allocations and diminished return flows, in many cases much to the detriment of already stressed surrounding natural aquatic systems. Many Spanish farmers are now using most if not all of their allocations, and even less is going back to maintain natural system productivity than did before billions were invested in irrigation improvements. Out of this circumstance has emerged a general public distrust of the selfish motives of the agriculture sector.

In 2007 the Ministry of Agriculture in Spain enacted a new law aimed at sustainable development of the rural environment. In accordance with the principles of "good ecological status of all water bodies" outlined in the EU Water Framework Directive, the law established regulations relating to environmental flows and recovery of over-abstracted aquifers. As per the EU Water Framework Directive, the law also reinforced the use of economic instruments for the temporary or permanent purchase of water rights. In passing this legislation, Spain made it clear that it was serious about integrating EU and national policies with respect to water resources management through the coordination of the action plans of its own national water, environment and agriculture administrations. The key lesson here is that public policy has to respond to each new obstacle in order to achieve some kind of practical, functioning harmony among internal interests. This must be done first at the national level before it can inform regional policy synchronization and reshape the activities of private interests.

The role of river basin authorities and irrigation associations in Spain

Spain has a long historical tradition of managing water resources on a watershed basis. The first single integrated basin management unit with competence in managing both surface and groundwater resources for all purposes and uses was created in the Ebro basin in 1926. This was some 75 years before anything similar came into existence in Alberta.

Since that time some 15 river basin authorities (RBAS) have been created in Spain, each with considerable organizational, functional and economic autonomy. The Water Act of 1985 enlarged the powers of the country's river basin authorities as unified planning and management units. The Act also introduced new environmental protection goals and gave additional powers to users at the decision-making level.

In addition to the 15 RBAS there are also some 7,000 irrigation associations in Spain. These associations are collectively responsible for the management of more than 90 per cent of all the irrigated lands in the country. Spanish irrigation associations have powers similar to those possessed by irrigation districts in Alberta. They are responsible for regulating water distribution, setting water use tariffs, resolving conflicts between users and providing input into basin watershed management plans. Because of the amount of water irrigators demand and the extent of the land they cultivate, irrigation associations are key stakeholders in water management processes.

The Spanish experience suggests that RBAS, as structured in that country, are well positioned, in principle at least, to respond effectively to the European Union Water Framework Directive requirements that demand a single unit management structure and public participation in the elaboration of water management plans. According to Consuelo Varela-Ortega, Spanish RBAS capably deal with supply and demand variability, climate change impacts and changes in water demand that have emerged as a consequence of agricultural policy reforms. River basin authorities throughout the country have also established participatory boards that invite direct, continuous input by irrigation associations and other water users toward water management decisions. The EU Water Framework Directive, however, requires a more complex, ecosystem-based vision of water resource management than is currently practised at the river basin authority level in Spain. The EU framework seeks better integration of hydrological, technical, socio-economic and institutional factors. The other main pillars of the Water Framework Directive are transparency in data and information collection, greater public participation in management decisions and expanded stakeholder involvement, all of which have required further action on behalf of the river basin authorities. Most of the river basin authorities are responding to these challenges and prospects of success are favourable, particularly in the more active basins. Adaptation to change, however, takes time.

Water markets

Economic analysis of water use led to a reform of Spain's Water Act in 1999 which permitted the revision of water concession rights to make transfers more flexible, which in turn stimulated the creation of formal water markets. Tailored specifically to issues of water availability and competition for water resources, a number of Spanish river basin authorities have established water exchange contracts, public tenders for purchasing water rights, and water rights exchange centres. Among water users, irrigators have been the most active in exchanging water rights. Most are interbasin exchanges that permit the transfer of water from the country's central basins to water-scarce areas in southeastern Spain. These southward-bound exchanges of water are expected to continue as long as they remain profitable for the exporting central regions. This, of course, will depend on the cost of water.

Because of the deeply entrenched system that existed at the time, these new regulations took considerable effort: it took seven years for these markets to begin to function as designed. The reforms opened up two avenues to enable rights-holders to lease out their allocations either to basin authorities or to other users. The very simplest of these exchanges required only the agreement of two rights-holders and a formal application to exchange rights. In order to facilitate such exchanges, basin agencies were required to respond within 30 days. Unless major technical, environmental or third-party difficulties were encountered, applicants could expect rapid approval.

The second avenue open to those wishing to exchange water rights came into existence through the creation of water banks, or exchange centres. Water banks in Spain are not independent organizations. In order to ensure transparency and to avoid third-party conflicts, Spanish water banks are hosted, operated and located within the basin agencies themselves. They appear to work, however, as farmers are now leasing out their full allotments from headwater resources that previously had been leased very inefficiently to other users who were not always located in the same basin.

Markets work both ways, of course. Water rights can be sold and they can be bought back. In areas where aquifers have been overexploited, river basin authorities have resorted to public tenders for repurchasing water rights either temporarily or permanently. The aim of these purchases is to reduce over-pumping and to restore aquifers to sustainable levels. Some water rights exchange centres have been created almost solely with the aim of repurchasing groundwater from irrigators.

In some basins, groundwater is also repurchased so it can be used to maintain and restore natural ecosystem function. At the time the Rosenberg was held at Zaragoza in 2008, prices offered to irrigators to sell their rights permanently and to return to rainfed farming have not been high enough to attract sellers. It is clear that while such markets do offer a vehicle for adapting to the requirements of the EU Water Framework Directive, the costs associated with buying back precious water resources is likely going to be very high. The cost for permanent water rights buy-back in Spain has averaged between €3,000 and €10,000 per hect-are, but even at these prices buyback will only work if enough irrigators sell. That has yet to happen.

From this we begin to understand how the myth of the humble and kindly family farmer was dispelled in Spain and why so much ill will is currently directed toward the country's irrigation sector. Though it provides products that are essential to human existence, agriculture at the scale practised in Spain is industrial in purpose and function. There is little that is altruistic about this kind of agri-culture. Farmers in Spain, just like the farmers in western Canada, are no strangers to hard times. They do not seek to feed a starving world. Spain is in possession of full understanding of blue and green water realities and the complexities of virtual water trade. Spanish farmers carefully choose the crops they grow on the basis of market price and seek the highest profit possible at the lowest possible cost of production, even if that sometimes means ignor-ing the long-term cost of environmental impacts. The Spanish agricultural sector sells food to people who can afford to buy it. The markets for their products are generally countries in which average incomes are at or above the incomes prevalent in Spain.

The increasingly industrial and commercial character of mod-ern European agriculture has resulted in a changing public perception of how much farmers should pay for water. Currently, farmers in most regions of Spain benefit from water costs that are so low that they barely reflect the cost of operating and maintaining the systems that deliver it to their farms. Water scarcity, however, invariably attracts public attention to heavy water users. In the last decade the notion that farmers use excessive amounts of water because it is sold to them so cheaply that there is no incentive to use it more sparingly has become deeply ingrained in the public imagination. While irrigation associations in Spain continue to vigorously promote the industry's important historical contribution to Spanish stability and prosperity, commitment to efficient water use and the benefits of maintaining irrigated farms in rural areas, these arguments have lost some of their force. According to Alberto Garrido, irrigation sector pronouncements are too often seen in influential circles as mere public relations.

While few would disagree that the evolution of the Spanish irrigation system depends utterly upon the ability of the public and private sectors to arrive at a unified vision of the future of the country, distrust of self-interest continues to stand in the way of progress. This is most unfortunate given how many billions of euros have been spent on agricultural reform and improvement of irrigation technology.

Water scarcity, drought and climate change

Water withdrawals in Spain increased on average by 2 per cent a year between 1997 and 2001, which represents a larger annual increase in water use than in any other southern European Union country. This heavy use makes Spain one of the greatest water-using countries in the Mediterranean region. Projections indicate that Spain is expected to increase its total water demand by 0.3 per cent annually from 2000 until 2025. By that time, water withdrawals in Spain are expected to be close to or beyond the average annual renewable volume of natural water resources. Parts of Spain are already using as much water as is available to them. Where additional water resources will come from after 2025 remains unclear.

Even under adequate rainfall circumstances and conditions, many areas of Spain face significant challenges due to the unequal distribution of water resources, which inevitably leads to conflicts among users and between regions. Recurrent droughts lead to the intensification of these problems, adding greatly to the complexity of water management. Moreover, droughts have become frequent in Spain since 1970, with economic and social impacts growing with each successive drought. Droughts do not just affect surface water flows. Not surprisingly, groundwater overdraft during drought episodes in Spain has contributed to the degradation of groundwater quality. In addition, important remaining wetland areas are affected during droughts by irrigation withdrawals, once again highlighting the difficulty of providing enough water to nature to maintain important biodiversity-based ecosystem productivity that over the long term may be as important to sustainability as surviving drought.

What is worrying is that commitment to bold water management reform threatens to break down in the face of more frequent and persistent droughts, and these are expected to occur even more often as a consequence of climate impacts on the entire Mediterranean region. Unfortunately, climate change projections, particularly in southern Spain, do not suggest that the water availability situation is going to be better in the future.

According to Dr. Alberto Garrido, climate change projections derived from global climate models project an increase in temperature of 1.5° to 3.6°c and a decrease in precipitation of 5 to 14 per cent by 2030 and from 10 to 20 per cent depending on season by the 2050s. In critical semi-arid areas, such as the south Mediterranean basins and the arid hinterland and island basins, water availability may be reduced as much as 50 per cent. Seasonal variability will be even more acute. Under these scenarios evapotranspiration water demand in agriculture in all the river basins in Spain is predicted to increase by between 5 and 10 per cent, which could reduce average water resources by 17 per cent.

Under every climate change scenario, water supplies decrease and irrigation demands increase in Spain, just as the models suggest they will on the Canadian prairies. In Spain the capacity of the irrigation sector to adapt to these changes is particularly constrained by the fact that climate change is occurring in tandem with high development pressures both in the country's most productive agricultural regions and in suboptimal regions where no economic alternatives exist for rural populations.

Droughts that have persisted through the 1990s to the present are already testing the limits of adaptation of socio-economic and agricultural systems in Spain. Some irrigation-dependent areas have simply ceased production. The fact that differences between the wide range of stakeholders with interests in water are only partially resolved has become a matter of wide public concern. Many now believe that drought and climate change issues are among the most pressing problems presently facing Spanish society. Many worry that despite huge efforts at reform, weak cooperation and the fragmented and often competing mandates of government departments, administrative regions and basin authorities result too often in conflicts and impediments to the implementation of existing legislation and agreed-upon innovations and management actions.

It is interesting to observe that these are exactly the kinds of problems parts of southern Canada are expected to experience under all projected population growth and climate change scenarios.

Lessons for Canada

1. Public awareness of water issues is growing

Balancing the trade-offs between water for food and water for nature is rapidly becoming one of the major challenges facing policy-makers, national and regional administrations and stakeholders in Spain and around the world. If what is happening in Spain is any indication of our future, we could be facing difficult circumstances for which we ought to prepare.

Societal awareness of environmental and water problems is

increasing in Spain. The Spanish public has begun to demand greater transparency in decision-making and more accountability in the management of the country's water resources. This mirrors what is happening in Canada generally and is highly emblematic of current developments in Alberta. It is as if water issues have suddenly been discovered by an astounded Canadian public.

Nowhere is Canadian attention on water more focused than on the Great Plains, where a growing number of interests are competing for a suddenly very limited water supply.

2. The importance of integrating national and regional policy direction

The Spanish case study offered at Rosenberg vi in Zaragoza points out how important it is to have all levels of government – starting continentally, then moving to national, regional and local levels – working clearly toward the same goals. Trying to match the national objective of assuring water services to all users while at the same time complying with the EU Water Directive Framework requirements of achieving "good ecological status of all waters" proved and continues to prove to be a difficult task even for the well-established and highly effective river basin authorities of Spain. It is not an easy job. Neither is the level of public participation the EU requires. Active involvement of stakeholders, however, is obviously central to successful implementation of such demanding policies.

3. The importance of integrating water and agricultural policy

From the Spanish example we also learn that in major food-producing countries water policies must be viewed as inseparable from agricultural policies. The key to balancing the trade-off between agricultural water use and water availability for other needs requires transparent, well-coordinated, collaborative design and implementation of integrated water management and agricultural policies at both national and regional levels.

The Spanish example also suggests that in countries where irrigation agriculture is the key sector supporting rural economic prosperity, the parallel, coordinated, integrated design and simultaneous implementation of agricultural and water policies is central to solution of water availability and quality conflicts.

This integration can only take place through transparent stakeholder participation and avoidance of policy contradiction and through support for synergies that reinforce common objectives.

In addition, it must also be recognized that the social and economic burdens associated with the implementation of water conservation programming must be managed through the parallel evolution of integrated rural and social development programs.

The integration of such wide-ranging elements within the larger framework of policy response to increasing water scarcity is presently the greatest challenge facing regional administrations in Spain responsible for the simultaneous implementation of both EU and national agricultural development and water management policies.

The Spanish example also demonstrates that such joint policy integration is not easy to achieve. Each new policy is likely to create a new and different set of problems that will have to be addressed by further policy innovation. While the process is clumsy, costly and time consuming, it is the only avenue presently available to prevent conflict over water quality, allocation and use between the agriculture sector and the people in cities it exists to feed.

4. The irrigation community in Canada may wish to avoid what happened in Spain

The irrigation community in Canada, and particularly in Alberta, would be wise to pay close attention to what is happening in Spain. After 12 centuries of irrigation production, the Spanish public no longer believes that irrigation is a given or that the dedication of the substantial amount of water currently supplied to agriculture is either efficient or equitable. Despite massive progressive public policy reform in Spain, it remains unclear where this public perception will lead next in terms of policy direction.

In Canada, and again particularly in Alberta, where public policy with respect to irrigation water allocation has not been altered significantly in a century, similar pressure for change is likely to emerge as water scarcity begins to attract greater urban attention.

Irrigators in Alberta and elsewhere in Canada should expect to be challenged on the price they pay for water and on their environment impacts; and everyone in the prairie West should expect longer and more frequent droughts.

Despite genuine collaborative progress in Spain, antipathy between environmentalists and irrigators makes it difficult if not impossible to build further on hard-won public policy improvements in water management. This is a situation we should do everything we can in Canada to avoid.

5. Charging the real cost of water will create conflict

We should expect exactly the same tensions should we in Canada decide to charge the real cost of water as it is supplied to agriculture. The mere notion of charging the agriculture industry the real cost of water would likely evoke an incendiary response from western Canadian irrigators.

Certain kinds of farming would no longer be possible if farmers were forced to pay the actual environmental and other costs associated not just with water supply but with the impacts associated with agricultural practices. But only when environmentally non-sustainable agriculture becomes economically non-sustainable do new possibilities emerge.

At the moment, at least, the Spanish example suggests that even the sincere co-operation of the agriculture sector in the development of enlightened new approaches to the sharing of water resources nationally may not be adequate to stave off growing criticism regarding the disproportionate amount of water allocated to irrigation. Just as occurred in Spain, the irrigation community in Canada could be harshly judged in the court of public opinion if it cannot convince urban neighbours that it is not only improving water productivity and reducing pollution but is measurably reducing total water consumption – and most importantly that water freed through conservation is actually being put to use for environmental and other purposes.

6. Basin authorities and councils have a role to play

In Spain the Ministry of the Environment is the national authority responsible for the management of water resources. Just as in Canada, however, autonomous regional governments are also involved in matters related to water resource management such as land use planning, agricultural policy, forestry operation and environmental standards.

Water institutions in Spain are, in principle, well positioned to adjust to the new policy setting and management expectations created by the European Union Water Framework Directive and by river basin management plans. Each river basin authority possesses considerable technical capacity, and many have demonstrated measurable success in the development of effective participatory processes that ensure collaboration with water users and interests. Just as in Canada, however, some RBAS are more active than others. The active authorities are working effectively. The less active ones need to concentrate on increased transparency, on improving data collection and increasing the effectiveness of information-sharing networks.

River basin authorities in Spain are becoming successful at encouraging more flexible distributions of water allocations among farmers and other users. These exchanges of rights, or, in the case of overexploited aquifers, the public purchase of water rights for environmental purposes, are central to creating sustainable water use practices. The Spanish example suggests that such demand-side solutions can be helpful in facilitating the adaptation process necessary for creating the kind of policy-setting environment that will be necessary if water policy and agricultural policy are to be effectively integrated on a national or continental scale.

7. It might be wise to consider further irrigation and agricultural renewal, but with some reservations

If it is possible to free up enough water to prevent the limiting of social and economic development in a dry country like Spain by simply improving the efficiency of irrigation agriculture, then surely the same must be true in Canada. The Spanish example clearly suggests that Spain experienced the same stubborn resistance to change in its agricultural community that we can expect in Canada. It follows, then, that the same solution that would work to address the problem of water supply in the dry regions of Alberta would also work in Spain and vice versa. But what was the solution?

One wonders if a similar kind of program to the irrigation renewal initiative undertaken in Spain might be worth considering in Canada, or at least in Alberta. If you take 1 acre to be about 0.4 hectares, our 1.3 million acres of irrigated land in Alberta works out to only about 526,000 hectares. Spain spent about c$9-billion to improve irrigation technology in an area roughly two-and-a-half times the size of what is currently under irrigation in Alberta.

This means it might cost somewhere around c$3-billion to orchestrate similar improvements in irrigation technology in Alberta and that is without taking into account the fact that some irrigation technology improvements have already been undertaken in parts of the province's southern irrigation districts.

The National Irrigation Plan in Spain has increased water productivity through an expensive nationwide irrigation modernization program. The plan has contributed to the reduction in environmental pressures on watercourses and has encouraged the integration of expanded data sets into river basin authority information networks. But despite its successes, the plan has not achieved its water savings goals in that water freed up for other uses is generally channelled toward guaranteeing water availability for irrigation and to a lesser extent to responding to the European Union Water Framework Directive goals of enhancing ecosystem protection.

In other words, the technology for reducing irrigation water use was made available but what wasn't created was the institutional means for ensuring that the technology was productively married to demand-management incentives such as the revision of water rights, volumetric pricing and simple mechanisms by which water rights could be exchanged in a timely manner.

Non-sustainable agriculture can become sustainable. The transition between the former and the latter, however, can be painful even when it is driven by good public policy and generous government support. Without carefully considered public policy and adequate, timely support for the agricultural sector, the impacts on people and local economies can be utterly devastating.

The lesson from Spain is that policy-makers must be tireless in their efforts to coordinate the parallel implementation of both EU and national policy directions to actually save water so that it can be put to use for environmental and other purposes.

Policy-makers must be very clear on final objectives. The decoupling of the EU's Common Agricultural Policy subsidies from production increases has not reduced the overall irrigated surface in Spain. It has produced a shift away from water-intensive crops such as maize in favour of less water-dependent crops, but it has not reduced overall agricultural water use in Spain.

Future options: Linking agricultural development goals to water availability realities

The question the Spanish example invites is how policy-makers can take the all-important next step from the creation of their much improved agricultural system toward actual water savings that can be put to environmental and other uses. It struck me that part of the answer to this question had already been formulated in Australia. In June of 2006, Paul Perkins shared a paper he had written on addressing the world water crisis through agricultural reform. As Australia was already facing serious water scarcity, Perkins was beginning to think seriously about how to reframe current resistance to change so that unproductive hand-wringing could be translated into effective action.

Perkins looked at the problem from a different perspective. His goal was to create a different scenario than the one in which Australia found itself so deeply entrenched. His logic in the end was very simple: given the World Bank's assessment of population growth and climate change impacts on world food production, which sees half the world's population deprived of water by 2030 but also sees Australia as one of the few regions (along with Canada, the US, Europe and parts of South America) capable at that time of "water export in the form of cereal grain, meat etc.," would Australia not be more productively engaged if it were to ask, How can Australia develop methods to produce twice as much food over 25 years, using, say, half the water?

Canada's situation is different from Australia's. Climate change impacts, while likely causing dramatic drying on what are now the Great Plains, are likely to improve mid-latitude agricultural productivity. But even so, limits to water supply could hamper this development. So the question Canada might ask might be something like this: How can Canada develop methods to produce four times as much food for export over the next 25 years, without increasing domestic food prices unreasonably and without upland watershed decline, while still ensuring enough water for environmental services, population growth and proportional industrial and technological development?

Reflecting on Paul Perkins's question, it could be proposed that part of the answer to how such a solution might emerge is through substantial Alberta investment of oil royalties in greater agricultural efficiency that does not simply rely on upstream storage development.

This investment will be necessary to ensure that individual farmers do not have to cut into already tight margins to restructure and improve irrigation practices in ways that will make them more efficient.

This investment also ensures that leading-edge irrigation technology and practices emerge that will allow the freeing up of large volumes of water from the agricultural sector that can be employed in specifically directed ways to ensure that water scarcity does not limit the social or economic development of the Canadian West now or in the future. If we were to undertake an approach like this, there would also be another advantage. We could export our knowledge and expertise to Spain, Australia, the United States and all the other places that face the same challenge.

Challenges we can expect as we work at the problem

If we want to avoid the kinds of problems other semi-arid regions such as Spain are facing, massive reform is no longer merely optional. It is an urgent necessity. Expect public policy to be difficult and time-consuming to develop and hard to implement. Expect such processes to require a great deal of collaboration and to take years to generate lasting results.

No single management action, legislative package or policy framework can respond to all of the problems that are presently converging around water availability conflicts, especially as they relate to the disproportionate amount of water demanded by irrigation agriculture in parts of Canada.

National and regional policies must be integrated and water strategies must somehow be merged into agricultural policies if water scarcity challenges are to be fairly and equitably resolved now and in the future.

Expect to have to manage conflict over allocation and water use priorities. Expect the shutdown of entire processes during droughts. Expect to have to keep refining policies and management directives in the face of the emergence of unexpected new developments and challenges. Expect this to go on for generations because the problems are likely to become more and more complicated as they converge around increasing global populations and climate change.

Expect to have to break down the corral fences that special interests try to build around what are essentially public water rights, in order to prevent singular interests from robbing Canada of the room it needs to move in order to become the first country in the world to manage its land and water resources sustainably.

CHAPTER FIVE

Water Teachings from Texas

TRANSCENDING THE TYRANNY OF THE LONGEST STRAW

While we were contemplating the impacts of prolonged drought in the Canadian West, Texas was in the midst of a huge flood. Driving to the Calgary airport, I heard on the radio that parts of the state had received more than 18 inches of rain during the night. In other words, Texas had got more rain in one night than large areas of southern Alberta typically gets in a year.

Earlier, when I'd called Jay Pulliam at the University of Texas in Austin to tell him of a planned visit by Dr. Dennis Fitzpatrick of the University of Lethbridge and myself, he was very supportive of our plan to have discussions with senior faculty on the subject of climate research. "We have more than enough water at the moment," he said, "but I am sure we will be up for a conversation on the subject of climate change adaptation."

Because of the storm, our flight to Dallas/Fort Worth was delayed. En route the pilot changed altitude and course often to avoid the turbulence left behind from what the cloud layers suggested was a very extreme weather event. It was still raining when we landed. Then a sudden thunderstorm froze everything. The airport closed down for an hour, with us sitting on the runway until the lightning passed.

The terminal was filled with passengers trying to make new arrangements to deal with delayed and cancelled flights. Though our Austin flight had not yet departed, it was overbooked by some 80 passengers. When at last we arrived in Austin, where we were met by Dr. David Eaton, we were told our luggage did not make the flight. We decided to wait to see if it might be on one of the two remaining scheduled flights to arrive from Dallas and found an all-night restaurant near the airport to pass some of the time.

Our luggage finally did arrive and we made it to our bed and breakfast at 2:00 a.m. The cooing of mourning doves and the song of frogs reminded me I was in a completely different bioregion. The frog song, no doubt a rejoicing at the heavy rain, would have lulled me pleasantly in and out of sleep all night had I not been so dead tired. In the end the only thing that disturbed my sleep was the roar of the air conditioning.

The storm had raised the humidity dramatically in Austin, and with temperatures in the high 90s Fahrenheit, walking out of the air-conditioned bed and breakfast was like stepping into a sauna. For those in temperate regions who wonder what a warmer world might be like, this is a good place to visit.

David Eaton collected us in his aging but still serviceable Subaru. After a brief stop at his favourite bakery we arrived at the Lyndon B. Johnson School of Public Affairs at the University of Texas at Austin. We set up in a boardroom where over the course of the morning we met with a number of senior administrators to talk about our proposal to create a Rosenberg-like forum on climate change that would be developed jointly by the University of Texas and the Western Watersheds Climate Research Collaborative at the University of Lethbridge.

The first person we met was Dr. Charles (Chip) Groat, who is the director of the Center for International Energy & Environmental Policy with the famous Jackson School of Geosciences at the

University of Texas. Dr. Groat is renowned in American academic circles for having served for ten years as the director of the US Geological Survey under both Bill Clinton and George W. Bush, no mean feat in such a politically volatile era.

Dr. Groat is a tall, slim, pleasant man who appears very much aware of everything around him. He listened very carefully to our ideas and then encouraged us to share them with senior University of Texas researchers who would be dropping by throughout the morning to meet us. There were many who did and each contributed positively to our proposal. Together they also had a great deal to tell us about the status of the climate change issue in the United States.

Aimed more at getting to know one another than arriving at any given conclusion, our initial conversations were wide-ranging. The faculty members we met appeared interested from the outset in having us understand the unique political situation in their state. These discussions served to put our own political situation in Alberta into relief. Property rights, it was explained, are central and fundamental elements of self-determination and the bulwark of conservative politics throughout the United States. Such rights are fiercely defended, especially in Texas. For this reason, we were told, it shouldn't surprise us that much contemporary state and federal legislation was being written by lobbyists. The defence of property rights was being viewed by this public policy institution as being central to the response to the climate change issue in this country. While some senior faculty members acknowledged that climate problems were simpler to understand than many Americans believed, a central concern was that solutions needed to be adopted across a wide range of economic sectors in which individual and corporate rights had already been clearly established. It was also put forward that a lack of federal policy was leading to the balkanization of individual states (which we see also in Canada) on climate change actions, forcing many US companies, particularly in the energy industry, to press the federal government for a unified national policy that would create the same playing field for everyone. A further point was made suggesting that it would likely be American corporations, not the government, that will alter the political landscape with respect to climate change issues in the United States. In this context, it was pointed out that major energy companies in the US were pressing for a carbon tax rather than a cap and trade system.

This, Dennis Fitzpatrick and I later observed, was not how American response to climate concerns was being portrayed back in Canada. Once again we were reminded of how important it is to find out what others are really thinking and doing on major public policy issues before moving or not moving forward on new legislation on your own at home.

The conversation then reverted back to the United States, and it was observed that resource speculators such as T. Boone Pickens and former US presidential hopeful Ross Perot have created a new resource play called "water ranching." While this practice was seen by some as incorporating all of the predatory elements of the free-market system into a single rather vile enterprise, David Eaton pointed out that this issue could not be so easily characterized. It was true that these speculators were buying big ranches both for the land and for the water rights. They develop choice parts of these properties to exploit the real estate value and then sell the leftover water rights to thirsty cities. It was important to note, said Eaton, that there was nothing in Texas law that suggested there was anything improper about such activities. The developers themselves argue that they are serving the public good by freeing up water that would otherwise not be available for urban areas while at the same time creating new wealth. This logic could hardly be contested except on the grounds that purely market-based responses to water availability and quality issues may not, in the end, create enduring or equitable solutions to growing water scarcity concerns, in the US or elsewhere.

Inevitably, talk turned, as it always does, to the weather.

One researcher explained that the big storm we had just missed was unusual only in its timing. The Texas record for rainfall is 31 inches in two days. This tropical deluge occurred just north of San Antonio in an area where fronts from the Atlantic and the Gulf of Mexico are often at war. The intensity of these often violent interactions is expected to increase as regional temperatures continue to climb as a consequence of global warming. The conversation then turned to water and then to groundwater. You can't talk about groundwater in Texas without talking about the Ogallala Aquifer. If there was ever a place where Alberta could learn from others, it is the Texas High Plains.

The Ogallala Aquifer: A rich bank account in overdraft

The Ogallala is one of the world's largest groundwater reservoirs. Sprawling from South Dakota to Texas, it contained at discovery enough water to fill Lake Erie nine times. As William Ashworth points out in *Ogallala Blue: Water and Life on the High Plains*, the 14 million acres of crops grown on the surface above this aquifer account for a full 20 per cent of the annual agricultural harvest in the United States. This is ten times the area of irrigated agriculture that exists in southern Alberta, the most intensively irrigated part of Canada. To support this cornucopia, however, some 5,000,000,000,000 gallons of water are drawn from the Ogallala every year. These five trillion gallons of groundwater account for about 30 per cent of all the groundwater used in irrigation in the entire United States each year.

As one would guess, this agricultural production is not insignificant. According to William Ashworth, the total value of the food and fibre generated from Ogallala withdrawals is in the range of $20-billion a year. The problem, however, is that this level of agricultural production cannot be maintained without taking water out of the aquifer faster than it can naturally be replaced. Ashworth points out that since pumping for irrigation began in earnest in the 1950s, 120 trillion gallons, or about 11 per cent of the volume of the aquifer, has been lost. This is slightly more than the equivalent of one Lake Erie. Ashworth points out – as the academics at the University of Texas did the day we talked – that this loss of volume was hardly accidental. Groundwater over-draft is being undertaken here in full knowledge of its potential impacts. It is fully understood and accepted that this resource is being mined for one-time use.

Groundwater overdraft is, in fact, a way of life on the American High Plains. It is undertaken consciously as a matter of public policy. The foundations of this policy can be traced to a New Mexico state engineer who, a quarter century ago, observed that there is noth-ing intrinsically evil about mining groundwater "as long as every-one understands what he is doing." The underlying argument here is that groundwater is essentially a mineral, which suggests that only by mining it can its value be realized. In adopting this logic, it is accepted that over time the amount of water in the aquifer will decline, which will have consequences for everyone who relies on that water for their livelihood. In deciding to pump the water out of the aquifer faster than it can be replenished – which is the decision that appears to have been made – water managers are acknowledg-ing up front that future generations will have to deal with what inevitably come next. Prolonged groundwater overdraft is always self-terminating in that at a certain point pumping the remaining water out of a diminished aquifer simply becomes unaffordable.

The decision to drain the Ogallala invites questions about allo-cation, water quality and the wisdom of interbasin transfers. The allocation issues are the same as everywhere else in the world where water is scarce. We face these same problems in Alberta as well. The principal issue relates to how you decide who gets how much for what use. Farmers compete with each other for water, agriculture competes with municipalities and industry, which compete with tourism and the environmental needs of aquatic ecosystems and local wildlife.

Questions about water quality can be more complicated, especially as the quality of the water withdrawn from the aquifer is diminished through annual overdraft over an extended period of time. The wisdom of water-saving technology is also being debated. It has now become obvious that such innovations in the end often lead only to more use rather than less.

Profiteering is also an issue. This is a particular problem in Texas, where antiquated water laws allow well owners the right to suck water from beneath their neighbours' land and sell it to the highest bidder. Under what is called the Rule of Capture, in Texas the longest straw wins. Here, greed is dignified under individual property rights laws that suggest it is perfectly reasonable – and therefore perfectly legal – to trade water wealth today for the risk of complete aquifer decline in the future. In fact, interests are encouraged to compete with one another to do so.

But as Ashworth points out in *Ogallala Blue*, the consequences of over-pumping the aquifer to the point where it is no longer economical to draw from it are far more complex than many presently understand. Springs will dry up, rivers will diminish, the numbers of kinds of plants and animals will be reduced and the High Plains landscape will become more arid. As this happens, pumping costs will rise as it becomes necessary to pump from lower depths. Land values will drop and food costs will increase. There will be bankruptcies, foreclosures and forced human migrations that usually accompany hydrological catastrophe. As Ashworth points out, the decision to drain the aquifer means that the current High Plains lifestyle cannot be perpetuated or even saved. All that can be done is to plan for the end of the current circumstances that exist in the Ogallala region.

Such plans have been considered. One proposal was to mine the Ogallala to the extent that only 50 per cent of the total water available at the turn of the 20th century would be gone in 50 years. Even this plan, however, was not found universally acceptable. Even if such meagre constraints were to be adopted, the water remaining in the aquifer will be deeper and increasingly harder to get. It will be more expensive to mine and likely of lower quality. Even under these circumstances there will be no guarantee that it will ever be possible to restore the aquifer. The geological forces that created this amazing hydrological feature are operative only over millions of years. William Ashworth's characterization of the situation is most compelling. Canadians would be wise to take notice of his description of what an aquifer is actually like, for it applies as much where we live as it does to the Ogallala:

> Don't be fooled by talk of underground rivers, of underground lakes, of veins and nodes and dowsing: aquifers are wet dirt. Water seeps rather than flows through them. They do not quickly change. The water that soaks the buried gravels of the Ogallala is largely the water of vanished rivers that put them there; most of it has been down there for at least three million years. It is sobering, and a little humbling, to realize that the glass of water you just drank was drawn from a stream that vanished about the time our ancestors first began to walk upright on the ancient savannahs of Africa.[25]

The Ogallala is presently being pumped – if Ashworth's statistics can still be relied upon – at a rate three times faster than it can be replenished. The aquifer is presently being pumped at a net deficit of 12 billion gallons a day, which is enough to supply the average family for more than 80,000 years.

Beyond simply over-pumping, damage is also being done to the purity of the three-million-year-old water being brought to the surface. Current agricultural practices can be characterized not as irrigation but as "chemigation." High Plains agriculture has created an industrial landscape in which fertilizers and pesticides are mixed with irrigation water. It should be no surprise that "chemigation" causes water quality issues relating to runoff. While the problem of agricultural chemicals appearing in Ogallala groundwater is presently minor, the future – as Ashworth says – is notoriously difficult to predict. The slow pace of groundwater movement may allow most pesticides, which are not stable over the long term, to break down into less hazardous substances before they reach an area of groundwater withdrawal. Ashworth further points out that layers of clay in the aquifer are both a barrier to groundwater movement and an absorbent for pesticides and other contaminants. It is unrealistic, he says, to think the Ogallala Aquifer will not be contaminated by agricultural chemicals. Effective public policy, as Ashworth points out, cannot be founded merely on hope – especially as it relates to water you can't easily see.

Two disturbing developments have been recognized. Agricultural contamination has been found in all areas of the aquifer that have been tested for evidence of their presence. While these chemicals do not appear to exist in anything more than minimum concentrations and only in the uppermost parts of the aquifer and not in all wells, their long-term impact on the aquifer remains unknown. A 1999 us Geological Survey study revealed that nearly 80 per cent of wells contaminated by agricultural chemicals were less than 200 feet deep. This could mean one of two things: either the natural structure of the aquifer protects it from this kind of contamination or its slow-moving dynamics simply haven't permitted contaminants to arrive in the lower reaches of the aquifer. Ashworth worries that the chemical buildup from recent agricultural practices has just begun its slow creep downward toward the water table but in time will make its way ultimately to the saturated zone at the base of the aquifer. Ashworth questions whether it is really a good idea to employ pesticides and fertilizers designed to be carried by water, especially in places where that water can find its way into important groundwater sources. This is a problem not just in the Ogallala but around the world.

In a sense, the decision to dispense pesticides in the water in this way could be seen as a triumph of cleverness over wisdom.

The decline of the aquifer will be slow and unnoticeable from the surface. But if the aquifer is being polluted at the same time it is being drawn down, water quality could deteriorate to the point where the water cannot be used without treatment. This is possible if only because Americans believe that overdraft and these agricultural practices are too important to their economy to demand that it be stopped. William Ashworth characterized the problem in a no-nonsense way that touches on the widespread problem of the disconnect that often exists between what we know and what we do:

> The thread that runs through all of these changes is an assumption that the Ogallala Aquifer will survive – at least for a while, at least in some form. All the new patterns require access to more water than plains rains can dependably supply. The Ogallala is the only other broadly available water source.
>
> For the most part, High Plains residents understand this. But there is a curious disconnect between what they understand and what they do. They forge ahead anyway, buoyed by the optimistic outlook, common to most human endeavors, that something will turn up – because it always had, because technology can create miracles, but mostly because what they are doing is too important to stop.[26]

Another interesting thing is happening. Users such as dairy farmers have begun to relocate from already water-scarce areas such as California to where they believe they can tap into reputably reliable Ogallala sources. The trend toward migrating away from stressed or scarce water supplies and toward reliable water sources has become global. But it is only a matter of time before many of these supposedly water-secure places – the Ogallala among them – will be unable to meet the demands being made of them. This migration will continue and likely accelerate as the impacts of long-term groundwater overdraft begin to be felt in places like India and China where groundwater overdraft is supported either consciously or by lack of effective regulation.

The similarities between what is happening on the High Plains and with groundwater management in places like Alberta are stunning. Despite inbound population migration, there is a growing sense that the certainties upon which even the immediate future is being modelled and projected have lost their validity. In parts of the region there appears to be considerable discrepancy between how much water there is on paper and how much there is in the ground. State engineers in High Plains jurisdictions have admitted they don't really know how much water is actually being withdrawn from the aquifer. This problem has much to do with the difficulty of measuring cumulative withdrawals from so many wells. As in Alberta, a conscious decision was made that it was not important to maintain accurate drilling records. Decisions were made to transport water from the aquifer despite the fact there is no reliable measure of how much water is being or has been withdrawn over time.

Though the US Geological Survey was finally brought in to begin monitoring withdrawals, all they have been able to do is create an island of data that is of limited use in long-term planning. Water managers now have only a crude handle on what is actually happening now in the hydrological regime defined and exploited by engineers over the last century. Unfortunately, just as in the Canadian West, there is no certainty that these same regimes will persist into the future as past and present climate warming express themselves in changes in recharge patterns in the aquifer. Meanwhile, just as in the water-scarce regions of the Canadian prairies, districts fight to keep the water they are presently allocated and they make constant demands for greater withdrawals to prevent others from getting water they might like to be able to use in the future.

There is nothing particularly equitable about the High Plains system. Restraint is impossible because management of the aquifer is defined by the lowest common denominator: the Rule of Capture that permits Texas residents to draw all the water they want from under properties in neighbouring states like New Mexico. As William Ashworth bluntly points out, there is nothing a property owner can do to prevent a long Texas straw from sucking their wells dry but watch. As a result of such laws, no one can preserve water even when it is fully understood that recharge is minimal. The only practical choice is to pump the water out of the aquifer yourself or watch someone else pump it out from underneath you. In the context of the Ogallala, the tragedy of the commons has become the American way.

So what, one might ask, were we doing visiting Texas if we wanted to learn about progressive ways of managing declining water resources? Ironically, the backward nature of the Rule of Capture approach to appropriation has forced Texas to become something of an innovator in groundwater management.

Groundwater management districts on the US High Plains

The first groundwater management districts in the High Plains region were created in Texas following the passage of the Underground Water Conservation Districts Act. It was interesting to ponder the enactment of that bill (in June of 1949, some six months before I was born) as we passed the Capitol building in Austin on the way from our bed and breakfast to the Lyndon B. Johnson School of Public Affairs, where our discussions about groundwater took place.

What is interesting about the Texas Rule of Capture is that it stipulates what state law has decreed about liability issues related to groundwater withdrawal but says nothing about its management. The law very clearly prohibits one from suing one's neighbour for draining all the water from underneath one's land. But it does not, as David Eaton points out, prevent you and your neighbour from coming to an agreement on how your joint water supply might be managed. In fact, the legislation – in an almost backhanded way – encourages joint groundwater management as the only way of preventing neighbours from entering into permanent destructive competition to take as much water as they possibly can so as to ensure you get yours before your neighbour does. A proper management agreement, if honoured, removes the hostile incentive to take yours before your neighbour makes yours his. While you still can't sue your neighbour in Texas for draining your well dry, you can enter into an agreement that makes all parties legally responsible for meeting mutually agreed-upon management conditions.

The first underground water conservation district in Texas came into existence in 1951. Centred in Lubbock, it encompassed six counties. There are now 87 groundwater conservation districts in Texas, 11 of which draw from the Ogallala. Only six of the state's 43 High Plains counties are not at least partially included within the formal boundaries of a groundwater district. Five groundwater districts also exist in Kansas and others have been created in Colorado. They have also been created, under a different name, in Wyoming, where they are known as Groundwater Control Areas. Nebraska, Oklahoma and New Mexico also have similar institutions.

How to create a groundwater district in Kansas:

- file a declaration of intent with the office of the Chief Engineer of Kansas
- be investigated and certified by the Chief Engineer
- file a petition for election
- hold an election and have the results certified
- file for incorporation with the office of the Secretary of State
- following incorporation, hold a meeting to elect a board and formally organize the district

The Kansas model may be of particular interest to western Canadians in that it permits groundwater districts to come into existence on essentially their own terms. Each district can make its own rules subject to the approval of the state engineer. These rules then become part of the Kansas Administrative Regulations, which makes them legally enforceable within the district. It is widely held that the strength of such regulations resides in the fact that they require little enforcement because they are created from within the district rather than enforced from without. While annual inspections are necessary, most operators in violation want to know how to fix the problem rather than contest the results of the inspection. But despite these obvious advantages, government oversight remains necessary to prevent collective self-interest from advancing groundwater management in directions that are not sustainable.

The problem with the Kansas approach – and the problem with all forms of self-regulation – is that parties that come together to create a groundwater management district can decide collectively to do things that may bring immediate benefit to themselves but over time may do harm to the aquifer and/or users in surrounding management districts. Local wishes may still take precedence over the larger common good. In the final analysis, state legislators retain ultimate jurisdiction over groundwater resources. State governments retain the right to impose specific regulations that groundwater management districts are legally responsible for meeting.

While imposing outside fiats on homegrown solutions devised at the local level can be politically explosive and potentially difficult to enforce, state governments have the authority to declare groundwater district mechanisms a failed experiment if they don't deliver sustainable long-term results. The problem, of course, is that by the time a state government knows about and acts upon a failed district system, damage to aquifers managed by these districts may already be irreversible.

There resides in this example an important lesson for Canadian provinces that extends beyond groundwater issues to include initiatives like Alberta's Water for Life strategy. If the creation of local watershed advisory groups and the downloading of local control does not yield appropriate and timely results, then the government must be prepared to impose its will.

It is worthwhile to compare the management of water on the High Plains with similar processes in Alberta for other reasons as well. It is interesting to note that there is no surface water irrigation on the High Plains, because by 1900 all of the rivers through the region had been siphoned off by upstream users. Where springs and remaining flows continued they were often badly damaged by allowing cattle to compact the soil and contaminate the water. As in Alberta, drilling records have also proven to be an inadequate source of groundwater information, for a number of reasons. First, irrigation and drinking-water wells are only drilled as deep as they need to go to find reliable supplies. This means that knowledge of the nature of the rest of the aquifer that lies below remains imperfect. There exists in Texas as well as in Alberta real concern about the quality and relevance of drilling data. Most well drillers keep logs only because they are required by law to do so. Most have limited interest in the formations and geological record beyond understanding the hardness and texture of the materials they must drill through. As William Ashworth reported in *Ogallala Blue*, it is held in some professional circles that well drillers are "basically mechanics who can keep a complicated piece of equipment like a drill working. Their job is to make a little hole in the ground and pull water out of it." It is a job drillers have done well, in both Texas and Alberta.

A lot of water is being pulled out of a lot of little holes drilled into the Ogallala, and not everyone is satisfied that local rules established by groundwater management districts are resulting in appropriate use of the groundwater that flows under the High Plains. Alarm over rates of withdrawal were expressed very bluntly by University of Nebraska water law expert David Aiken at a major symposium on the state of the Ogallala held at Texas Tech University in Lubbock in 1984. William Ashworth quotes Aiken in his book:

> Texas . . . has followed the politically convenient local control approach to groundwater management. The result is virtual economic depletion of irrigation groundwater supplies in

Texas by the end of the century and the associated reduction of agriculture and related economic activity. High Plains irrigators have thus far attempted in vain to obtain a source of supplemental water to rescue themselves from their failure to control groundwater depletion. . . . Texas serves as an example to other states [and I should say provinces] concerned with groundwater depletion, not of how depletion should be controlled, but rather what will happen when depletion is not controlled.[27]

Will a cultural shift toward water thrift be sufficient?

Against all odds, a dramatic decline of the Ogallala has not yet occurred. Water table and well yields continue to drop but the rates of decline have slowed. Agriculture remains viable in many places that were projected to run dry by the end of the 20th century. The principal reason why these declines have not appeared is that major shifts have occurred in local attitudes about the importance of water conservation. These shifts in attitude have also been mirrored in agricultural practices in western Canada. Less water is wasted between the well and the crop, and tillage practices have been improved. Wastefulness is now seen as more than just carelessness; it is considered a social and economic blunder.

Reprieve brought about by cultural change, however, may not be occurring soon enough. The predicted Ogallala apocalypse may well have been delayed but it has not been prevented. Many observers argue that rapid decline of the aquifer could resume at its old alarming speed at any moment. The reason for this is that greater water use efficiency often leads to greater actual use justified by the need to pay for expensive improved conservation technology. In the end, water conservation doesn't always mean water is actually conserved. As we have seen with advances in irrigation technology in Alberta, business opportunity usually trumps conservation, and the same crop production with less water invariably leads to more production with the same water and no actual net reduction in use.

We seem to have a habit of tricking ourselves into thinking we are doing the right thing when in fact we just doing something different. Too often, gains in water availability achieved through new conservation technologies don't end up as net conservation. Instead, the water that is supposedly conserved is simply used to meet previously unmet demand. This happens on the High Plains; it also happens elsewhere in Texas; and it happens all the time in Alberta. Efficiency-minded irrigators in southern Alberta, for example, have put forward that they don't need or want more water. But they are not prepared to use less.

Though rising costs are beginning to make deeper pumping of the Ogallala uneconomical, political pressure continues to grow as a result of further demands for withdrawals, all of which should be of interest to anyone living in the water-scarce regions of the southern plains and the semi-arid regions of southern Canada. New extractions include those associated with bottled water production, which offers high premiums for water use; the continuation of limitless withdrawals based on the Rule of Capture in Texas; tanker pipelining to adjacent dry areas; and river flow augmentation to meet the requirements of interstate water compacts and treaties.

This last use is of particular interest because of recent court rulings that political boundaries within the United States cannot be a constraint to the movement of either surface water or groundwater. As a result of these precedents, groundwater is now being treated as an article of interstate commerce. This legal requirement to treat water as transient now holds no matter whether the water in question is groundwater or surface water *and* whether or not there happens to be an interstate compact in place that governs the second but says nothing at all about the first. Such considerations clearly ought to inform any developing plans for deeper integration of Canada with the United States through proposed initiatives such as the Security and Prosperity Partnership, as these could have huge impacts on our country's sovereignty with respect to our water resources.

It is interesting to note, especially given our reason for visiting Texas, that modelling has not been able to fully reproduce the complex dynamics of the Ogallala Aquifer. While the capacity of models continues to improve, legal precedents are being established that are beginning to have impacts far beyond the High Plains region. A settlement related to developments that dried up the Republican River, which at one time flowed over top of the Ogallala Aquifer in Kansas, has led to a legal precedent that recognizes that groundwater pumping in one state can affect the water supply in another, and damages should be awarded accordingly. As a result of the Republican River settlement, Nebraska has declared a moratorium on new wells in the Republican basin and has begun installing meters on all existing wells. The lessons here are very clear. Even on large aquifers such as the Ogallala that were once thought to be inexhaustible, all wells have to be monitored if you want to manage water efficiently over the long term. But even with efficient water management, groundwater over-pumping in one jurisdiction can and will affect water supply in surrounding jurisdictions. It is only a matter of time before Alberta and Saskatchewan, for example, will have to deal with such issues over the 19 known aquifers in which these two Canadian provinces share access.

Another far-reaching implication of Ogallala management concerns relates to who decides what constitutes beneficial use. We learn from the Ogallala that it is no longer a question of whether or not any specific use will be continued; it is a question of whether or not any given aquifer can in fact survive, especially when greed enters the picture, which in Texas it clearly has. The Panhandle Groundwater District tried to put some kind of lid on overdraft in 1998 when it put into place what was called the 50-50 Rule. While far more complicated than even William Ashworth was prepared to describe, the essence of this rule is that the saturated thickness of the section of the Ogallala that is found within this groundwater management district may not be reduced by more than 50 per cent during the 50 years the agreement was to remain in place. The supposition here was that well owners would only be allowed, under the conditions of this rule, to pump water from the top half of the aquifer. Not everyone agrees that saturated thickness is an appropriate measure, but even critics accept that it was better to try something – anything – than simply continue the overdraft problem and hope it goes away. As one astute observer was quoted by Ashworth, the 50-50 Rule was "all they could get away with," hopefully on the way to a more durable solution. That durable solution has yet to present itself.

Whatever happens to the Ogallala, it is not likely we will see a sudden collapse of the aquifer. The depletion of the aquifer will be gradual, and as it unfolds the region will slowly return to dryland agriculture, which will mean dramatically lower productivity. The decline of the aquifer and the region it once supported will likely not be big news while it is happening, as we will be facing even more pressing water scarcity issues elsewhere in the world at the same time. Other North American aquifers are expected to be in difficulty as well. One of the other places in Texas where aquifer mining is imminent is in the Hill Country in the southern part of the state west of Austin and north of San Antonio. While the Ogallala is more famous, the Trinity Aquifer is of special interest to David Eaton and the Lyndon B. Johnson School of Public Affairs at the University of Texas at Austin. It was the opportunity to explore the connections among Eaton, the University of Texas and the Trinity Aquifer that formed our main purpose for visiting Austin.

The Trinity Aquifer

The Trinity Aquifer is an important source of groundwater supply for agriculture, industry and municipalities in the Hill Country region of Texas. Substantial development and recent droughts have together heightened local concerns about groundwater availability in the aquifer. Regional water planning groups are now required by state law to plan for future water needs under drought conditions, but there are other problems facing this aquifer. Landowners in northern Bexar (pronounced "bear"), Bandera, Kendall and Kerr counties who get their water from the Trinity Aquifer want to know how pumping and drought affect water levels, groundwater availability and the environment generally.

In 1990 exploding growth atop the Trinity Aquifer and concern over regulation of water withdrawals led the Texas Natural Resource Conservation Commission to designate the Trinity region as an area where critical water shortage is occurring or expected to occur in the next 25 years. The region's special status as a Priority Groundwater Management Area, or PGMA, has provided county officials with authority to regulate development over the aquifer to the extent that developers can now be asked to prove there is enough water available before planning new construction. From this we are reminded once again that southern Alberta is far from the first place in North America where water scarcity has already begun to limit economic and social development.

Although the Trinity Aquifer is recognized as important to the state of Texas, yields from it are often small compared to surrounding aquifers. The Trinity can hardly hold a candle to the Ogallala in the northern part of the state. Though it remains vitally important locally, average yields from the Trinity are barely 1/250th of average yields in the Edwards Aquifer farther south. But water is water and reliable sources are important no matter where you live in Texas. Lower yields, slow recharge, fluctuations in level and greatly increased pumping have demonstrably decreased the reliability of the Trinity Aquifer during periods of drought. There is also growing concern that heavy pumping, especially during dry periods, has caused water level declines and an increased potential for encroachment of poorer quality water and depletion of base flows in nearby streams. Given that Texas is just a little farther downstream in the same groundwater exploitation continuum we are following in water-scarce areas in southern Canada, provinces like Alberta can learn a great deal from what has happened and is happening to this aquifer.

It has been observed that unlike the Edwards Aquifer farther south, the Trinity recharges very slowly and water moves more slowly through it than through the Edwards. It is estimated that only about 6 per cent of the rain that falls over the area above actually ends up recharging the aquifer. It has also been discovered that the Trinity and Edwards aquifers are to some extent linked. So even though water users in the Hill Country use the Trinity, they are caught up in controversies associated with the Edwards. Hill Country groundwater districts must manage not only their own withdrawals but developments and discharges that might eventually affect the quality of the water that ends up as Edwards Aquifer recharge.

As is often the case with major aquifers, there are actually several sub-aquifers that make up the Trinity. For much of the Trinity, current rules and regulations resemble those that existed for the Edwards Aquifer before the state legislature passed a Senate bill that for the first time imposed groundwater withdrawal controls on a Texas aquifer. Despite this groundbreaking legislation, Senate Bill 1477 applies only to the Edwards Aquifer, which means that the Rule of Capture still prevails in Texas outside the Edwards Aquifer region. As is the case elsewhere, few restrictions remain on using groundwater or drilling wells into the Trinity Aquifer. Overdraft continues at an alarming rate. This has led to some of the most bitter and divisive debates in the history of Texas, a fact that policy-makers would be wise to examine carefully in the interest of avoiding similar circumstances in places such as Alberta's water-scarce south. What is happening with the Trinity illustrates how wrong things can go before they are no longer tolerable or acceptable and have to change.

The Rule of Capture continues to fuel bitterness over the

manner in which water appropriations from the Trinity Aquifer are allowed. There are cases where wealthy developers have forced nearby residents to have to haul water after their wells went dry because they didn't have a long enough straw to prevent golf courses from taking their water from right beneath their feet and putting it to uses that affected not only the Trinity but the neighbouring Edwards Aquifer. The only way the residents could fight back was to create groundwater management districts with the power to craft legally binding water sharing agreements that would protect the viability of the aquifer to whatever extent possible.

By July 2001 nine groundwater districts over the Trinity, including those in Comal, Kendall, Hayes, Bandera, Blanco, Gillespie, Kerr, Medina and Travis counties, had joined the Hill Country Alliance of Texas Groundwater Districts. Members of this alliance favour local control over the creation of a more formal external authority such as the one formed to regulate withdrawals on the Edwards Aquifer. They fear that such an authority would put control of their water into the hands of water marketers and people who do not have the best interests of the communities at heart. In order to come to terms with the future of their aquifer, they began working with the Jackson School of Geosciences, the School of Law and the Lyndon B. Johnson School of Public Affairs at the University of Texas at Austin to determine the desired future conditions they would like to create for managing the Trinity Aquifer. To our great delight, Dennis Fitzpatrick and I walked in at a crucial moment in the evolution of this groundbreaking process.

A New Texas Model

Using computers to understand desired future conditions

After our morning discussions, we had lunch at the University's elegant Faculty Club with a number of Dr. Eaton's colleagues before returning to the Lyndon B. Johnson School of Public Affairs to observe how a group of 24 water managers from India worked with an eerily familiar Texas groundwater management situation employing a computerized model initially created by the Texas Water Development Board that Dr. Eaton and his colleagues had adapted for the use of Groundwater Management Area 9, which the Hill Country Alliance is part of. Eaton and company had created a software "wrapper" for the complex Texas Water Development Board model that allowed users to employ it more easily. These modifications included simplified inputs and the capacity to alter what the outputs of the model can be. They also incorporated into the Texas Water Development Board template the capacity to run the model frequently in real time so as to create optimization tools that could be used to arrive at better, mutually acceptable results.

What is remarkable about the simplified University of Texas model is that it invites participants in the training program to try to beat the game instead of beating one another. In the case of Groundwater Management Area 9, it was the choice of the participants to go beyond the training the model provided to put possible solutions into tangible relief. This they did voluntarily, as David Eaton pointed out, because they could. As we were about to see, participants quickly became so interested in beating the game that when they lost they immediately demanded better tools, more accurate data and more information about how the game really worked. Each run of the model, each new attempt at beating the game, brought participants closer to more complete common knowledge of the aquifer and toward new solutions that became apparent through shared exploration of the problems presented by their own demands and expectations.

The latest improvements to the "wrapper" were to be tested by water managers visiting from India in preparation for a much-anticipated session of game-playing scheduled with the members of Groundwater Management District 9 the following day.

The exercise was organized by graduate students Michael Ciarlegio and Marcel Dulay, who outlined the ground rules for the Indians, who were in Austin for a three-week course on public policy at the LBJ School. Their introduction was consistent with William Ashworth's observations on the Texas groundwater situation, which was very familiar to the Indians by virtue of the problems they faced at home.

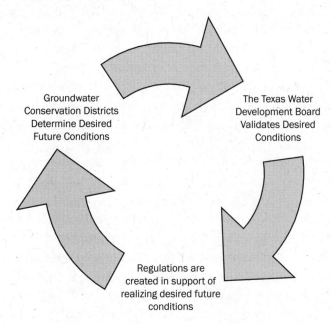

The first step was to establish desired future conditions. Desired future conditions are defined as quantified groundwater circumstances at a specified time in the future. An example of a future desired condition might be that spring flows be no lower than 10 per cent of mean flows in perpetuity. Desired future conditions can also be defined, as they have been in parts of the Ogallala, as a percentage of water remaining in the aquifer over a period of time, say, 50 per cent over 50 years.

The LBJ School has employed a technique called "narrative codes" in assisting the Hill Country Alliance to come to terms with desired future conditions. Narrative codes are really little more than situational stories that participants in the process share so as to establish a common understanding of the collective problem they are trying to resolve. The Indian water managers were very interested in these codes. It was fascinating to observe that the narrative codes being employed in the collaboration to find common ground with respect to groundwater withdrawal in Texas are the same as those that form the foundation for a similar process we hope to advance on the South Saskatchewan River basin in southern Alberta. Suddenly I could see that this narrative approach could help unify common interests around more inclusive management of the most troubled watershed in the Canadian West. I soon discovered, however, that the narrative codes were only the beginning of what was different – and very promising – about the LBJ process.

Bench-testing the beta

Prior to our arrival, the members of Groundwater Management Area 9 had been working for months to create the model the Indian water managers were invited to examine in our presence that afternoon. Hoping to anticipate any problems with the "wrapper" of the model prior to the "game" scheduled for the next day, Eaton and company introduced the same constraints the Texas Water Development Board had imposed on Groundwater Management Area 9. They could manipulate the model in any way they saw fit to arrive at ideal outcomes based on local management decisions for the period beginning in 2000 and extending to 2050. Essentially participants in the process could manage the Trinity Aquifer in any way they saw fit, with only one proviso: whatever management regime you adopted, it had to incorporate the capacity to withstand circumstances imposed upon the aquifer by at least one multi-year drought.

As the Indians quickly discovered, there were also other limitations implicitly imposed by the model. While the model was capable of testing a great number of variables and an automated search function worked very quickly to find the best criteria to satisfy the needs of all jurisdictions, the amount of groundwater presently being extracted from the aquifer put serious constraints on the range of management options still open for exploration by the groundwater management area.

It was amazing to see how effectively the model worked. Individual participants were invited to tell their laptop computers what they wanted the average drawdown of the aquifer to be and, in concert with the model, the program would determine whether the requested drawdown was possible and what the potential impacts might be on surrounding groundwater districts. If individual or collective drawdown requests were greater than what the aquifer could deliver, the model would fail to converge on a solution. If this happened, the computer graphic would display the part of the aquifer in which the problem occurred and outline how and when the overdraft caused its capacity to collapse.

While we were only observers, we too were invited to follow the process on our own laptop. Dennis Fitzpatrick of the University of Lethbridge and I both observed how easy the model was to use. We could see the Indians were very eager to learn from it, so it wasn't long before they were all clustered around their laptops plugging in demands for ever-increasing withdrawals. It was soon clear that they were vigorously hoping to beat the model so as to demonstrate to their American hosts that they too knew how manage water. As there was a great deal of similarity between the Texas situation and the groundwater overdraft situations they were familiar with at home, there was no small of amount of peer pressure among them to see who could triumph over the model first. The ambient noise level quickly began to rise as each group of two or three entered and re-entered new drawdown expectations and measured their demands against the impacts on agreed-upon ideal long-term outcomes. It wasn't long before the classroom sounded very much like the arrivals area of a major Indian train station. It wasn't long either – as one might expect in a ground-water situation as complex as the one that exists in the Trinity Aquifer – before there was frustration and then disagreement. The nature and intensity of the disagreement proved to be more telling than I ever could have imagined.

In less than an hour the Indians began to see that no mat-ter what they did, they could not achieve ideal future conditions that assured water availability for all users, the maintenance of flow regimes in springs and the simultaneous maintenance of groundwater flow levels over 50 years if they had to take planning for a five-year drought into account. A long drought anywhere in the time sequence simply made it impossible to meet current and future average drawdown expectations that were required if the ideal outcome of assured water availability to all users was to be achieved. This was hardly surprising to Dr. Eaton or his colleagues. Certainly it would not have surprised the Texas Water Development Board, which sees long-duration drought as a serious enough threat to the reliability of water supply in the state to demand that drought planning be mandatory in all future groundwater management plans. What happened next, how-ever, was even more interesting. When confronted with limita-tions of a multi-year drought, the Indians simply demanded that this limitation be removed as a modelling and management constraint. They then presented their reasons for making such a demand.

The Indians' logic went something like this: "As a user I should have the right, especially given that I have been charged with the maintenance of the resource, to ignore the threat of drought if I choose and pump the aquifer without factoring this threat into withdrawal projections. If I want to take the drought factor out of the modelling formula, I should be granted the right to do so." When their right to do so was set against the parameters set by the Texas Water Development Board for the modelling exercise, the Indians had a ready answer. Their point was they should be permitted to ignore the threat of drought disaster in management plans, provided that everyone involved agreed that they will establish and stand by separate protocols that come into play the moment a drought appears.

I must admit that I found this attitude alarming. It seemed to me that what the Indians were doing was relegating drought to an outside domain so that they did not need to include its likely prospect in the formula through which everyone's allocation expectations were to be realized. The notion here was that a new, higher level of regulation would suddenly come into play when drought appeared that would divorce its impacts from the management processes upon which users relied to supply the water required in any given area under normal conditions.

Atomizing risk by sleight of hand?

This proposal put the cat among the pigeons, so to speak, with respect to the role played by drought in the management of increasingly scarce water resources. In the court of engineering application, it is perfectly reasonable to atomize risks until the elements are small enough to be managed technically. This works well on paper at least. The Indians proposed that the best way to manage drought was to relegate it to a separate management subset divorced from day to day management consideration. With the issue of drought out of the way, at least temporarily, the model could be put back together again so that it appeared that the risk of drought had been managed. The next step was to continue to build withdrawal capacity into the system as if the risk of drought were a remote concern that would receive special attention only if and when it presented itself as a risk.

While this is a widely accepted practice worldwide, it struck me, as an observer, as a very risky way to manage water, especially where populations were large and needs great as they are in places like India. Saying you will manage water differently in a drought does not mean you are addressing the threat drought poses to the reliability of either surface or groundwater sources. In fact, it increases the risk of quite the opposite happening. By dismissing the risk and continuing to increase pressure on the system by intensifying withdrawals to the very limit of the system's delivery capacity, you in fact increase to near certainty the chances that drought will cause serious disruption. The risk is no longer that only some users will be without supply in an extended drought. By relegating risk to a separate domain and increasing withdrawal demands as if the risk were somehow remote from the management process you are modelling, you amplify the risk far beyond what would have existed had the withdrawals been limited to what the aquifer can produce in less than optimal circumstances. Drought will come – it always does to places like India and Texas – and when it does, a greater proportion of the oversubscribed system will be vulnerable. Management of the drought will require not just partial shutdown of parts of the system as it would if water availability were subscribed only to the lower limit of productivity, but quite possibly a complete shutdown of the entire system. Depending upon the intensity and duration of the drought, disruption of agriculture and industry could be widespread. This is not risk management or even risk aversion, except in name only. To push the very limits of withdrawals as a matter of course is to put everything on the line every time there is a drought. What kind of management, I wondered, is that? I waited to see what Dr. Eaton and his colleagues would do.

It soon became clear that neither Dr. Eaton nor any of his modellers felt it was their place to tell users what to do. Their function, as they saw it, was to put their dispute resolution process and their modelling capacity at the disposal of those playing decision-making roles in the computer game and let them arrive at whatever public policy choices they could agree upon. Had they commented upon the choices the Indians made, they would have compromised their complete neutrality and the valuable leverage it provided in putting new and better shared water management decisions into relief over time.

The Indians, however, had given Eaton and company a great deal to think about in anticipating how Groundwater Management Area 9 might respond to the model they helped created when they met to play the game in less than 24 hours.

Testing the software for real

The next morning, Dr. Eaton arrived to collect us at 8:30 p.m. We arrived at the LBJ School just as the first representatives of the Hill Country Groundwater Alliance began to file in. In their cowboy hats, jeans and boots and their casual, friendly demeanour they resembled any one of dozens of farming and ranching groups in Alberta. This meeting could just as easily be taking place in Lethbridge as in Austin.

When everyone was assembled in front of their laptops, the Indian water managers filed in to sit as observers of the process they had experimented with the day before. Once again, David Eaton's graduate students Michael Ciarlegio and Marcel Dulay officiated but did not constrain the proceedings. They explained that the purpose of the day's gaming exercise – as already agreed upon – was to create a 50-year plan for the management of the Trinity Aquifer over a period that began in 2000 and ended in 2050. It was also pointed out that the Texas Water Board had prescribed that the model be constructed in such a way that it would be able to respond to a drought, between 2043 and 2050, of a duration that mimicked the longest drought of record – seven years – which had occurred in Texas in the 1950s. Pumping estimates in the model were to be based on regional water planning group projections, which in turn were to be based on estimates determined by a recent survey of water users. The time step portrayed in the model was one year. While growth projections were already built into the "wrapper" of the model, the software would also allow users to examine the effects of different future pumping rates in each of the model zones.

It was already well understood that the Trinity and Edwards aquifers are highly sensitive over the long term to very small changes in baseline pumping values. For that reason the modellers built in a provision that permitted users to vary the increase and decrease of withdrawals in any given district by increments of only 10 per cent in each model run. Michael Ciarlegio quickly discovered, however, that the members of Groundwater Management Area 9 had come to the table with much higher expectations of future withdrawals than the modellers had anticipated. County representatives were not satisfied with the prospect of mere 10 per cent increases in groundwater pumping over time as permitted by the model. Some were looking for 200 per cent to 300 per cent increases in the amount of water they could draw from the aquifer in each of their districts. Neither were they satisfied with the idea of gradual increases in the delivery of their expectations. They wanted these large increases as soon as they could be accommodated. With Dr. Eaton's quiet encouragement, Ciarlegio and Dulay handled the situation perfectly. Making no judgment at all on the nature of these expectations, they simply allowed the game to speak for the capacity of the aquifer to meet their demands.

Because of the stress the aquifer was already under, especially in Comal and Bexar counties, the model found it impossible to converge on a solution for such high withdrawal demands. An error signal came up on each participant's laptop, indicating that the model could not comprehend such an extraordinarily high level of projected pumping. The facilitators calmly explained that, in order to accommodate such high levels of projected withdrawals and portray their effect visually, it would be necessary to redesign the model to give it the capacity to assess the broader consequences of much larger drawdowns. But a crucial point had already been made by the model itself. The aquifer would clearly fail under much lower pumping scenarios than any of the districts had anticipated. Even under current use, the model depicted huge areas of the aquifer where all the water would be pumped out by 2050.

Though the participants were astounded, there was no one they could blame for the failure of the model to process their expectations. Nor was there a need for blame. No one was negotiating for real. There was nothing tangible at stake. It was only a game. It was they who had, in essence, constructed the parameters by which the model operated, so there was no need to blame the modellers. Ciarlegio and Dulay had made no judgment whatsoever on the nature of each district's excessive future withdrawal demands. They were just facilitating the game. It would be hard to blame the government, for it was through the Texas Water Development Board that local management responsibility had been placed right where the districts wanted it – in their hands. The only avenue left was to do their collective best to see if they could beat the model in search of other ways to arrive at more desirable future outcomes. It was at this point that the game took on some stunning new dimensions. Suddenly participants began demanding more information, better data and a clearer picture of how the fundamentals that made the model work. They wanted to keep playing until they beat the game.

It is exactly this development that Dr. Dan Sheer of Hydrologics Inc. had explained was the signature of a successful real-time computer-assisted collaboration on water allocation and use. This development in the gaming process marks a huge divide where interests cease blaming others for limitations to current water management processes and begin competing, not with one another, but against the very model they collectively built with the aim of truly arriving at the most desirable future outcomes. It was precisely this result that we hoped to achieve by applying a similar process to the future management of the South Saskatchewan River in Canada. There was no longer any doubt in our minds that such a process could succeed in Canada. We had seen it work right in front of our very eyes in Texas.

The power and potential of this process reside in the fact that participants are able to visualize real circumstances and possible future scenarios on their own terms. They can see what mistakes look like before they make them. As each new realization is internalized, one more step is taken toward transcending past adversarial entrenchments. As all participants go through the same revelations at the same time, the process quickly puts into relief the urgency of working together to explore the widest range of use patterns, operating rules and technological options that are currently available or that might be available in the future.

The numbers don't lie: There is no free lunch

When the first model-run based on increased withdrawal expectations crashed, no one present needed any explanation of what it meant. It portended nothing less than a water crisis in the Texas Hill Country. As one participant said, "This is a great way to cut to the heart of the matter!" The ongoing value of the process is that each participant comes to their own conclusions on their own but can also continue to play the game against the model, independently or with others, to determine how best to arrive at future desired circumstances. It is here that the real collaborative breakthroughs are often made.

As the Groundwater Management Area 9 representatives continued to work the model, some of them determined that if they worked together they might be able to manage up until 2040 in a manner that would allow them to prevent being wiped out by a drought of the duration of the drought of record that occurred in Texas in the 1950s. They did, however, make the same point the Indian water managers had made a day earlier about how in a drought separate rules come into play that demanded reduced pumping regardless of the kinds of agreements that may exist within or between water management jurisdictions. To my astonishment they too demanded to remove the risk of a drought of record from the modelling formula. It was pointed out that – because of the Rule of Capture – a great deal of pumping is an unregulated right in Texas even in drought. As some of the participants reminded themselves, however, pumping can be limited even at the unregulated level if a drought management plan existed to permit it. It was in order to facilitate the creation of such plans that the Texas Water Development Board now demanded both a water conservation plan and a drought plan if any given groundwater water conservation district expected funding from the state. In the meantime others were continuing to run the model projections of scenarios they desired. The same participants who had earlier hoped for withdrawal increases of 200 to 300 per cent found it impossible to arrive at anything even close to the future desired circumstance – which they now pronounced to be a drawdown of no more than 35 feet in the aquifer – *even if they reduced future uses by 50 per cent.* They also began to see how excessive use in one county could very much affect future water availability in surrounding counties.

As participants explored possibilities, circumstances appeared in which it became clear that even if one county cut projected uses by 50 per cent and surrounding counties didn't, the aquifer in that county would fail even though withdrawals were dramatically reduced. The aquifer, it was discovered, was already so heavily tapped that only one of the nine counties had even the remotest potential to increase withdrawals in the order of 300 per cent and still come anywhere near the ideal desired future conditions.

Without any intervention by the facilitators the participants soon came to an independent understanding that every one of the groundwater districts had to reduce their expectations or none of them would be able to achieve desired future conditions. All of this became apparent without even yet requiring calculation of the effect of a drought of record or incorporating climate change projections into the model.

It was put forward that perhaps the best way to rethink management options for the Trinity Aquifer was to imagine the world as it might be like in 2050 and then work backward to ensure this was not the world that groundwater management districts created in Texas. It was then pointed out that counties at the downstream end of the aquifer must figure out how much water they currently need and will need and determine which of their upstream neighbours would sacrifice some of their water to ensure the downstream users had enough. Suddenly it was put forward that the Texas Water Development Board data may be inadequate to the extent that it may represent pumping rates as being less than what actually occur. There were demands for more accurate data and immediate improvements in the model. The members of Groundwater Management Area 9 came to consensus on this issue independently by comparing their own modelling results. By lunchtime they were in the midst of agreeing to return to their constituencies intending to explain that local expectations of two- and threefold increases in withdrawals from the Trinity Aquifer were simply not possible. They were ready to report that, in fact, even current withdrawals in many areas were likely not sustainable.

While historically it has always been difficult for representatives in a collaborative process to return to their constituencies with bad news, these participants had the unique advantage of being able to recreate exactly what happened during any given computer-assisted scenario exercise because they could take home with them on their laptop the very model upon which that scenario was simulated. By learning how to play the game themselves, they could then show the folks back in their county exactly how they arrived at the conclusions they were reporting. They could also model additional scenarios to test further hypotheses about how to achieve desired future outcomes in their groundwater district and throughout the aquifer withdrawal area. I know of only one modelling application being used in western Canada that possesses these same qualities of flexibility, adaptability and transparency – for either groundwater or surface water management – and that is the one Dr. Dan Sheer developed in association with his colleague and friend David Eaton. This is the Hydrologics Oasis model the University of Lethbridge has proposed to employ to engage interests in Canada in new ways of thinking about how we might manage the South Saskatchewan River basin.

Following the modelling demonstration we walked to a very elegant restaurant attached to the campus football stadium in which 90,000 University of Texas fans congregate to watch their beloved Longhorns play each fall. Following a very successful lunch follow-up meeting with senior University of Texas administrators, David Eaton took us on a tour of the city. Austin is surrounded by hills. Each possesses grand views of the Capitol and the downtown business district. Many looked down upon the Colorado River Valley, the source of surface water that makes this hot area habitable.

Dr. Eaton delivered us to the Austin airport in plenty of time for our flight home to Alberta. We could not thank him enough for his generosity, both intellectually and in terms of his kind hospitality. I can honestly say I have never seen anyone in a university – except perhaps for Dennis Fitzpatrick at the University of Lethbridge – who was more committed to ensuring that their university was involved in initiatives that really matter in a directed and practical way in the world.

On our flight to Denver, I tried to plot out all I learned from this brief but very intense experience. These two days changed the way I think about the preciousness of our resources and the ways in which they could be valued and managed. I can now appreciate how changes in attitude and habit can actually be effected. I also have a much clearer idea now of how gaming based on carefully developed computer models can be made to work in the hands of serious stakeholders. Though I knew there would be obstacles, I hoped that we could use what we learned in Texas to get going on our long-delayed project on the South Saskatchewan River basin.

Pitching the new techniques to the folks back home

We returned home very excited about what we had learned. Unfortunately, not everyone, especially in the Alberta government, shared our enthusiasm. Our first meeting was with scientists and graduate students at the University of Lethbridge. Though it took us more than three hours, we were able to resolve their concerns about collaborative processes of this kind, which largely related to whether the gaming method worked and how they themselves, as researchers, might be able to benefit from it. They were not prepared to support such a process collectively until they were satisfied the collaboration would be driven by scientifically defined performance measures. Another concern was the need to be able to publish findings related to the process in academic journals, which, we were reminded, are the stock in trade of serious academic credentials.

Once these obstacles were overcome, faculty members began to offer important observations on current circumstances related to the management of the South Saskatchewan River basin. One highly respected researcher pointed out that empirical and modelling data were at last converging within this important watershed. The South Saskatchewan, he offered, is fast becoming a sentinel for climate change impacts in the interior of North America. Of real concern to these scientists was aquatic ecosystem health. It was also pointed out that one important performance measure being proposed for the Red Deer River, a tributary of the South Saskatchewan, was that aquatic ecosystem health would require no less than 85 per cent of the natural flow of the river. If such a performance measure were to be adopted as a regulatory management standard, the Red Deer River would instantly be fully allocated if not overallocated in terms of current permitted uses. We have not yet defined minimum in-stream flow needs for any watercourse in southern Alberta. The point was very clear. There was a lot of work that needed to be done to ensure optimal management of the South Saskatchewan River.

Our next meeting, with Alberta Agriculture, was very positive. Senior people in the department's Lethbridge office understood clearly that what we had seen in Texas had real application in the water-stressed South Saskatchewan basin. They pointed out a number of emerging concerns that could perhaps be addressed in a creative way through computer-assisted collaborations of the kind we described. Their concerns were straight-forward. They wanted the process to proceed based on the flexibility and transparency of the model and the desirability of exploring consensus regarding science-based performance measures that would improve management of the river over the long term. They wanted to make sure everyone involved recognized the important work already done by Alberta Environment. They did, however, agree that an alternative hydrological model would be helpful especially in the context of managing climate change.

Alberta Agriculture experts explained that, at present, optimal water availability for crop development takes precedence in the management of water resources in the South Saskatchewan River in Alberta. They observed that flow recession curves after the spring freshet are crucial to aquatic ecosystem health, and that aquatic ecosystem concerns are not presently considered in the management of flows in the river. They explained that with higher temperatures – like those we were experiencing during my visit to Lethbridge – will result in higher rates of evaporation. Higher evaporation rates will mean that water managers will no longer be able to optimize crop development without more storage. Even with more storage, however, it will be difficult if not impossible to optimize the growth of some of the crop types presently favoured in southern Alberta. Alfalfa was mentioned as an example, as even today farmers cannot keep up with the supply of water needed to optimize production of this crop. Farmers must stop irrigating alfalfa crops so as to allow them to dry so they can be cut and baled. But even under present temperature conditions, current irrigation systems cannot supply enough water to restore optimally productive conditions. This situation and others like it, Alberta Agriculture worries, will be exacerbated by further climate warming.

It was put forward that an overhaul of the water management process is overdue, especially given the prospect of longer drought projected to occur in all current climate change models. Such an overhaul, Alberta Agriculture offered, would be greatly assisted by the availability of leading-edge computer-assisted modelling collaboration tools of the kind Dan Sheer and Hydrologics were offering.

It was also pointed out that the tensions that would emerge during a three- to five-year drought could shatter co-operative relations in southern Alberta. Any modelling exercise we could employ now to prevent that from happening would be of inestimable value.

We thought everyone in Alberta would be thrilled with the news we were able to report from Texas. They were not. Alberta Environment had their own model, and even though it didn't have anywhere near the transparency of the Texas model, that was the end of the story.

It did not appear that it had occurred to anyone in Alberta Environment that the openness and support provided by the State of Texas in the process we observed at the University of Texas in Austin was just what the Alberta Water for Life Strategy promised but was obviously not ready to deliver.

For months after our return, Alberta Environment continued to stand in the way of exploring the new possibilities we had witnessed for managing conflicts over water use in Texas. In time it became apparent that for all our celebrated political and ideo-logical similarities, Texas is in fact different from Alberta. Texas has antiquated water laws but is attempting to employ stunning new modelling processes to work around those laws. Alberta, at the time of this writing at least, just has antiquated water laws.

Unfortunately, water concerns in western Canada are not going to go away. In order to prevent water availability and quality issues from limiting our economic and social future, we have to change the way we think about, manage and share responsibility for our water resources. Fortunately, there are tools already devel-oped by others that could help us do just that. All we have to do is start using them.

CHAPTER SIX

Our Cold Amazon

THE OTHER WEST

Even in the most senior professional water circles, there is a bias in Canada toward an east/west way of thinking about our country. With the advent of the train, the car and the plane Canadian notions of place have been slowly subverted by linear thinking. Many of us have lost connection with the reality of landscape and watercourse and become lost in self-centred myth. Though we know better, most Canadians act as though our country really does exist along an east/west axis that extends from sea to sea in a neat, straight line from Victoria to St. John's along the plane of the American border. The sensuous, sinuous nature of our watercourses, however, tells us something quite different. While most of the people in our country live along the imaginary line that is our boundary with our US neighbours, comparatively little of our water flows due east or due west. While the overwhelming majority of Canadians live in the south, that is not where most of our fabled water resources are found. Many of the greatest rivers in this country flow north into northern seas. We are a country that really does extend from sea to sea to sea.

Heading north of 60

On a flight to Yellowknife with Henry Vaux I wondered what we might have to offer water resource managers in the Northwest Territories. The NWT is so different from the rest of Canada. It is remote and expansive and unique in that it has abundant water where other parts of the continent do not. The answer to that question lay, we concluded, in the fact that the NWT is so large and so few people live in it. With only 42,000 residents in an area three times the size of France, the government must of necessity be small. There are not many who have a full grasp of the state of the Territories' water resources, which are considerable. There is also a problem with the scale of the region and the cost of transportation in the far North. If you want to go anywhere in this eternity of lakes and rivers, you have to fly and even then it can take a very long time to get anywhere.

Then there is the problem of just comprehending the main hydrological feature of the region. The Northwest Territories is essentially composed of a single river basin, the 1.8 million square kilometre Mackenzie system, a basin so large it encompasses one-fifth of the entire area of Canada and contributes 60 per cent of the fresh water that flows into the Arctic Ocean from sources in this country. The system is so big that not even very many locals have seen its full extent. Though its peak discharge of around 35,000 cubic metres per second is about the same as the St. Lawrence, its drainage basin is nearly twice as large. Though it is one of the great rivers of the North American continent, it is so distant from any population centres that fewer than one in a hundred Canadians have likely ever even seen it. For most Canadians, the mighty Mackenzie is as much myth as it is fact; part of our history and historical identity, maybe, but separated by a vast distance from people's everyday reality. The Mackenzie is a cold and brooding silence somewhere "up there" that Canadians don't think much about except maybe in connection with the energy resources that exist there that we will some day have to exploit if we want to sustain the prosperity that permits us the luxury of not knowing where we live, beyond knowing the names of our most important rivers. All that, however, is about to change – and that is why Henry Vaux and I were invited to Yellowknife.

Our climate is warming and nowhere is this more apparent than in the North. As an opportunistic species we have been ignoring the potentially problematic effects of this warming and concentrating only on potential benefits. These include more hospitable winters, more readily accessible northern natural resources and the potential of using the fabled Northwest Passage as a shipping route. There seems to be only one problem: the pesky locals who live in the North do not want their way of life compromised by the damage warming is causing to the landscape they depend on for their livelihoods and way of life. They have seen enough of poorly regulated resource development and don't see much benefit for them if their frozen North melts away into soggy soil soup as a result of permafrost loss.

As a consequence of birthright and long intergenerational connection to place, many northerners are highly sensitive to the economic value of functioning natural ecosystems and have a strong sense that what they are sitting on will become a lot more valuable to the world in its intact state as natural systems continue to disappear at an accelerating rate over much of the rest of the globe. At present, however, locals face two problems. Many northerners reject out of hand the notion that a monetary value can be put on their culture and way of life. Even if they accept that such valuations might be useful, they aren't sure they know how to put an appropriate dollar value on the ecological services the Northwest Territories provides to the country. Their second problem is that even if they were sure of their estimates, they doubt the rest of the country and particularly their unruly southern neighbours in Alberta would recognize that value, especially if it was estimated to be far more than anyone would have anticipated. Our goal in visiting NWT was to see if we might not be able to marshal some outside intellectual resources that would help address these two problems.

Northern voices, northern waters

We are by no means the first to bring such sensibilities northward. A great deal is known about the Northwest Territories and in particular about the Mackenzie River system. Much of this information has come into existence and been made accessible through the efforts of the Mackenzie River Basin Board, which was created to implement the Mackenzie Basin Transboundary Waters Master Agreement signed by the governments of Canada, British Columbia, Alberta, Saskatchewan, the Northwest Territories and Yukon in 1996. The Mackenzie River Basin Board brought forward its first "State of the Aquatic Ecosystem" report in 2003. An overall finding of the report was that there was a need for improved monitoring, compatible data collection and more comprehensive evaluation of results in order to translate findings in support of the aquatic ecosystem health of the river. While this could be said of most river systems in Canada, what is different about the Mackenzie is that ways of understanding this environment include large elements of traditional knowledge and local experience and appreciation of place that is seldom taken into account anymore in southern Canada. It is important to note, however, that most of the traditional and local knowledge considered in the 2003 report had been gathered before 1995. While this may have been a moot point in periods of relative ecological and climatic stability, it may not be moot now. Nearly two decades have passed since much of that data was collected. In that brief period of time, the landscapes of the Northwest Territories have changed more than they have in generations. Many First Nations peoples have already experienced more change than they wanted to see.

In previous visits we had gotten an earful concerning what First Nations thought about landscape compromises that linger for generations as a result of short-sighted resource extraction practices. We also heard a great deal of concern about climate change. There was no small rancour surrounding the role southerners have played in the warming of the North by way of extravagant lifestyles and excessive greenhouse and other emissions in upstream locations such as Fort McMurray in Alberta. That dialogue was to continue during this visit.

Though the first meeting we attended in Yellowknife was very polite, all of the non-governmental organizations represented held much the same view as First Nations with respect to the primacy of environmental integrity over economic interests in the North. Perhaps because so many of those attending the meeting were young there was a great deal of idealism in the room. That idealism was kept in close check, however, by the fact that there were so few voices in the Northwest Territories, while there were millions of people to the south who had become very comfortable with the prosperity brought about by tar sands developments at Fort McMurray and elsewhere, and who didn't know or very much care about the impacts these activities might have on their downstream riparian neighbours to the north.

The rest of our meetings in Yellowknife, including those with government agencies, followed these same themes. Certain activities in the south were having huge impacts on the North. Many of these impacts were already beginning to tell on local climate and water. But with so few voices, how could this truth be told?

Great Slave Lake

The following afternoon, as perfect as any to have ever existed in the history of this planet, was spent flying over parts of the Northwest Territories that had been affected by the changes to which our hosts had introduced us. Our guide, that is to say the person on the flight charged with pointing out landscape features we were flying over, was a NWT government conservation officer named Fred Mandeville. Mandeville knew the region intimately and demonstrated the informed casualness that many northerners exhibit when invited to share deep knowledge of places they care a great deal about.

In a landscape of the scale we were exposed to during our three-hour flight, there are no simple statements, statistics or standard tour guide ploys that can make an outsider feel as though they should be even remotely comfortable here. During the flight I saw the immensity of the East Arm of Great Slave Lake with my own eyes but I can't say I came anywhere close to comprehending it. Reflecting even now on what I saw on that perfect autumn afternoon causes my mind to slow in utter awe. Great Slave Lake is an enormous natural feature and we only saw one arm of it. I still have to chip away at its dimensions so I can even have a hope of coming to terms with its scale. The lake is 480 km long and from 19 to 109 km wide. The total area of the lake – depending upon the source you pick – is between 27,200 and 28,400 square kilometres, which means it covers an area a third larger than the country of Israel. Imagine much of Israel and neighbouring Jordan under a single lake and you get the picture. And this is only a small part of the Mackenzie system.

Though it is the ninth largest lake in the world, Great Slave Lake still isn't the biggest body of water in the Northwest Territories. Great Bear Lake is bigger yet. But what Great Slave lacks in area compared to Great Bear Lake, it makes up in depth. At 614 m – 2,014 feet – it is the deepest lake in North America. This is where Canadian water goes to live. In this single enormous natural reservoir are 2090 cubic kilometres (500 cu. mi.) of fresh, clean Canadian water. If all this water were to disappear, northerners would be left with a valley that was far below sea level. If there were still a lake in that valley, it would be like the Dead Sea.

The volume of water in Great Slave Lake is a meaninglessly large number unless it can be put into a relevant context. I live on the banks of the Bow River in southern Alberta. The Bow is a small river but an important one. Though its waters represent only 3 per cent of Alberta's annual river flow, a full 30 per cent of the entire population of the province relies on its waters for drinking, growing food and sustaining industry. The average annual recorded discharge near the mouth of the Bow is about 2.8 cubic kilometres of water. At its current annual rate of flow it would take the river that flows through the town where I live 746 years to fill Great Slave Lake to its current level.

The first question that may come to mind might be this one: how did so much water end up in just one lake? As John Vallentyne and David Schindler observed in their book *The Algal Bowl*,[28] the eastern part of Great Slave Lake is considered ultra-oligotrophic, meaning it is low in nutrients and has only small algal populations, traits that are typical of lakes left behind after ice age glaciers melted.

As Vallentyne and Schindler point out, most of the lakes that exist today in the world, and all of the lakes in the Northwest Territories, were created only very recently in geological history. Most, including Great Slave Lake, were created as a result of the scouring of the landscape by continental glaciers that ground across vast areas of both the northern and southern hemispheres as recently as 10,000 years ago. Wherever the scouring created an impermeable basin or natural dam, lakes came into existence.

Schindler and Vallentyne demonstrate how readily this can be validated by looking at a map of the former distribution of glacial ice and comparing it with a map that shows where lakes exist today. Nowhere is this more obvious than in the Northwest Territories. There is a clear line between the western part of the region surrounding Great Slave Lake, where almost all the water drains into this one huge basin, and the eastern part, which includes the East Arm. This eastern portion is underlain by igneous hardrock rather than permeable sedimentary rock, which means the surface water has nowhere to go but into pools on the land's surface.

Before we got on the plane we were each given maps that illustrate this phenomenon perfectly. When I folded the map of the Yellowknife region in half vertically, the left side was dominated by Great Slave Lake proper. Almost all the water in this area is concentrated in the lake. When I look at the right side of the map at the East Arm, however, almost all of the water is concentrated in small lakes that appear to exist everywhere on the landscape. There are literally tens of thousands of them. The landscape is one part land, two parts water and – in summer – one part mosquito.

The seam that separates the Jekyll from the Hyde of this landscape is the Taltson River which, as Fred Mandeville pointed out, demarcates the boundary between two major geological provinces – the hard rock of the Canadian Shield to the east and the calcareous region to the west where soils have formed to at least some depth that allows water to be absorbed and where relief allows the bulk of the water to flow into the basin that contains Great Slave Lake.

Because so much of Canada was scoured by glaciers in the way we saw below, there are countless lakes in this country. Though no one has actually counted them all – and all you need to do is to look at the map of the East Arm of Great Slave Lake to know why – estimates suggest there are likely between two and three million lakes in Canada. It wouldn't surprise anyone up here if half a million of them were in the Northwest Territories.

A lot of the water that is so obvious on maps of the Northwest Territories is not renewed each year. It is water left over from an earlier and wetter geological period. One of the reasons it is still here is that the Northwest Territories is so cold. The winters are often long and bitter and northern summers brief. Even the nearly 24-hour days of midsummer cannot warm all the water sitting on the land as lakes, wetlands, fens and muskeg. There is just too much water to heat, and of all the common compounds on Earth water takes the most energy to change its state from solid to liquid to vapour. But all that may be changing.

Researchers have discovered that permafrost is disappearing in the Northwest Territories at rates no one could have imagined a decade ago. One study conducted by researchers from Wilfrid Laurier University[29] indicates that most of the permafrost in this part of the Arctic is at a mean annual temperature of -0.1 to -0.2°C. At the rate of melt observed between 1947 and 2000, it would take an estimated 90 years for the permafrost in the study area to disappear. At the rate of melt witnessed between 2000 and 2008, however, the permafrost in the study area is not expected to last more than 30 years.

Permafrost is the foundation of the hydrology of vast regions of the North. The rapid and increasing rate of its disappearance means that the hydrology of the Northwest Territories has begun to change. As northern climates warm we will not be able to rely on cool temperatures to keep water in the lakes, wetlands and muskegs. Vast areas of the North are already exhibiting signs of drying out. As John Smol at Queen's University and Marianne Douglas at the University of Alberta have learned, lake levels are dropping, stream flows are diminishing and the landscape is changing in response to what all that water is doing differently than it did in the past.[30]

Smol and Douglas observed that, as measured against the backdrop of paleolimnological records, some ponds and attendant ecosystems have dried out as a result of a warming climate. As these ecosystems represent the most common habitat in many polar regions, their desiccation may represent a threshold that has been crossed with respect to climate change effects on polar regions. Smol points out that while the desiccation of small, shallow ponds is of ecological significance, what is of real interest is that even larger ponds are disappearing completely. Not only has the standing water evaporated, but the land in the area of these former ponds has dried to the point where it is easily ignited. This suggests that parts of the Arctic are ceasing to be carbon sinks and are instead becoming carbon sources. In a sense, Smol's work confirms what many scientists have feared most. Permafrost loss is only one problem. A larger, related problem is that warmer temperatures are evaporating surface waters and drying out the tundra, turning the Arctic into a three-million-square-kilometre "horizontal smokestack" belching CO_2 from the underworld into an already dramatically altered atmosphere. As Smol points out, a key "tipping point" has been passed. Arctic ponds that were permanent water bodies for millennia are now ephemeral. Smol worries that the ecological ramifications of these changes could be devastating. It was these changes that the NWT government and their federal colleagues at Indian & Northern Affairs Canada wanted us to see.

What Fred Mandeville took such pains to show us also confirmed, through comparative first-hand observation, all that Henry Vaux has been saying for a decade about the end of the hydrological stationarity upon which we have built the foundation of water resource management in our time. For a hundred years we have expected hydrological regimes to act within known ranges of variability and to allow themselves to be confined within the parameters of established engineering control. But as we were shown while looking down at Great Slave Lake, that stationarity no longer exists. Northern waters are on the move and the scale of that movement appears to be enormous.

The people who live in the Northwest Territories can clearly see these changes and are afraid that climate change will undermine, perhaps utterly, the relevance and validity of traditional and local knowledge. This will happen because what occurred in the past will no long be a reliable guide to the future. They are afraid that no matter what is done now, they will no longer have it in their power in the future to keep what they have or bring back the conditions that once were the foundation of traditional cultures and relationship to place. Southerners may eventually see that what we are doing to First Nations in the North, we also doing to ourselves. But by then it may be too late. By filling the sky with our invisible emissions we are cutting ourselves and all future humanity off from the past. We are setting ourselves adrift on an ocean of change, bound, it would appear, for the rocky shores of a future we neither intend nor desire.

Before this flight I had an intellectual sense of what even a minor increase in temperature might mean in the North from talking with researchers, reading the scientific literature and examining scenarios created by climate models. But until I flew over Great Slave Lake mine was only an intellectual conception of what might be happening. For Fred Mandeville, landscape change is not an academic concept. In effect, his house is on fire and though he remains calm about it he is not the kind of man to stand around watching as it burns. Fred also has other problems besides the fire. As one would expect, all his northern friends have responded with equal concern and efforts to help. He fears that his upstream neighbours to the south, who many suspect contributed to the conditions that led to the climate change fire, may be spilling so many contaminants into the water and so much carbon into the air that the water he pumps onto his house will only cause it to burn hotter still. His concern was hard to dismiss. On this flight we could see evidence of how hot the climate change fire was becoming and how hard it would be to put it out if neighbours to the south didn't turn down the heat.

The moral and ethical dimensions of climate change effects on the North

Unlike those who live in southern cities, who are often oblivious to what climate change is doing to the landscapes and natural processes around them, the people in the Northwest Territories, Aboriginal and otherwise, are close enough to the land to observe what is going on. This fact in itself makes climate change a moral and ethical rather than academic issue among these people. It is an argument, however, that is only slowly coming to the fore in the climate debate.

The philosophical and moral dimensions of climate change impacts are only now being considered more widely in southern universities and other institutional circles. One of the first popular works of note to appear on this subject was a book by James Garvey.[31] The book is interesting in that it put some of Fred Mandeville's voiced and unvoiced concerns into plain language. At Great Slave Lake, Garvey's ethical arguments converge at the landscape level.

Not surprisingly, the very public debate that has been raging around the climate change issue over the last two decades has largely been carried on by climate scientists, economists and to some extent politicians. Noticeably absent from the tumult until now has been the thoughtful and logical voice of philosophers. Philosophy is the branch of human knowing that concerns itself with practical moral problems. It is the discipline that allows us to systematically analyze the moral implications of inaction and the moral adequacy of action choices with respect to concerns related to the human condition.

While philosophy departments in universities around the world have been examining the moral consequences of the climate change question for some time, most of this analysis has not made it out of academic circles into the broader public domain. For this reason, philosophy has appeared, from the outside at least, to be almost silent on the issue of how we ought to frame global warming arguments within the context of individual and collective morality. This has been regrettable. Science can only tell us so much. While climatologists can explain what is happening to our planet and may even be able to predict what might happen in the future, what we do about what science tells us will depend utterly upon what we think is right, what we value and what matters to us most. This, as James Garvey points out, is the domain of philosophy.

The fundamental tenet of Garvey's philosophical analysis of the global warming threat is that there is no uncertainty where it counts with respect to climate change science. It follows then that denial stands in the way of appropriate moral evaluation of the problem. Garvey also points out that the most important climate change variable is not the rate of glacial melt, the extent to which the oceans can absorb carbon dioxide or the frequency or effect of sunspots. It is us. It is what we do – and not what nature does – that matters. Within this context, there are three philosophical questions that need to be answered: What is happening? What are the causes of what is happening? And what should we do?

Garvey proposes that proper philosophical inquiry into the global warming question demands first of all that we recognize the role of morality in decision-making concerning the issue. This means that actors in decision-making processes that aim to determine appropriate human responses to the climate change threat should be held accountable for giving reasons for their beliefs. Philosophy argues that personal biography and history are not valid or even necessarily relevant in establishing appropriate moral direction as to how we should respond to the effects of global warming.

Garvey begins by laying down the fundamentals of his philosophical tradition. He argues, as have so many philosophers before him, that if life is to have meaning, we have to invest it with that meaning. Within this context, not acting in accordance to moral reason is considered worse than meaningless. It leads to recklessness and even viciousness. Without meaning to inspire and direct us, we are nothing at all or at least much less than we might be.

Determination of the morality of a given climate change response, Garvey offers, might well be founded upon notions of justice. One of the fundamental principles of justice is that harming the innocent is unjust. If one subscribes to this principle of justice, then inaction on climate change is in itself unjust, because it results in harm to the innocent.

The innocent in the context of the Northwest Territories could be considered those who have not been granted choice or agency in decisions related to how the landscapes around them are changing as a result of the impacts of outside others. The innocent also include those to whom no benefits flow even from positive consequences of decisions related to how climate change will be managed in their time. The innocent are the most vulnerable in that they have the fewest resources. The innocent in this regard do not enjoy distributional equity in that decisions related to the extent to which climate change is addressed elsewhere only widens existing economic gaps and other divides that separate them from the general prosperity of the society of which they are only peripherally held to be part.

Garvey goes on to suggest that climate change raises a number of difficult moral questions go beyond established notions of justice. Some philosophers, Garvey tells us, have proposed that an entirely new ethic is required to answer these questions. It may not be harm to other humans only that should be considered unjust. We may, for example, find it necessary to redraw our moral circle to include much more than humans or even animals. If we decided to follow that moral direction, new values would become necessary. We might even be forced to rethink ethics and the nature of valuation.

Garvey, however, is very clear on the challenges climate change presents with respect to making wise decisions concerning morally appropriate action. Climate change presents problems of a complexity that humans have never had to face before. Three aspects of climate change make it particularly difficult to address.

First, the relevant causes and effects of climate change and the agents behind them are spatially dispersed throughout the globe. The fact that different peoples, governments and businesses act in different ways in different places compounds the problem of doing something about climate change. Actions set in motion in one hemisphere have effects on the other side of the world. The way land is used here affects flooding over there. The fuel burned over there changes the effects of El Niño, which causes a drought somewhere else. Wherever these impacts occur, it is often those who have the least who suffer first and most.

Second, the relevant causes and effects of climate change and the agents behind them are also temporally dispersed; which means that effects and impacts will present themselves at different times in different places over intergenerational time spans. It takes time for our actions to be translated into noticeable effects on the climate. By the time we see some of the effects it may be too late to do anything about them. Worse than this, from the point of view of coming to grips with the moral dimensions of climate change, responsibility and consequences are spread over long periods of time that extend from the past into the future.

Finally, reflection on the problem of climate change is much hampered by our theoretical ineptitude. Given the complexity of the climate change issue, it is no wonder that the third aspect of the problem, our theoretical ineptitude, should make matters worse. We are not very good, according to Garvey, at thinking about our long-term future, non-human animals and nature, the value of persons who might never exist, events separated in space and time and so on. We have been able to go about our business as a society without worrying about any of this, so now, when it really matters, we lack both the wisdom and the theory to deal with it.

Citing Stephen Gardiner, Garvey worries that our theoretical failure can lead to a moral failure, a kind of deception in which we focus on one part of the problem and not on others. Garvey worries, as many working today in the field of climate change do, that the complexity of the global warming problem can be an excuse – a morally problematic excuse – for doing nothing at all.

Garvey argues that Canada and the United States should be the object of global moral outrage. He believes that the only way we can only address the global warming problem is through just redistribution of burdens and responsibilities. He makes the moral argument that the better placed an individual or a nation is to do what is right, the greater the onus on that nation or person to do the right thing. Justice in this context would require that North Americans shoulder additional responsibilities to compensate for the unjust distribution of benefits and burdens associated with the disproportionate volume of our emissions and the impact of these emissions on innocent others.

According to Garvey, we should, for example, be forced to pay for sea walls elsewhere. He argues that the global carbon sink must be viewed as a planetary commons as valuable as the planet's freshwater resources.

Garvey goes on to demand reassessment of contemporary notions of stewardship. Based on broader moral perspectives, ideas related to human responsibility for stewardship do not stand up well against the notion that a recent arrival on the planetary scene may not matter that much to the Earth's long-term prospects. Garvey goes so far as to claim that notions of stewardship are in fact a fallacy. "I don't see why a primate, recently down from the trees, gets to be in charge," Garvey writes. This is something to think about.

Throughout his book, Garvey challenges us all to think more seriously about what climate change means to us, ethically and morally. He recognizes that the moral weight of so many miserable future lives can be crushing. He exposes the "expense" dodge by putting into relief the fact that putting costs first is to get things exactly backward. Our real choices, according to Garvey, are moral and therefore come before economics.

In conclusion, Garvey identifies ten expressions of denial and examples of moral weaseling that from a strictly formal philosophical perspective should be considered suspect whatever their source. The weasel words Garvey identifies are ones with which every Canadian will be familiar.

The ethics of climate change get real up North

The first question Fred Mandeville might ask Garvey if ever they might meet is, What might all this fine philosophical reasoning mean in the context of real and dramatically changing circumstances in the Northwest Territories? To what extent should moral and ethical issues come into play when people like Fred Mandeville or local leaders like Michael Miltenberger or Trish Merrithew-Mercredi struggle to address climate change impacts where they live?

One thing that comes immediately to mind – and it is something that comes to mind widely in places that do not generate significant greenhouse emissions but are nevertheless subject to substantial emissions-related impacts – is how unfair it is for people living in the south to deny that anything is happening or that humans are the cause. Climate change denial stands in the way of appropriate moral evaluation of the problem. If southerners simply deny that climate change impacts exist, then they don't have to face the moral consequences of destroying the landscapes and livelihoods of their northern neighbours.

One of the most fundamental of all moral tenets, however, is that the harming of others is unjust. In the context of what is happening in the Northwest Territories, this makes southern inaction on climate change both immoral and unjust. As James Garvey points out, unless some morally relevant considerations intervene, justice means that the benefits and burdens of society should be distributed among people equally. That is clearly not happening in the Northwest Territories where people are saddled largely with the burden of the impacts of southern prosperity but few of its benefits. Thus we find, as Garvey illustrated, that economics alone is not an adequate tool for evaluating the complex questions that arise from climate change. For the people we were with on this flight, moral and equivalent environmental values ultimately trumped issues related to prices, rational self-interest and cost/

benefit analysis. Northerners, nonetheless, remain in a vulnerable position, for until values other than economics matter upstream they stand to lose much of what is important about where and how they live without much recourse to values other than those imposed upon them from the outside.

The people of the North know that sustainability demands something from everyone. But it won't be long before they grow weary of being among those of whom sacrifice is tacitly expected but to whom few benefits flow. Many are already angry that the south isn't doing anything about threats to their beloved rivers or about global warming. They understand that they have to be pro-active about such matters. Failure to do so in the past has already taught them all they want to learn about the crushing moral weight of being responsible for the misery of future generations. Having wrestled with such issues since the arrival of European settlement, First Nations have a lot to teach the rest of Canadian society. Unfortunately, what they have to teach may not be what many southerners will want to learn.

While I continued to think my way through the moral dimensions of climate change denial, Fred Mandeville pointed out further evidence of the impacts of global warming on the landscapes of the Northwest Territories. As we flew over where the Slave River entered Great Slave Lake just north of the community of Fort Resolution, Fred commented on the influence the Bennett Dam in British Columbia had on the health of both the aquatic and terrestrial ecosystems that compose this famous delta.

There are two great river deltas in this area of Northern Canada. Both are renowned for their waterfowl populations, their biodiversity and for what they do to maintain that biodiversity elsewhere on the continent. The first of these is the Peace/Athabasca delta. It is located just below the Alberta border, where the Athabasca River pours out into Lake Athabasca near Fort Chipewyan. Even more remote but just as important is the delta we saw below us where the Slave pours into Great Slave Lake. Both deltas, however, are being starved of water because of the Bennett Dam and because of large water withdrawals to support bitumen mining and processing at Fort McMurray. Mandeville pointed out the impacts. Flood channels that no longer received water were being colonized by vegetation. Riparian habitat was disappearing rapidly as the flood channels filled in. Muskrat numbers had dropped dramatically and waterfowl habitat was vanishing.

As the Bennett Dam stores the waters of the Peace and moderates stream flow over the course of the year in order to provide a reliable source of electrical power, the pulse of annual flow in the river has been altered. The spring flood is much reduced and less variable in volume and seasonal flows are regulated within ranges that make it impossible to sustain optimal biodiversity in the delta. In addition, substantial withdrawals from the Athabasca system exacerbate this effect. Activities in the Fort McMurray area also pose the additional threat of catastrophic failure of toxic-waste containment systems, which could seriously damage aquatic ecosystems, at least as far downstream as Great Slave Lake and perhaps farther. No one knows the exact parameters of this threat, as credible studies of how contaminants might disperse in the event of a dike failure at Fort McMurray remain to be done.

What Fred Mandeville showed us reminded me of the aspen forests in the lower Bow River Valley in Banff National Park that had been spared the influence of wildfire for nearly a century as a result of human aversion to fire in and around tourism facilities in the mountain parks. These forests today are still beautiful, just as the Slave delta was, in the oblique fall light, but there is something wrong. What is wrong with the aspen clones in Banff is the same thing that is wrong with the Peace/Athabasca and Slave River deltas: they are slowly dying because human activities have halted or reversed natural ecological process and succession. We are strangling these deltas from afar, at great potential cost to our collective future.

Henry and I also noticed circles of birch trees splayed in dead circles in pools of dark water. These appeared everywhere and looked from the air like wooden-spoke wheels broken and discarded in black pools dotting the boreal. What is happening here is related to but not quite the same as permafrost loss.

The death of the birch trees is evidence of the melting of ice lenses in the glacially derived soils. A lens of residual ice perhaps a metre or more thick melts, the ground slumps and fills with water, which drowns the birch trees trapped in the hollow. This has been happening, of course, since the end of the last ice age. But the process is accelerating because of warming and is likely to continue accelerating until the remaining ice lenses are gone. The fear is that the process won't simply stop there. As temperatures continue to rise, as they are expected to do in every climate model, evaporation will increase. Eventually – if we don't do something to regulate constantly rising temperatures – all the permafrost, ice lenses and surface moisture will evaporate and the great northern lakes will begin to disappear. The right-hand side of the map, of the East Arm of Great Slave Lake, will begin to resemble the left-hand side, for at some point all the remaining standing water will be gone. We may then discover that the fragile and much-abused Canadian boreal is by biogeographical disposition similar to the tundra upon which it is presently encroaching, in that at its heart it is or can easily become a desert.

As the dryness spreads south to meet the desert that has been created around Fort McMurray, the two aridities will join and march south to meet the northward advancing prairies. Unless rising temperature trends reverse, they will meet in the middle of the pine bark beetle-devastated West of the mid-21st century. If that happens the northern interior of this continent will be on its way to becoming a Sahara. What then might we think of the moral weight of being responsible for so many miserable future lives?

Upstream impacts on the Peace/Athabasca and Slave River deltas are economic externalities in the truest sense in that they represent damages to the world caused by economic interests that have determined that all of society should contribute to their short-term profits. BC Hydro does not include the cost of damage to the Peace/Athabasca and Slave River deltas in the calculation of their electricity tariff. They automatically assume the people of the Northwest Territories don't mind picking up the tab for the costs of this damage through a diminished landscape and reduced way of life. Tar sands operators do not include the cost of the damage they cause in what they charge for the oil products they produce. Because these impacts are likely to occur downstream in the sparsely populated North, the companies hope no one will notice they are profiting in the short term at the potential long-term expense of vital ecosystem function and diminished quality of life downstream. Few will admit that this is a market failure of the order that brought about our current economic collapse. People do live up here, and the health of the ecosystems they depend on for their livelihood matter to them and to the rest of planet.

Developments of this kind would never be permitted at the headwaters of Canada's other great river, the St. Lawrence, but they are permitted here in this cold Amazon because in this country out of sight means out of mind. Fred Mandeville clearly cares about what is happening here but BC Hydro and the oil cartel at Fort McMurray pretend that Fred and people like him don't exist. This public relations strategy is working for the moment, but when you listen to the people of the Northwest Territories, it is clear that ignoring damaging economic externalities until they become political issues at the territorial, provincial and federal level is an invitation to conflict.

The no-longer-frozen North: Pine Point and other digressions

Many in the North are saying they have had enough of paying the environmental costs of southern prosperity, a subject that could not be dismissed as we flew over what southern resource development interests left behind after they made all the money they could at Pine Point. Pine Point is an abandoned lead and zinc mine located on the south shore of Great Slave Lake roughly halfway between Hay River and Fort Resolution. Though activity at the mine came to an end in 1988, the mine has an interesting history that has come alive again in the wake of some interesting recent developments that have brought back some bad memories in the Northwest Territories.

History records that significant lead and zinc deposits were first noticed at Pine Point during the latter part of the fur trade era. As is typical of so many resource discoveries in Canada, Aboriginals told traders at Fort Resolution about the unusual ores and traders hustled to Pine Point to see for themselves. Word somehow got out that there was silver at Pine Point, too, which proved untrue after Klondike prospectors rushed in to stake claims. The rumours about the lead find, however, were true but little could be done to develop the site because of its remoteness from southern markets and the absence of transportation to haul the heavy ores.

The extent of the find did not come to be known until the late 1920s when a number of short shafts or "glory holes" were sunk into the deposit. The Great Depression, however, halted the development of further mining. It was not until after the Second World War that interest in the site was revived. A Canadian mining company, Cominco, had developed a number of new theories relating to how lead and zinc deposits trended in the geology in which they were embedded. By 1955 Cominco geologists had accurately mapped the Pine Point lead/zinc deposits, which extended over a 20-square-kilometre belt. The deposit was so rich that Pine Point would within a couple of decades be heralded as the largest and most profitable base metal mine in Canadian history.

The Great Slave Railway, now part of the Mackenzie Northern Railway, was completed from Grimshaw, Alberta, to Pine Point in 1964. The mine went into full production the following year. Cominco built its own town on the site, which in its heyday grew to a population of 1,200 fully and happily employed souls. In the 23 years the mine was in full operation Cominco produced and shipped 10,785,000 tons of lead/zinc ore south from Pine Point. After the ores were processed at Cominco's smelter at Trail, BC, they yielded some two million tons of lead and seven million tons of zinc. When the profitable ores were exhausted, the one-industry town was dismantled and the houses were sold for a dollar each to people who could move them to Hay River.

When the dismantling of the town was complete, only the roads and some related infrastructure remained – at least visibly. But there were less-visible residues that came back to haunt the site. Land and water were contaminated and full restoration of the site remained incomplete. As is often the case in this age of evolving technology, enough unmined lead and zinc also remained to make the site interesting to 21st-century mining interests. This would hardly be worthy of notice except perhaps locally were it not for one small matter. One of the principals in the mining operation that has since taken over the Pine Point site had also been involved in the abandonment of the Giant Mine near Yellowknife. Many consider the Giant Mine the most environmentally egregious and notoriously expensive mine failure in Canadian history.

Located just a few kilometres from Yellowknife, the Giant opened in 1947. Its name derives from the fact that it remains the largest gold mine ever worked in the history of this country. At full operation, it employed 700 to 800 people and for decades was the mainstay of the Yellowknife economy.

Everyone wants a gold mine in his or her life, but not everyone realizes that a lot of damage can be left in the wake of all the glitter. Mining gold, as the locals soon came to understand, is a dirty process requiring the careful management of hazardous by-products. Arsenic exists naturally in the hard rock of the Canadian Shield.

As a result of the milling that separates gold from the rock it is embedded in, arsenic trioxide becomes concentrated in the tailings. Arsenic trioxide is a problem in that it is one of the more poisonous substances on Earth and it also happens to be water soluble, which can present serious trouble with groundwater.

The gold milling involved "roasting" to melt the gold out of the ore. In the early years of the mine, the arsenic trioxide from the milling simply went up the smokestack and was rinsed off the surrounding rock by rain and snowmelt. Soon, however, every living thing around the mine began to die. Scrubbers were then put on the roasters to remove the arsenic trioxide, which was bagged and stored in old tailings and workings. But soon there was so much of the deadly poison that special below-ground storage chambers had to be built. The storage chambers were called stopes. These stopes were protected by 5 to 100 metres of surrounding permafrost. Some 270,000 tonnes of arsenic trioxide was disposed of in this way, enough arsenic, one local water expert joked, "to kill every man, woman and child on Earth three times over."

The engineering thinking behind this solution is interesting. It was held that the permafrost would reclaim the stopes, encasing and freezing the arsenic dust in ice. This was thought to be a brilliant solution. As so often happens, however, not all the necessary considerations were fully thought out. Not taken into account was the amount of heat entering the storage stopes by way of the mine workings, which eroded the permafrost from below. Another consideration not taken into account was that the arsenic trioxide dust was still hot from the roasting when it was bagged and stored, which caused permafrost melt to radiate outward from the stopes. The melting was further exacerbated by a decision made in the hard economic times of the early 1980s to permit open-pit instead of underground mining of the ores. While the decision to allow surface mining made it cheaper to access the gold-bearing ores, temporarily saving the economy of Yellowknife, the open-pit system began to erode the remaining permafrost from above.

The milling of ore ceased in 1999 and in 2004 the company that owned the Giant Mine declared itself bankrupt and walked away from the problem. The principals of the company went successfully on to other ventures, including the redevelopment of Pine Point. But the permafrost did not stop melting. What exists now at Giant Mine is a series of storage stopes containing enough arsenic to poison the entire Mackenzie system from Great Slave Lake to Inuvik. The poison is water soluble and therefore potentially highly mobile. The only thing presently standing in the way of that mobility is the fact that the dust and its surroundings are only a few degrees below the freezing point of water. But as we clearly observed on our flight over the East Arm of Great Slave Lake and south to Fort Smith, permafrost is disappearing quickly in the Northwest Territories. If the current rate of melt continues into the future as is projected much of the permafrost in this region could be gone in 30 years.

No one knows what will be mobilized by streamflow when the permafrost is gone. The only thing certain is that it will be harder and far most costly to prevent more than a quarter of a million tons of arsenic stored at the Giant Mine from dissolving and being washed downstream. It may be something we can't prevent at the Giant or at dozens of other unreclaimed mine sites all over the no-longer-frozen North.

The people of the Northwest Territories have been left holding the bag. The government of the Northwest Territories and the government of Canada are now faced with having to artificially refrigerate the water-soluble arsenic trioxide stored in the stopes to prevent it from being mobilized by groundwater. The land surface around the abandoned mine and even the tailings can be remediated, but the stopes and the surrounding permafrost will require constant artificial refrigeration and monitoring at huge public cost, probably forever. No wonder the people of the Northwest Territories want a new deal with their neighbours to the south. The deal they have now could eventually kill them.

Restoring the flow: Intergenerational equity and the future of the Northwest Territories

On an earlier visit we met with youth leaders from both Aboriginal and non-Aboriginal communities. Many had strong opinions about the importance of protecting water as a means of protecting the larger landscape integrity upon which so many cultural traditions depend. Though few fully understood just how difficult it will be to resolve current water-related problems, especially as they relate to the North's relationship with its upstream neighbours in Alberta and British Columbia, they had an idea of what to do.

Members of this group had learned much from a mock negotiation of a transboundary water agreement in which many had participated in a recent educational forum. The NWT team, though well armed with superior moral and ethical ammunition, were no match for the team chosen to represent Alberta, who did not deviate in their negotiation from a hard position of economic self-interest and perceived legal rights. It was noted with interest that the fact that NWT is the only Canadian political jurisdiction that has actually legally declared clean water to be a fundamental human right didn't carry much weight with those arguing for southern interests. That the Alberta team could so dominate the discussions on the strength of economic and legal arguments put into relief for everyone present that without other supporting arguments, high moral ground can be a hill to die on.

The mock negotiation enabled participants in the forum to understand just how much preparation must go into any form of negotiation or public policy evolution. Not one of the participants failed to see just how thoughtful you have to be and how hard you have to work if you want to effect real change. It proved you have to know the facts if you wanted to carry the day in political debate, especially if the debate is between sovereign states. Another thing the mock negotiation put into relief was how difficult it was to decide when to use the most important advantages you may possess in consolidating internal support for public policy changes.

Youth leaders in the Northwest Territories believe it is important to establish justice and equity as the foundation for further development of the relationship between British Columbia, Alberta and the Northwest Territories with respect to shared water resources. Rivers, they believe, must be recognized as public resources, and as such, no one should be allowed the right to compromise them. One jurisdiction can't be allowed to make unilateral decisions that affect the quality or quantity of river flows or the enjoyment or use of the river by others. Impacts on water resources are not confined to rivers; they also affect land and wildlife. In a literal and figurative sense, everything drinks from the river.

The forum was also valuable in raising awareness of water issues in NWT and strengthening understanding among the next generation of leaders about how these issues need to be framed, debated and ultimately resolved in a very rapidly changing world. These young leaders recognize that knowledge and fact will be crucial elements in the development and defence of a durable new transboundary agreement over the water resources of the Northwest Territories that have their origins in Alberta and in British Columbia. They recognize also that the people of Alberta don't even know where the Athabasca River flows and most think the impacts of the oil sands are localized.

This view was supported by a major Council of Canadian Academies report on the state of the country's groundwater resources, published in 2009, in which experts drew particular attention to the groundwater problems yet to be fully characterized in the oil sands development region. The report noted that oil sands deposits are relatively close to the surface, which means that mining operations have real potential to damage groundwater regimes. The report also cited the threat posed by large tailings ponds where what is left after the oil is separated from the sand can leach petrochemicals into the surrounding groundwater. The report pointed out that Alberta's regulatory regimes were being challenged by the scale and rate of oil sands development. While environmental impact assessments were being used in development planning, the study observed that such assessments were generally limited to the lease area. In the opinion of the panel of Canada's most respected groundwater experts, Alberta's environmental assessments failed to address large-scale impacts and often neglected cumulative effects of other operations. The report concluded that groundwater use in the oil sands development area was not sustainable as defined by contemporary standards relating to wise use of Canada's groundwater resources.[32]

Youth leaders in the Northwest Territories recognize that before any changes will be possible it will be necessary to educate southerners about these effects and to make Albertans aware that they can't keep threatening the North by way of these developments without eventually impacting themselves. It also had to be understood by northerners and southerners alike that environmental impacts such as those occurring on the scale of the oil sands not only have impacts regionally but are of a concern continentally and globally.

They argued that northerners need to ask their southern neighbours to consider whether they would accept tailings ponds in which dangerous toxins take as long as a hundred years to settle out to be situated where they live. As Michael Miltenberger, the deputy premier of NWT, once famously said, "How would Albertans feel about Fort McMurray if the Athabasca River flowed the other way?" It was important also to point out that the potential impacts of such operations and the full costs of these impacts continue to remain unknown. It was held that new transboundary agreements have to recognize not just the fact but the evolving complexity of these problems.

Youth leaders recognized that the tar sands issues were not static. They observed that the Alberta government had approved and continues to approve major oil sands projects with the promise that technology would be developed that would guarantee proper treatment of contaminated water in tandem with expansion of production. They observed that this has not happened and that as a consequence there are now more than 100 square kilometres of toxic tailings ponds containing billions of cubic metres of contaminated water that no one knows how to treat within any meaningful timeframe. The huge volumes of contaminated water generated by oil sands projects will be a hazard for centuries or until the long-promised treatment technology comes into existence. It was noted, however, that poisoned water was only one of the many problems southerners were creating for themselves and the world in and around Fort McMurray.

The challenge of restoring a boreal forest to any semblance of its original condition when it has been disturbed to the extent and on the scale it has in northern Alberta is as significant a restoration project as has ever been undertaken on Earth. The fact that only a few square kilometres of the hundreds destroyed to date has been restored to even a semblance of its original pristine state does not offer much hope in the context of a future that is likely to be redefined by climate change. Many northerners fear that in the end the long-standing mining tradition in northern Canada of stripping out the profits and leaving a contamination catastrophe for future generations of Canadian taxpayers to clean up will prevail in the oil sands. There are also growing fears that Alberta is about to do with climate change the same thing it has been doing with oil sands water.

Northerners noted with interest that the government of Alberta has decided to address climate change threats not by reducing emissions, which would be impossible without terminating oil sands projects, but by relying upon as yet unproven carbon capture and sequestration technology. The plan is to bury the province's CO_2 garbage in deep geological formations. Unfortunately, just as in the case of the long-promised oil sands water treatment technology, there is no clear evidence that existing carbon capture and sequestration technology will work as effectively as promised in current or projected circumstances. Once again public policy has advanced far beyond the development of the technology required to support it.

The fear in the North is that if the government of Alberta is as successful at implementing carbon capture and sequestration as it has been at fulfilling the promise of protecting water quality in the oil sands, then the resulting damage to Alberta and ultimately to the rest of the planet should be expected to be substantial. No one in the North expects the oil industry or the government of Alberta to respond to such concerns.

Considerable concern was expressed in this context about Canada's international reputation. It appeared to some that a point had been reached in international circles where dangerous questions were beginning to be asked. It seems Alberta could afford anything, but unless some policies change there may come a time when the world will not be able to afford Alberta. The debate centred on the question of how much damage to the planet a single selfish jurisdiction should be allowed to create. This was a question that, given the impact of Canada's disproportionate and growing greenhouse emissions on the rest of the world, young leaders expect to be asked more often.

The dialogue, however, was not just about the South. Youth leaders argued that before the government of the Northwest Territories engages Alberta over oil sands impacts on the Athabasca River, it must move simultaneously toward fixing some of its own environmental problems. They pointed to examples in NWT, such as the Giant Mine and Pine Point, of failure to demand proper reclamation of resource extraction sites. They held that the Northwest Territories must learn from much more successful later developments such as the BHP and Diavik diamond mines in order to improve its own record so that its transboundary water resources management demands will be credible in the eyes of its upstream neighbours and the rest of the world.

They further recognized that efforts to establish workable relations with upstream neighbours over water resources cannot succeed without local public support. In order to assure that support, residents of NWT, and young people in particular, need a better understanding of what is happening to their own environment. This, they observed, will not be as simple a project as it might appear. Youth leaders recognized that young people don't presently have or make time as they did in the past to learn about the northern landscapes around them. The outside world monopolizes their time and attention by way of popular culture and entertainment – and that had to change.

Our dialogue with young leaders was both refreshing and enlightening. Our conversation put into relief that for two generations we have been moving largely in the wrong direction in North America with respect to sustainability. But there is still reason for hope in the future. The people of the Northwest Territories don't want to stop progress, but they would like to stop the northward advance of short-sighted southern water resources policy dead at their border. They want to reform that policy based on sustainability principles from which the people of the North have never deviated. And once they have perfected that policy direction they want to send it back south again fully invigorated, with the hope it will help their southern neighbours regain the sustainability they have lost.

Because of what we have saved in terms of ecological and cultural vitality in Canada's cold Amazon, this may be possible. What we have saved could now save us.

CHAPTER SEVEN

Avoiding the Perfect Storm: Toronto, Great Lakes Water Woes and Climate Change

The principal reason Canadians believe they have more water than anyone else in the world – and therefore do not have to worry about wasting it – is because so much is contained within the Great Lakes. Lakes Superior, Michigan, Huron, Erie and Ontario are collectively one of the great wonders of the world. Within the basin that contains these five lakes is just under one-fifth of all the fresh water on the surface of this planet. Lake Superior is the largest lake on Earth. It alone contains half of the 8700 cubic kilometres of water stored in the Great Lakes. Four of the Great Lakes are among the largest lakes in the world as measured by surface area. In these five lakes is enough water to cover all of North America under a metre of fresh water. These five lakes are so large they create their own weather, so huge they are considered inland seas. But astoundingly there is still not enough water in all the Great Lakes to satisfy the 40 million people who rely on the lakes for all the things they want water to do for them. A full understanding of why this is so will shatter for good the myth of limitless water abundance in Canada.

Understanding the Forms of Scarcity

Physical scarcity vs. economic scarcity

Astounding as it may seem, the people who live in the Great Lakes basin are running out of water. Not because there isn't any; there's plenty. They are running out of water because there isn't enough water for them to do all the things they want to do with it when they want to do them. Though they have more fresh water available to them than anyone else in the world, they use it so thoughtlessly and profligately that even the water they have may never be enough. This puts into relief the main forms of scarcity that we find in our increasingly thirsty world. Physical water scarcity can be defined as a circumstance in which water use is approaching sustainable limits of supply – that is, where more than 75 per cent of the flows are abstracted for agriculture, industry or domestic use.[33] Within the context of this form of scarcity, dry areas may not be water scarce if there are adequate supplies to meet all demands. At present some 2.8 billion people – about 40 per cent of the population of the world – live within basins that face some level of physical water scarcity. Nearly half of the rivers on the planet are degraded to some extent, and flows in a number of major river systems no longer reach the sea. It is anticipated that by 2025 over three-quarters of the people who live on Earth will be facing some form of physical water scarcity.

There is, however, another form of water scarcity that can affect regions that have abundant water supplies. Economic scarcity occurs when human, institutional, infrastructural or financial limitations prevent people from having access to all the water they need or want even though there is enough supplied locally to meet all human demands. Economic scarcity exists when the management and delivery of water services is out of alignment with water supply. Shortages of water in these cases arise from growing economies, increasing populations and changing lifestyles, which in combination result in growing competition for water. Economic scarcity occurs – just as it is occurring now in the Great Lakes basin – because the way abundant water resources are managed is not sustainable.

Economic scarcity and Great Lakes water

As a consequence of growing economic scarcity, water resources in the Great Lakes basin have become vulnerable to overexploitation and pollution and, for all their abundance, are becoming increasingly scarce relative to current and projected demands. The people in the basin want to use water for too many things, and too much water is being made useless for other purposes because it is polluted. Growing demand and increasing competition for water mean that choices have to be made with respect to allocation for various purposes. In the Great Lakes basin, water is needed for drinking and sanitation, hydro-power generation, food and fibre production and for industrial use. If too much water is allocated for these purposes, there will not be enough left in the Great Lakes and connecting rivers to sustain transportation. Water is also required for maintaining ecosystems and their services.

Hard choices also have to be made in the ways water is used. The choice between whether water should be valued for all its uses or simply exploited for the benefit of a privileged few has yet to be made. Choices also remain to be made between wasting and conserving, between polluting and protecting and between over-extraction and managed sustainable use.

Unfortunately, much has been invested in current management systems, and established precedents are hard to alter. The sudden realization that nature needs more water than is presently being provided to it – and the fear that outside others could put a big straw into Canada's shared water resources – is moving basin governments in the direction of change. These fears are driven in part by a general distrust of government, on the part of citizens on both sides of the border, and a lack of faith in governments' capacity to protect the environment.[34] Years of collaboration on water quality agreements and water management compacts between the eight US states and two Canadian provinces that share the basin have yet to yield entirely satisfactory results.

The "State of the Great Lakes" report for 2009[35] indicated that while inflows of bioaccumulative toxic chemicals appear to have declined generally, concentrations remain high in some near-shore areas where the Great Lakes remain receptors from sources such as municipal and industrial wastewater, air pollution, contaminated sediments and contaminated groundwater. As in Lake Winnipeg, algal growth is a problem in some areas as a result of nutrient overloading. The report noted some progress in water quality as it affects human health. Data from over 1,600 beaches along the US and Canadian coastlines indicated that 67 per cent of these beaches were only closed for 5 per cent of the swimming season because of pollution. There were still a great number of problems, however. The report indicated that a total of 185 aquatic and at least 157 non-native terrestrial species were now found in the Great Lakes system. At least 10 per cent of these nearly 350 species are considered to be invasive in that they negatively impact ecosystem health.

The report also commented on water resource utilization. It noted that less than 1 per cent of the Great Lakes waters are renewed each year through precipitation, runoff and groundwater infiltration. At this rate, the net basin water supply is estimated to be about 500 billion litres, or about 132 billion gallons, per day, which is approximately equal to the discharge of the St. Lawrence River. In 2004 water was being withdrawn from the Great Lakes Basin at a rate of 164 billion litres, or about 43 billion gallons, per day, with 95 per cent being returned and 5 per cent being lost to various consumptive uses. The report further noted that parameters such as population, geography, climate and trends in housing size and density all affect the amount of water consumed in the basin and that urban sprawl is changing not only the landscape but the way water moves across the landscape, which in turn is altering seasonal flow regimes. In other words, human use is changing the hydrology of the Great Lakes Basin.

In short, pressure on water is expected to continue to be exacerbated by further population and economic growth as well as by climate change. Experts fear that in some areas of the basin at least, economic scarcity will eventually become physical scarcity. Certainly this is the view of some hydro-power interests. It is also the view of communities that have had to turn to groundwater to assure reliable supply.

As is happening in so many other parts of the world, technological innovations and new sources of supply never seem to be able to keep up with growing demands of an ever-increasing population and the new ways in which people want to use water for their own ends. At present the Great Lakes supertanker appears to be heading full speed toward a future no one anticipated or desired. Crew members are fighting for the helm as the ship heads for rocks exposed by receding waters. Observers on the shore find it almost impossible to comprehend how such mind-boggling historical abundance could suddenly be transformed into scarcity.

Scarcity amid abundance

In the last two decades, residents have begun to realize that water is not as abundant in the Great Lakes basin as they once thought. The principal reason for this is that, just like in the North, most of the water in the Great Lakes is left over from an earlier, wetter period in the Earth's history. Less than 1 per cent of the water in the Great Lakes basin is considered renewable – that is, renewed annually by the hydrological cycle through rain and snowfall and groundwater recharge. In other words, only 1 per cent of the water in the basin can be used if we do not want to diminish the total volume presently in the lakes and the natural systems that supply them. We are already using that 1 per cent and much, much more. In a report released in 2000, the International Joint Commission noted that "if all the interests in the basin are considered, there is never a 'surplus' of water in the Great Lakes system; every drop of water has potential uses." [36]

If we keep drawing down more water than the system renews we can expect lake levels to fall, which will affect transportation; we can expect aquatic and terrestrial ecosystem decline, which will affect water quality as well as cause declines in fisheries. We can expect greater and greater tension among national, state and provincial governments over who should be permitted to use water for what purpose. As cities, farms and factories vie for ever larger shares of water, ecosystems are likely to be the big losers. To continue to provide the broadest range of services, natural regulation and cultural benefits, ecosystems need clean water. This demand by nature itself, however, is not always taken into account when water is abstracted from lakes or when lakes are used as sewers. If this situation intensifies we will wake up one morning facing evidence that for all our abundance in Canada, we have managed water no better than anyone else in the world. The evidence will be that we will be facing the same problems that exist so widely elsewhere.

As economies are intimately linked to the efficiency with which water is used, managing water is now seen as an economic and environmental imperative rather than a luxury available only to those who can afford it. Until recently, water conservation was not a high priority in the Great Lakes basin. It was widely held that there was so much water that no one had to concern themselves with reducing use. As a result, water was undervalued, which led to misuse and abuse. Fortunately, that view is changing, but much more has to be done to dispel this country's myth of limitless water abundance.

Too little water in the Great Lakes basin is only one problem. There can also be too much. Dispelling the myth of limitless abundance is going to be complicated by the fact that climate change is likely to create more circumstances where there is too much water in the midst of longer trends of lesser overall water availability. The reality of what is happening to the world's water resources is counter-intuitive in the context of the way we normally think about natural resources. If our population continues to grow and our demands continue to increase it is not unreasonable to expect scarcity even in the midst of apparent water abundance. Similarly, if the mean temperature of the atmosphere continues to rise we should expect floods in the midst of droughts. And that is exactly what is happening.

WARMING & WATER: A TEMPESTUOUS MARRIAGE

An extreme weather episode: Toronto, August 2005

Many Canadians still misunderstand the climate change threat. As the former chief economist of the World Bank, Nicholas Stern, noted in a recent book, the danger from climate change lies not only, or even primarily, in heat. Most climate change damage is from water.[37] On one hand there is too little water, which manifests itself as drought. On the other, there is too much water, in the form of storms, floods and rising sea level. Too much water is a big problem, especially in areas where infrastructure has been designed to manage lesser extremes.

Many of the world's greatest cities find themselves trapped by infrastructure that was designed to work within far less wide-ranging climate variability than has already come into existence as a result of warming mean global atmospheric temperatures. Climate change impacts on urban structures have become a serious concern in Canada. As the City of Toronto discovered in 2005, many of these impacts relate in one way or another to water.

At the Pacific Northwest Economic Region Summit held in Vancouver in July 2008, Michael D'Andrea, the director of water management infrastructure for the City of Toronto, gave a presentation based on a paper he and three other urban infrastructure experts had presented at the International Symposium on Flood Defence held in Toronto the previous May.[38] The essence of D'Andrea's presentation was that, in the experience of the City of Toronto, there is no question that global warming is in fact increasing the frequency and intensity of extreme weather events and that this increase is already causing enormous damage.

D'Andrea pointed out that in the 20 years between 1988 and 2008, Toronto and the Greater Toronto Area, or GTA, has experienced eight extreme storms that exceeded a 1-in-25-year frequency of intensity. All eight of these storms were of an intensity well in excess of the conventional design capacity of local storm drainage and sewer systems. One of these storms, which was of an intensity expected once in a century, rivalled the impact of Hurricane Hazel in 1954, which devastated Toronto and caused many deaths. The storm that hammered North Toronto in August 2005, dumped 150 millimetres of rain and caused $400-million in damage in just two hours. A major four-lane arterial road collapsed as a result of the washout of a culvert beneath it; other roads suffered significant damage; streams overtopped their banks, causing flooding and erosion damage including the washout of a major sanitary sewer system and a major sewage spill into the watercourse; and some 4,200 homes were flooded. But this, D'Andrea argued, was the only the beginning of what climate change is capable of doing to our major cities.

The graphics he used to illustrate where and how infrastructure failed were unforgettable. The areas hardest hit by the storm had been built in the 1950s and 1960s, with sewer systems typically designed for a 1-in-2-year or 1-in-5-year storm return frequency with no overland flows that would exceed the sewer design. Orthographic modelling illustrated how building in hollows and along the natural courses water used to take before the city was built over top of the natural landscape had resulted in most of the flooding. Stormwater initially ponded in dips in the road and in low-lying areas before backing up onto private property and ponding around foundation walls. The computer graphics showed how roof downspouts connected to the sewer system, poorly graded lots on which lawns sloped toward building foundations, and down-sloping driveways further exacerbated flooding by directing additional flows to already overloaded sewer systems. The audience watched in awe as water flooded drainage and sewage lines and backed up through floor drains to ruin basements.

D'Andrea noted that infrastructure in his city, as in so many others, was designed for less extreme weather variability than is presently occurring, which is making Toronto highly vulnerable to more extreme rain- and snowfall events. Doing nothing about this problem, he argued, was not an option. As is typical in established North American cities, about 11 per cent of Toronto's sewer system is more than 80 years old. Some 4 per cent of it has been in service for more than a century. Fortunately for Toronto, the areas where this infrastructure is still in service were not hit by the storm. But it is not just older infrastructure that was being damaged as a result of more energetic storms. Depending on topography and hydrology, even newer areas are being heavily impacted, especially in intense rainfall circumstances.

What's more, the damage from such incidents can be very extensive to reputations as well as property. D'Andrea pointed out that the Toronto experience proved that public confidence in urban infrastructure managers can be significantly eroded in such circumstances and that this confidence can be difficult to restore. The increasing frequency of such events poses significant questions related to how public policy should respond to the kinds of challenges a warmer, more energetic atmosphere will create in our cities, not sometime in the future, but now.

The Toronto experience made it clear, D'Andrea argued, that the huge costs of adaptation to climate change effects will mean that infrastructure replacement strategies in Canada's major cities will have to be reconciled through different design standards. Adaptation to changing climatic circumstances, he concluded, is likely to demand that municipalities partner with similarly vulnerable other organizations such as the insurance industry to develop appropriate risk management protocols and educate citizens as to their role in helping address the problem.

The Perfect Storm in myth and fact [39]

The notion of a perfect storm emerged into popular culture in 1997 with the appearance of Sebastian Junger's non-fiction work of the same name, which was also made into a popular Hollywood movie. The book is about the "Hallowe'en Nor'easter" as the locals called it – a storm that struck the east coast of North America in October of 1991. The story revolves around the crew of the fishing boat, the *Andrea Gail*, who were out for swordfish nearly a thousand kilometres off the coast of Massachusetts when the storm formed. It is a riveting story based on the hard facts of autumn seas.

It should be noted that it wasn't Junger who first referred to the 1991 tempest as "the perfect storm." It was the US National Weather Service that gave it that name and created its legend. In the history of American weather observation, no one had ever seen anything quite like it. The National Oceanic & Atmospheric Administration (NOAA) still maintains a webpage explaining the nature and character of that remarkable combination of weather events. [40]

Late October and November are months when the eastern United States often experiences a rapid transition in weather. To the west, large cold-air masses from Canada begin to pour south into the Midwest. To the east, the Atlantic Ocean is slower to lose its stored summer heat than is the land mass adjacent to it. These two conflicting conditions often help hurricanes to form over the warm waters farther south in the Caribbean. The contrasting temperatures and dynamics of the two very dissimilar air masses also occasionally result in the formation of massive storms just offshore of North America. These tempests are called "nor'easters" in the Atlantic states and provinces and are known to have caused considerable damage in the past.

It was on October 28, 1991, that this particular extratropical cyclone developed along a cold front that had, in typical fashion, moved northward off the northeast coast of the US. By the end of the day, this low was located a few hundred kilometres east of Nova Scotia. It did not take long, given the support of upper air masses, for the low to rapidly deepen to become the dominant weather feature in the western Atlantic.

This low, however, wasn't the only storm blowing at the time in the great expanse that is the Atlantic. Hurricane Grace, which had formed on October 27 from a pre-existing subtropical storm, was moving northwestward. Grace took a longing look at this new storm and decided to introduce herself. Responding to the strong, westerly deep-layer flows that formed the southern flank of the developing extratropical low, Grace made a hairpin turn to the east and headed toward the low-pressure cell.

Grace was a large system, and though she remained far offshore, she was already generating five-metre swells off North Carolina. At first it looked like she would just stay out there until she lost strength and dissipated, but then something unusual happened. Late in the day on October 29, the cold front from the developing extratropical low undercut and quickly destroyed Grace's low-level circulation. As the low pressure continued to intensify, Hurricane Grace was reduced to a secondary contributor to the phenomenal sea conditions that developed in the western Atlantic during the next few days. If Grace was looking for trouble, she had found it.

An NOAA weather satellite observed that after their brief introduction Grace immediately took more than a passing interest in the stormy stranger that appeared to be dangling before her the prospect of a tempestuous union. As they reached out to one another, the remaining mid- and upper-level moisture from Hurricane Grace entwined with the outer part of the extratropical storm. It was as if the two storms were holding hands. The next day they embraced. The extratropical storm absorbed the hurricane and the two were suddenly one.

The combined storm was a colossus. The centre of the expanded extratropical low drifted southeastward, then southwestward, deepening with each passing hour. Its inner core then developed into a topical storm and later turned into an unnamed hurricane with winds gusting to 65 knots that created waves 12 metres high. It was a storm of uncommon duration. North Carolina's coast was blasted for five consecutive days. Wind gusts of above-hurricane force pounded the New England coastline. The captain and crew of the *Andrea Gail* were not the only ones surprised and then overwhelmed by the hurricane's intensity.

The storm combined with high tides to cause extraordinary damage to infrastructure not designed for such extremes. Coastal flooding occurred along the Atlantic shoreline from Canada all the way down the US coast to as far south as Puerto Rico, the Dominican Republic and the Bahamas. But it was not just the damage that impressed itself on the public imagination. Never before had weather and climate scientists on this continent seen so many seemingly disparate circumstances come together so perfectly to create such violent weather on such a massive scale.

The 1991 Halloween Nor'easter became the public's notion of a "perfect storm." It remained so until 2005 when Hurricane Katrina flattened 250 kilometres of the Gulf Coast before turning the Mississippi River back on itself, destroying much of New Orleans. Some will argue that's a different story. But perhaps it's not. Perhaps it was a warning of other storms to come. That certainly was how it was viewed in Toronto.

Overshadowed by Katrina: Toronto's Perfect Storm

As Michael D'Andrea so often points out, many aspects of natural resource management in the more heavily populated regions of Ontario are undertaken through watershed-based agencies known as conservation authorities. The Toronto & Region Conservation Authority is such an agency and has jurisdiction over water management in watersheds encompassing some 2,500 square kilometres along the north shore of Lake Ontario. The importance of the conservation authorities' role in watershed management is well recognized even where watersheds extend beyond multiple municipal boundaries. In the Toronto area, for example, all but one of the six watersheds within the city extend well beyond Toronto's city limits.

The City of Toronto is the largest municipality within the jurisdiction of the Toronto & Region Conservation Authority and is home to about half of the five million residents in the GTA. While the conservation authority operates flood control infrastructure to reduce flood impacts and provides information and advice to municipalities through its flood forecasting and warning program, the primary responsibility for emergency planning, response and recovery rests with the City of Toronto.

Had it not been for the storm of August 19, the summer of 2005 would have been remembered in Toronto at least for its bouts of torrid heat, smog and insufferable humidity. It was, in fact, one of the warmest and driest summers on record. In a summer that had had less than 70 per cent of normal precipitation up to August 19, the storm suddenly delivered nearly twice the historical average for August in just less than two hours, which once again suggests that traditional averages don't matter when climate variability increases.

The weather system

According to official sources, a warm front running almost north to south entered southwestern Ontario on the morning of August 19, moving rapidly eastward at about 80 kilometres per hour. As the day progressed, severe thunderstorms, which in the forecast included the threat of tornadoes, were anticipated along this warm front due to a very unstable air mass. In advance of the main warm front, a smaller and weaker system entered the GTA, depositing moderate rainfall of 5 to 15 millimetres. All indications from weather forecast models and analysis indicated that the weather system had the potential to create severe weather over a large portion of southern Ontario. However, the speed of the warm front's passage was anticipated to result in only 15 to 50 millimetres of precipitation.

At about 2:00 p.m., a narrow band of thunderstorms associated with the warm front approached the Toronto area and passed over the Niagara escarpment, encountering cooler air over the west end of Lake Ontario. While the overall movement of the front was not appreciably slowed, the system began to back-build, resulting in a relatively narrow east to west band of severe storms trailing the leading edge of the warm front. This narrow band of severe storms crossed over the Toronto & Region Conservation Authority's jurisdiction in just over one hour, during which most of the heaviest rain fell.

The entire system associated with the warm front continued eastward, with all precipitation passing the Toronto area completely by 6:00 in the evening. Although a severe weather system was expected, the intensity of the thunderstorms and corresponding heavy precipitation along the front were not predicted.

Precipitation analysis

The collection of rainfall information from various monitoring stations began immediately following the storm. Data was collected from Environment Canada, municipalities, surrounding conservation authorities and the Toronto & Region Conservation Authority's extensive gauge network. These efforts yielded data from 92 tipping-bucket gauges that collected rainfall throughout the affected region. The co-operation of these agencies resulted in an unprecedented amount of data, allowing for the storm to be accurately mapped and detailed rainfall analysis to be undertaken. An analysis of radar information from both Environment Canada's King City site north of Toronto and from the us National Weather Service site in New York State allowed Environment Canada to undertake a quality assessment of the data provided. The data confirmed that the storm exceeded all previously recorded rainfall intensities for the Toronto area.

Mapping of the total precipitation revealed the storm's track of heavy rainfall, extending from west to east, across the GTA. The maximum precipitation was first experienced in regions northwest of the city.

As the storm moved eastward, however, its centre tracked southward, extending across the north end of the city and then over the Highland Creek watershed. Along the storm track, rainfall of 3 to 4 millimetres fell in as little as five to ten minutes. Rainfall totals in the range of 70 to 120 millimetres were common along the storm path.

A comparison of intensities in millimetres per hour at various sites along the path of the August 19 storm with the historical intensity/duration/frequency curves available for the Toronto city gauge showed that this storm exceeded virtually all past rainfall intensity records.

Flooding rivers

Storm rainfall intensities and urban runoff exceeded all infrastructure design standards along the path of the heaviest rainfalls. The amount of flooding varied widely across the city. The larger watercourses in the west end (with combined urban and rural land use within their watersheds) experienced flows ranging from the one-in-five-year to one-in-ten-year return period levels in the reaches downstream of the path of the storms.

In contrast, flooding of smaller urban streams at the east end of the city measured close to one-in-100-year return period levels. In many locations, the accumulation of debris aggravated local flooding and erosion.

Across the northern portions of the city, where storm rainfalls exceeded municipal drainage designs for major systems, almost every road interchange was flooded to some degree. Low-lying areas with no outlet for flood waters were the hardest hit, with many areas experiencing flood depths of more than 1 metre. As a consequence, transportation was virtually paralyzed for several hours until the water receded. Dozens of vehicles tried to navigate these interchanges regardless, resulting in stranded vehicles and people needing rescue. In many instances, numerous fire and police vehicles were required at each site, severely taxing the city's emergency services. Many of these flooded areas had damage to road surfaces that required emergency repair or reconstruction.

In one location outside of the city, a large sinkhole caused the collapse of an arterial route a month after the storm, leading to concerns of similar issues elsewhere. It would take months to determine how much unseen damage had been done to major roads and other infrastructure.

Most of the 4,200 basement-flooding complaints were received from the north end of the city, where the storm exceeded a one-in-100-year return frequency. Unfortunately, this area already had a long history of basement flooding complaints, dating back to 1986.

System improvement works in the past have focused almost exclusively on the sanitary sewer system through the elimination of hydraulic bottlenecks with oversized pipes, and by constructing in-system storage facilities to provide protection against a storm equivalent to the 1986 storm, which represented only a one-in-25-year return frequency. These improvements proved insufficient to guard against larger, more intense rainfall events, such as the one that occurred on August 19, 2005.

Studies show that the incidence of basement flooding complaints was commensurate with the severity of the rainfall event, when the sewer systems are overloaded and there is significant ponding of stormwater on public and private property. In areas prone to basement flooding, the roads are very flat or have low-lying areas with no place for stormwater to go and therefore typically do not provide a continuous flow route. In these areas, stormwater entered the sewer system through sanitary sewer maintenance hole covers, overloaded foundation drains at their connections with the sanitary sewer system, and entered basements from cracks in foundation walls and window wells and where stormwater was intercepted by floor drains.

This problem is further exacerbated by storm sewers, leading to overloading of the storm systems that service individual properties and thereby creating a high water table around foundation walls, with water entering through cracks in the walls and through floor drains.

Despite all the flooding problems, traditional flood control infrastructure such as dams, dikes and channels held, much to the relief of the city, resulting in an overall reduction in flood risk and damages. Nevertheless, these systems were stretched to their performance limits during the storm and had little or no capacity left to control additional stormwater.

In spite of the performance of the flood control infrastructure, flows in the river valleys resulted in considerable impacts to municipal infrastructure, including road crossings, sanitary sewers, water mains, stormwater management ponds, pathways, footbridges, public park buildings and stormwater outfalls. Responsibility for response was spread over numerous departments within the City of Toronto, including Parks, Forestry & Recreation, Transportation Services and Toronto Water.

The most noteworthy damages in the city's river valleys as a direct result of the storm were the catastrophic failure of a culvert beneath Finch Avenue at Black Creek and extensive stream erosion in the smaller urban watersheds. The collapse of the Black Creek culvert and of a major trunk sanitary sewer and the exposure of several other sections in Highland Creek due to erosion required emergency attention and millions of dollars to repair.

The Finch Avenue collapse at Black Creek

Directly beneath a major four-lane arterial road in the north end of Toronto called Finch Avenue, Black Creek passes through a four metre by three metre corrugated-metal arch culvert. During the August 19, 2005, storm the roadway collapsed at the upstream end and partially crushed the culvert opening. This resulted in a buildup of floodwater that overtopped the roadway and eroded the roadway embankment from the downstream side until complete washout occurred.

The collapse of Finch Avenue resulted in the closure of the roadway for 14 months, causing major traffic issues including rerouting of public transit and impacts to utilities such as hydro, gas and telecommunications. Multiple agencies were involved in the recovery and remediation, including the Conservation Authority and the federal Department of Fisheries & Oceans. Within the city itself, numerous departments, including Engineering, Transportation, Water and Parks & Recreation, were involved in the redesign of the crossing and channel restoration efforts. Direct costs for the reconstruction of Finch Avenue totalled $4.5-million. Indirect costs have yet to be fully calculated.

A total of 80 sites across the city were identified as having stream erosion related effects. Forty sites had major damage, about 25 were classified as minor works and 15 needed further investigation. Stabilization works were completed for four sites by the end of January 2006 and at another four by the end of May 2006. Remediation of the most severe sites was estimated at $1.7-million to the end of 2005, and another $8-million was spent through 2006 and 2007. Development of repair plans for the remaining 32 major erosion sites are in progress, involving a multi-disciplinary team of geomorphologists, aquatic biologists and water resources and design engineers.

What did the City of Toronto learn from this storm?

Toronto learned a great deal from this experience. The primary thing learned was that future climate change impacts may be more costly in terms of damage to infrastructure than anyone had previously imagined. August 19, 2005, was, in fact, the most expensive natural disaster to have occurred in the new millennium so far.

Repairs to infrastructure damaged during the storm will continue for several years. Unlike in New Orleans, however, they are likely to be completed. Past experience derived from remediating stream erosion caused by a big storm of slightly lesser intensity in 2000 suggests that about 60 to 70 per cent of the erosion problems could be addressed within five years of the event.

The City also learned to its relief that its regulatory approval process worked to provide the rapid response and decision making needed in emergencies. The reason the process worked in 2005 was because a special emergency works protocol had been put in place after the big storm of May 2000. The damage caused by the 2005 storm did, however, highlight the need to assess infrastructure within the valley system for vulnerability to stream erosion, particularly during major storms. Rather than reacting ad hoc to individual erosion site conditions, an adaptive management approach for the entire GTA was adopted that strives to protect critical infrastructure and includes a geomorphic systems analysis along with an ecological analysis of the entire valley system.

Adaptive management

Michael D'Andrea and his colleagues at the City of Toronto now have a new respect for how climate change will affect urban environments. D'Andrea has not been reluctant to warn other major North American cities of the lessons Toronto learned during that hot, dry and then suddenly very wet summer of 2005. D'Andrea maintains that past management of extreme weather events in urban areas has generally been reactive. Such management has operated largely on an emergency basis. Reactive management of storm events will no longer be adequate in a world that will be 3°c warmer than at present.

Public institutions are starting a journey of learning how to practise adaptive management in the face of a warming climate. In Ontario this type of approach is commonly applied to stream restoration projects. Using natural channel design principles, the goal of identifying opportunities to create fish habitat and enhance ecosystem health of the system while maintaining the stream's overall function under varied and changing flow regimes is pursued. These designs are premised on an adaptive management approach, in recognition that the system as designed and constructed is not permanent, but rather is expected to change and adjust over time, both in terms of stream meander and channel cross-sections, as the stream continues to adjust to the various impacts of land use and climate change. The adaptive management approach draws on the evolving state of science and practice and is linked to changes in community vision and governance. Now, the same approach has to be employed proactively to deal with large storms.

The key advantage of this type of approach is that it helps direct and prioritize resources to mitigate future urban flooding from more frequent extreme storms. An adaptive management strategy to help guard against future incidents of basement flooding is being advanced in Toronto using an integrated systems approach. The cost implications of this systems approach in terms of infrastructure redesign in Toronto are enormous.

Source or individual property level controls being advocated include installing sanitary sewer backwater valves; disconnecting roof downspouts; capping off storm sewer laterals; and installing sump pumps for foundation drains for every house in threatened areas in Toronto. The advocacy measures also include promotion of proper lot grading and a ban on construction of any new reverse-slope driveways.

At the sewer system level the response to the increased frequency and duration of extreme weather events will demand the identification and elimination of illegal sewer connections contributing stormwater; sealing maintenance hole covers in low-lying areas; and system rehabilitation to reduce extraneous sources of infiltration into the system.

Enormously expensive changes in the design and function of major overland flow systems will also be required. It will be necessary to create overland flow diversion channels where that is still possible, particularly in areas containing watercourses. It will be necessary to commit to significant road regrading, coupled with the construction of overland flow diversion channels on many existing roads and in future road reconstruction. It will also be necessary to build new stormwater storage facilities in the form of aboveground dry ponds where open space is still available, and underground storage as necessary where surface storage is not possible.

While the implementation of such changes to future infrastructure will be expensive enough, retrofitting a major system design in fully developed areas presents the most significant challenge in terms of cost, scheduling and disruption to the local communities. For that reason D'Andrea and his colleagues at the City of Toronto and at the Toronto & Region Conservation Authority propose that the implementation of the major infrastructure elements be prioritized based on cost-effectiveness, where a base metric to be considered is cost per "benefiting" property. Projects that fall outside of this criterion are to be implemented only as appropriate funding opportunities become available through other infrastructure renewal programs. In Toronto, early estimates of system infrastructure improvements to provide (where possible) storm drainage control to a one-in-100-year return frequency storm in flooding-prone areas have been estimated at several hundred million dollars. This presents a huge financial strain on a municipality dealing with a water and wastewater infrastructure backlog already estimated to be $1.8-billion.

In other words, it will not just be New Orleans that will be unable to afford the growing costs associated with infrastructure damage brought about by increasingly intense storm events that are projected to occur more frequently as a result of climate change. As Michael D'Andrea told a rapt audience in Vancouver, every city in North America should be concerned about the threat. Circulating dangerously around the climate change threat are all the interpenetrating elements required to create a perfect storm of cascading global environmental, economic and social cum political circumstances. It is the duty of our generation to do everything we can to avoid creating that storm and to minimize its effects if we can't prevent it.

What the City of Toronto is doing about climate change

There are few people at the City of Toronto who doubt that climate change is happening and what it means. In March 2007, the City released its "Change Is in the Air Plan," which outlined the City's formal commitment to an environmentally sustainable future. The plan committed to reducing greenhouse gas emissions by 30 per cent by 2020, based on 1990 levels. It committed to an 80 per cent reduction of these emissions by 2050. The City also committed to reducing smog-causing pollutants by 20 per cent by 2012. Even if the City of Toronto actually achieves these goals, however, it may be too little too late in terms of avoiding unimaginably expensive climate-related damage. At the ground level the challenges associated with upgrading Toronto's infrastructure to deal with dangerous and very expensive storm events remain overwhelming.

An assessment of the impacts and the actions taken during and after the storm of August 19, 2005, refocused efforts of the Toronto & Region Conservation Authority and the City of Toronto on the need for better understanding of the potential response of local rivers and streams, as well as our urban drainage infrastructure to extreme storm events. Analysis of what worked and what didn't has allowed for improvements in the Toronto & Region Conservation Authority's flood forecasting and warning program, including increased staffing and staff training to deliver the program, updates to dam operational procedures, and enhanced methodologies for the collection and assessment of weather data. The actions taken will be used to provide more specific severe-weather information to assist municipalities, including the City of Toronto, in responding to future events. Development of a comprehensive monitoring network was clearly defined as a critical component in understanding such events. Improvement and maintenance of this system was deemed a priority.

Unfortunately, however, such improvements have yet to be funded. The growing fear in Toronto, and in many other North American cities, is that there may simply not be enough money in our economy to prepare our cities for what is waiting in the wings in a warmer world. Michael D'Andrea did not have to explain this to his Vancouver audience. Similarly intense but less destructive storms had been already experienced in Calgary, Edmonton, Vancouver, Victoria and Seattle. No one had to be told what these storms meant in terms of damage to urban infrastructure. There was also serious talk across the country about the increasing incidence of tornadoes. To those who run our major cities, climate change already looks very much like a perfect storm.

Going Over Niagara Falls in a Barrel: The Urgent Need for Water Policy Reform in Canada

FACING OUR GLOBAL SITUATION

As a civilization we may have painted ourselves into a corner. Our agriculture and resource needs have become so substantial that they are shutting down other life-support processes upon which the entire global system depends for stability and sustainability. We can see clearly what is happening but we can't do anything because no one wants to be the first to make compromises or sacrifices, for fear that those who won't make those same sacrifices will triumph over them economically or politically.

If there was ever an area of social science research that needs urgent attention it is this form of environmental cum economic brinkmanship that ignores the obvious impacts of rapid population growth, encourages agricultural practices globally that we know are non-sustainable, acknowledges that biodiversity losses are compromising the state of our global life-support systems and yet takes only token steps toward preventing such loss; and knowingly starves nature of the water it needs to provide services to people that we cannot afford or do not know how to supply for ourselves. While many describe this madness as strategic or calculated brinkmanship, that view in the end may prove to be only a form of collective delusion.

We may not be able to get much further as a society until we know what it is in our collective character that permits us to act in such a dangerous manner on one hand, and how it is that we have almost universally come to accept the consequences of such behaviour on the other.

It may be that until we can understand why we are like this, more research into the damage we are doing to ourselves by what we are doing to the world will not yield meaningful results in the form of changed habits or effective action.

The social science research we need to undertake must explore elements of our nature that would allow us to make apparently rational choices that support the constant pushing of every environmental constraint and limit until the system breaks down and has to be replaced by costly but inferior artificial solutions which in turn we again push to the limits of failure.

Looking into the blinding eye of policy truth

In the preface to his remarkable book *Governing Water*, policy scholar Ken Conca compares the manner in which we address the larger policy issues related to the global environment to the manner in which we deal with the problem of viewing a solar eclipse.[41] If Conca's view of how we address global environmental governance were to be applied at a national level to the governance of water issues in Canada, our current situation might be characterized, with apologies to Ken Conca, in the following way.

Like those fearful of looking directly at the sun, we avert our gaze from the heart of governance issues in water matters in Canada. Instead of seeing the problem in global or even continental terms, we view the problem virtually through the intellectual equivalent of a cardboard pinhole camera. This allows us to see the shape of the problem we don't want to face directly, projected onto the comfortable surface of established federal/provincial relations.

We pretend that the limited instruments at hand, including those relating to existing laws and regulations, water apportionment agreements, inter-governmental relations and established levels of federal and provincial oversight, are up to the task. We allow environmental degradation and transboundary pollution to appear on the interprovincial and federal agendas only when they cross socially constructed borders or impinge on a euphemistic "commons" such as our shared climate, which we envision as somehow lying outside our borders.

We avert our gaze from these problems because staring directly at them would do serious damage to the lenses through which we normally view interprovincial and federal/provincial relations. These intellectual lenses encourage us to see a country characterized by the assumed legitimacy and effective function of current federal/provincial relations all properly standing up against the thin institutional veneer of a world system based on what Ken Conca calls a "gradually maturing anarchy." To gaze at the real world – in which provinces are authoritarian and self-interested in instinct, incompetent in practice and lacking collective rationale, and in which our entire governance structure is embedded in a global-scale politics that is deeply institutionalized around capitalist ideology focused almost maniacally on markets – would be to damage these lenses beyond repair. To prevent damage to our lenses we remain satisfied to gaze at the forms of intergovernmental relations relating to the management of our water resources that we see projected onto our time through a pinhole of momentary self-interest.

A few limited and transitory successes in the last decade have created the illusion of success, but our water resources problems and what they may ultimately mean to our environment and our economy remains largely out of focus. As a consequence, we fail to ask the larger questions, and those who know enough to be genuinely concerned about the future of Canada's increasingly besieged water resources find themselves returning year after precious year to negotiation tables armed with better and better science only to find themselves confronted time and again with the same flawed and ineffective institutional forms. We have created an unreality from which we cannot seem to escape.

SUSTAINABILITY AS A FOUNDATION OF DEMOCRACY

We have seen that development can clearly improve the lives and circumstances of people in poor countries and can do much in some cases to simultaneously improve general ecosystem health and agricultural productivity. It seems, however, that once we reach a certain level of development, we often start moving again in a direction away from sustainability – whatever one takes sustainability to be.

It was the view of many water experts attending the Sixth Biennial Rosenberg International Forum on Water Policy in 2008 that contemporary discussions about sustainability were largely irrelevant because we do not as a society act on a common vision of what sustainability means. Sustainability has been generally defined as development that meets the needs of the present without compromising the ability of future generations to meet their own needs. That said, many expert participants lamented the superficial manner in which the term "sustainability" had been appropriated by so many public and private interests today. There was a sense that, in the absence of a common understanding of the meaning of the term, we have adopted by default a consensus view of what we want sustainability to be like that once again does not reflect reality.

It is rather like the Spanish farmers who want to have their cake and eat it, too – who want huge public support for revitalizing irrigation infrastructure but are unwilling in return to give back any of the water which that revitalization saved so that even a drop could be used for other purposes such as the restoration of aquatic ecosystem health. It is also like Canadian farmers who want on one hand to keep their first-in-time, first-in-right licences granting them access to disproportionate volumes of water for agricultural purposes supplied by way of publicly funded infrastructure, but on the other hand also want to be able to sell those rights to the highest bidder for non-agricultural use as if the public had granted them not licences but full and complete ownership of the water. Such circumstances support the global unreality we have created.

Increasingly we find ourselves living in our own fantasy. Too many of us in Canada believe our own outmoded myth that the rest of world perceives our country as a model of environmental responsibility. That myth died in the late 20th century and any hope of restoring it is nipped at the bud each year we put off appropriate action on the climate change threat and by each additional project approved in Alberta's oil sands that is not supported by adequate environmental protection measures. At present we are viewed widely abroad as a complacent, self-satisfied people who don't care about the impacts our prosperous lifestyles have on own environments or on the commons we share with rest of the world. In the eyes of others our way of life is not sustainable. In fact it is threatening to the sustainability of the rest of the world.

What has "sustainability" come to mean?

The issue of sustainability may already be so urgent that we have to overlook the fact that the word itself has been appropriated and made meaningless through manipulation of its connotations by corporate and political interests. We have to wrest the term back rather than wasting years creating and putting forward some new term that means the same thing. We may need to insist on firm local and contextual definitions and meanings and be on high

alert in preventing weasel words from sidling up to the pure concept and robbing it of its forcefulness and integrity. As public
relations interests will inevitably try to cast a net over its pure
meaning, it will be necessary to be uncompromisingly persistent in defending sustainability's highest ideal from those who
would torque its meaning out of shape in the service of their own
interests.

The only impetus that appears to inspire real and timely
change is crisis, but even crises do not always carry us across the
threshold to new ways of thinking and acting. We so very often
go right up to or even over the threshold of change but turn back
the moment the crisis is over. We know there are limits but we just
keep pushing them. The moment we achieve even a modest sustainability gain, we cancel it out or create new problems for ourselves through further population or economic growth.

This suggests that we have not yet established in the public
imagination the link between sustainability and democracy. In
the context of contemporary governance with respect to the management of our water resources, it is not clear whether Canada's
democratic institutions are ready to contemplate that link yet, but
that may soon change.

Toward revitalized governance for sustainability

Though it often appears that governance in our time has either lost
its focus or has spread its focus over too many often contradictory or self-cancelling interests, we know that governance can be
revitalized by focusing on a single unifying urgency. That urgency
is not the marketplace. The market tends to take care of itself, often
sucking so much air out of the room by doing so that there is no
breathing space left for anything else. Rather, the urgency we must
address is sustainability, and only by addressing it can markets be
brought into line with any hope of creating an equitable and desirable future for those who will occupy the planet after we are gone.

Many who have been forced to look into the blinding sun of the world's growing water crisis are beginning to see sustainability as a dauntingly fundamental human value that is every bit as important to fight for as democracy, and that is as central to who we are or who we must be as the right to life itself. It is also a struggle that, like democracy, will be one we never entirely win and that once achieved will have to be diligently protected and defended. Moreover, sustainability may well prove to be central to the perpetuation of democracy itself, for whenever and wherever ecosystem health declines to the point that economic prosperity is no longer possible, that is when human despair creates circumstances antithetical to human rights and dignity and tyranny establishes itself and becomes lodged in our most important institutions.

In order to prevent erosion of civic participation in our democracy we need to recognize that our current institutional system is no longer adequate to deal with the problems we continue to create for ourselves. As the internationally respected water policy scholar Helen Ingram has pointed out, some of the water resources management processes in which we have taken great pride, have not worked.[42] The list of these innovations is long. Breakthroughs that had their day in the sun include revitalized water management principles and standards, centralization of decision-making, devolution and decentralization of decision-making, multi-objective planning, coordinated river basin planning and management, watershed management, privatization of water services and reliance on newly created water markets. It should not be said, however, that these efforts have been outright failures. These ideas often corrected errors and made things better in some areas, but each in turn proved to be no panacea for the problems associated with water governance in other, broader contexts.

Our current hope, in Canada at least, is integrated watershed management and adaptive management, which envision more collaborative governance and a more flexible and engaged role for science. Dr. Ingram offered, however, that there was a lot of old wine in these bottles. She notes that in spite of the high hopes and expectations of the academic and professional water community with respect to integrated water resource management and the adaptive management practices associated with it, the actual prospects for the delivery of purported benefits are no better than fair.

Ingram argues that while integrated water resource management and attendant adaptive management have great appeal to specialists, actually delivering on these ideas presents a number of political, institutional and equity issues. A big part of the difficulty of integrated water resource management is that the scope and scale of its ambitions may be too great to achieve. If each of the single elements that have composed integrated water resource management ambitions were in the past difficult to achieve individually, then all of the other components in combination pose an almost insurmountable implementation challenge. These include the recognition of the full range of uses of water; the recognition of in-stream flow needs; the desire to integrate water policy and land use policy; and the flexible, equitable allocation of water rights. Undertaking all of these together is huge challenge, especially in the face of so much historical precedent. When you can't even do one of these things well enough to ensure achievement of whatever you define as sustainability, how are you going to reform entire water management systems in ways that will permit implementation of all of these elements simultaneously?

Seen in this light, a common definition of sustainability becomes the bedrock upon which all future possibility must be built. New understanding about how ecosystems generate and purify water will also become part of that foundation. Until these new ideals drive our national and provincial water legislation and policies, we are, from a public policy perspective, continuing to pretend to live in a time that no longer exists.

THE GREAT WORK OF THE NEXT GENERATION

If Helen Ingram is right, our clumsy, time-consuming public processes can barely comprehend environmental decline, let alone turn that decline around to achieve any meaningful level of sustainability. What Dr. Ingram suggests is that we are going to have to improve our fundamental institutions while at the same time pressing at every opportunity for greater clarity in our definitions related to what sustainability actually means in the context of being human. Decades of work must be committed to understanding our impacts on our own life-support systems and in creating mechanisms for responding to those impacts by changing our habits, adjusting our expectations and improving our technologies.

This clearly is "The Great Work" of our generation, as Thomas Berry[43] called it, and of every subsequent generation that wants to possess anything close to the prosperity we have enjoyed. Unfortunately, it is not likely to be the kind of work that will create Hollywood-type heroes. As Helen Ingram points out, this work will take place in town and city council chambers, in meeting rooms and in endless dialogue aimed at arriving at a more durable consensus about the future than exists today. For the most part it will be done by volunteers.

The challenges for watershed basin governance models

Unfortunately, the situations under which straightforward forms of governance exist and are capable of managing increasingly complicated and pressing water issues appear to be becoming less common worldwide. This unhappy circumstance is likely to be even more common as populations continue to grow, greater pressure is applied on existing water supplies, and climate change increasingly affects the timing and extent of precipitation over large parts of the globe. The suggestion here, then, is that, unwieldy as they often may be, collaborative watershed basin management processes are going to be needed more than ever, to address issues of trust and to create a forum in which concerns and potential conflicts can be forecast and at least the possibility of preemptive resolution outside of courts can be preserved.

The widespread challenges associated with watershed governance, Ingram offered, is going to be made even more difficult by the fact that new energy production processes are taking up ever-greater volumes of water in many parts of the food-producing world. This, in tandem with growing concerns about the need to share a great deal more of the water we presently use with nature so as to maintain other critical biodiversity-based ecosystem functions, makes much of the current news about future water availability less than encouraging.

Growing concern over water availability globally underscores even more the critical trust-building role that watershed basin councils and authorities can play in building consensus about how to manage water resources in the future. But simply creating a forum for trust-building will not be enough to allow watershed basin councils and trusts to win enduring public and political support. It is absolutely essential to explore every avenue available for making basin councils more effective in the actual final implementation of better policies and practices. This perhaps represents the most important lesson Canada could learn from the proceedings of the Rosenberg Forum with respect to the revitalization of governance.

It is not enough to simply collaborate on the subject of possible public policy evolution and changes in practice. Talk generated within the collaborative framework created by any given watershed basin council has to be translated into action if it is going to mean anything over the long term. In order to ensure that recent investments in the development of watershed basin councils in places like Alberta are not wasted, we have to acknowledge the substantial gap that presently exists between promise and practice, and we must move immediately to fill that gap. This demands careful, honest evaluation of why recommendations of basin councils and trusts are not acted upon in a timely manner by government, agriculture or industry. It also requires clear articulation of what must be done to remove current obstacles to measurable progress. This may mean deep and perhaps uncomfortable examination of gaps or conflicts in jurisdictional accountabilities and the identification and individual naming of conflicting outside interests and political influences. It may also mean asking difficult questions about the ultimate motives of representative interests participating in basin activities. Such an evaluation should not be undertaken, however, without a commitment to also undertaking the final, difficult but crucially important step of cultivating the political will required in order to break out of current bureaucratic and political constraints that stand in the way of the ultimate success of the basin councils in achieving their established goals.

While this may appear a painful step to have to take, the consequences of failing to properly and truthfully evaluate the reasons for poorer than expected performance of watershed basin councils in terms of actually changing water policy and practice could be even more painful.

Revitalized water governance: filling the gap between promise and practice

Helen Ingram reminds us that the multiple and complex ways in which humans relate to water suggests that individuals and groups can be moved to change behaviour or take action as a result of impulses and motivations that transcend simple self-interest. She points out that while analysis of water politics has in the past tended to be viewed as a struggle among various user groups to obtain specific advantage, issues of identity, moral grounding and fairness can in certain instances be more persuasive than appeals to self-interested rationality in changing orientations and allegiances.

There are examples from all over the world that suggest that out of the shared experience of loss of opportunity, security and control over water resources, powerful forces can emerge to change water governance. Ingram points out that the collective "sense of we" can animate and mobilize ordinary people cognitively, emotionally and even morally to take common action. This seldom happens, however, without some form of leadership.

Getting things done in politics requires effective leadership, and in virtually all cases where real change occurs with respect to water resources, success can be traced to the involvement of people skilled in politics. It is important to note that Ingram identifies the need to involve political operatives, not just politicians. As former Alberta Environment Minister Dr. Lorne Taylor has indicated many times, changing the way we value and manage water will simply not happen in Alberta or anywhere else in Canada without full, productive and continuous political engagement.

Those who would seek to reform public policy with respect to water management must clearly understand that leaders are not attracted to policy areas unless there is a potential for public support beyond just the experts and professionals. This means politicians must be connected to people in the larger water community whom they trust for advice and support. Lorne Taylor agrees with Helen Ingram that political leaders need access to new ideas, especially if public support for change prompted by water-related crises can no longer be satisfied through time-worn solutions such as the large-scale dams and diversions that used to be offered up as a panacea every time water became scarce.

Political operatives are those who can engage politicians in meaningful dialogue about the policy options that might be explored in order to ensure orderly change. Real leaders, as Ingram indicates, do not stop with simply exploring public policy choices. They make the leap from promise to practice. In other words, they cross the line from concept to effective implementation.

The lesson here is that the real leaders in water resources

management are not just those with power but those with the ability to influence power. Being in that position, however, requires clear focus on larger, long-term goals; careful attention to detail and accuracy; and a strong sense of political reality, possibility and opportunity.

With each passing year governments around the world are becoming more and more paralyzed by the cumulative weight of past decisions, commitments and loyalties. Our society's ability to move around inside the straitjacket of established precedent is constantly decreasing. Already we can see that the past mechanisms for breaking free of political impasses through acts such as territorial expansion and war only make things worse. Every problem we face comes back to one single issue: we, as a species, are running out of space and resources, and as a consequence we are unavoidably on our way to global environmental and economic decline.

At present it takes real genius and huge energy to effect meaningful public policy change. That is why such change occurs so seldom. As our ever more populated world converges on trade-offs that will have to be made between our way of life and our survival, we should expect it to become even more difficult and even more time-consuming to positively affect public policy reform. Support for effective leadership will no longer be optional. It may be our only hope.

To achieve sustainability we need to continue the ongoing project of constant reform of our governance structures; recognize the crucial importance of leadership; recognize that equity is becoming increasingly important in decision-making; and design solutions for real-world situations. Most importantly, we have to cross the line that separates intention from action – and after we have crossed that line, we have to stay there.

A great deal of territory has already been staked and a great deal of ecosystem function appropriated. Getting that territory back for life support function may be one of the most important challenges we will face as a civilization.

From promise to practice: a cautionary tale from Arizona

People with widely divergent interests in far-flung places are responding similarly to feelings of risk and insecurity generated by "impenetrable and unaccountable" water resource decisions that appear to be made elsewhere by expert others, through market forces they did not know existed, or in response to interests or circumstances they do not know anything about. Helen Ingram believes that this is no longer a scientists' or policy-makers' game. Citizens with a sense of place are becoming involved in the recovery and restoration of riparian habitat. Greater concern over the equity of water resources decisions is leading to a quiet groundswell that seeks to transcend the engineering focus on "doing things right" toward a broader focus on "doing the right thing" in evaluating water resource options. The difficulty, however, is keeping up with our manifold impacts. She offers a telling example.

In the American Southwest, overexploitation of water resources may be close to the "tipping point." According to the Arizona Auditor General, the three most populous management areas will not reach water safe yield by 2025, even though that was the specific goal of the highly touted Arizona Groundwater Management Act. Even so, widely respected water commentators in the state write that the Act is a success largely because of its innovative water banking provisions that make full use of Arizona's legal entitlement to the already overstressed Colorado River. Ingram completely disagrees. She points out as a matter of fact that while such water banking actions do reduce groundwater overdraft for about 15 years, the aquifer depletion problem escalates after that because of relentless population growth. She also points out that resistance to conservation regulations remains common; that many wells are exempt wells; and that drought continues to contribute to dwindling surface water supplies. From this it can be seen that exemptions from regulations, lack of enforcement of existing laws, and drought make the terms and conditions of the

Arizona Groundwater Management Act impossible to fulfill. In Dr. Ingram's opinion, all the public relations spin in the world is not going to change this fact.

In Helen Ingram's estimation, it is important that water policy scholars and practitioners consider the Arizona experience as a cautionary tale. The visionary language of contemporary reforms is not the same as performance. The Arizona system is biased toward business as usual, and only if political leaders see either threats or opportunities in current failed circumstances are real changes likely to occur.

The lesson for Canada is that we may wish to examine what worked and didn't work in the Arizona circumstance so that we can avoid spending billions of dollars on public policy actions that appear to reform water resource management habits but in fact only perpetuate current circumstances while worsening scarcity in the future.

If the gap between promise and practice is not filled, enthusiasm currently generated by the creation of new watershed basin councils will wane, volunteers in these organizations will become disillusioned, burn out or lose faith, and the public may abandon trust in government's capacity to fill the gap between practice and the great promise that is being made by way of new water strategies in many Canadian provinces.

On the other hand, if the government of Alberta, for example, were able to break through what appears to be a barrier that exists globally between collaboration and action on water issues at the watershed level by carefully cultivating truly effective basin-based institutions, it will not only succeed with its Water for Life strategy, it will have something very significant to showcase and share on the world water resource management stage.

Notes

1   See Max H. Bazerman & Michael D. Watkins. *Predictable Surprises: The Disasters You Should Have Seen Coming and How to Prevent Them* (Boston: Harvard Business School Press, 2004).

2   Donald A. Wilhite, ed. "Drought as a Natural Hazard," in *Drought: A Global Assessment* (New York: Routledge Hazards & Disasters Series, 2000), 1:4, 5.

3   For more on these economic perspectives, see Nicholas Stern, *The Global Deal: Climate Change and the Creation of a New Era of Progress and Prosperity* (New York: BBS Public Affairs, 2009).

4   See "It's about People: Changing Perspectives on Dryness, A Report to Government by an Expert Social Panel" (Canberra: Commonwealth of Australia, 2008).

5   This section is adapted from a presentation prepared for the Improving Water Security through Integrated Observation and Prediction Networks conference held in Canmore, Alberta, in December 2008. The original paper was written by Bob Sandford; John Pomeroy of the University of Saskatchewan; Mike Demuth of the Geological Survey of Canada; Gordon Young, president of the International Association of Hydrological Sciences; and Paul Whitfield of Environment Canada.

6   See C. Spence, S. Hamilton, P.H. Whitfield, M.N. Demuth, D. Harvey, D. Hutchinson, B. Davison, T.B.M.J. Ouarda, H. Goertz, J.W. Pomeroy, P. Marsh, "Invited Commentary: A Framework for Integrated Research & Monitoring (FIRM)," *Canadian Water Resources Journal*, 34, no. 1, Spring 2009.

7   See Henry F. Diaz and Jon K. Eischeid, "Disappearing 'Alpine Tundra' Köppen Climatic Type in the Western United States," *Geophysical Research Letters* 34, L18707 (September 27, 2007).

8   See Brian Luckman & Trudy Kavanagh, "Impact of Climate Fluctuations on Mountain Environments in the Canadian Rockies," *Ambio* 29, no. 7 (November 2000), 371–80.

9   Donald Worster, *Dust Bowl: The Southern Plains in the 1930s*, 25th Anniversary ed. (New York: Oxford University Press, 2004). Worster is also the author of two other books that have had a profound influence on the way I think about the North American West. Both of these, *Rivers of Empire: Water, Aridity and the Growth of the American West* and *Under Western Skies: Nature and History in the American West*, touch heavily on the importance of water to the identity of those who live in the dry heart of the North American continent.

10 David C. Jones, *Empire of Dust* (Edmonton: University of Alberta Press, 1987).

11 Worster, *Dust Bowl*, 29.

12 Worster, *Dust Bowl*, 219.

13 Jones, 220, 221.

14 Worster, *Dust Bowl*, 119.

15 Wallace Stegner, Introduction to John Wesley Powell (1878), *Report on the Lands of the Arid Region of the United States, with a More Detailed Account of the Lands of Utah* (Cambridge, Mass.: Belknap Press, Harvard Univ. Press, 1962), xi, xii.

16 Mohamed T. El-Ashry & Diana Gibbons, eds. *Water and Arid Lands of the Western United States* (UK: Cambridge University Press, 1988), 33.

17 For a Hollywood interpretation of the William Mulholland legend, see the 1974 movie *Chinatown*, starring Faye Dunaway and Jack Nicholson.

18 William Kahrl, *Water and Power: The Conflict over Los Angeles' Water Supply in the Owens Valley* (Berkeley: University of California Press, 1982), 90.

19 Kahrl, 182.

20 Kahrl, 375.

21 See Los Angeles Department of Water & Power, "Securing LA's Water Supply," May 2008. Accessed 20090725 at www.ladwp.com/ladwp/cms/ladwp010588.jsp.

22 Readers or researchers with specific interest in the proceedings of the Rosenberg International Forum on Water Policy are invited to view all of the papers presented at Zaragoza, Spain, in 2008 and at earlier Rosenberg forums, at http://rosenberg.ucanr.org/forum6.cfm.

23 The article indicated a figure of 92 million cubic feet, which we later determined was an error. The actual units were cubic metres.

24 See Carlo Giupponi and Mordechai Shechter, eds. *Climate Change in the Mediterranean: Socio-Economic Perspectives of Impacts, Vulnerability and Adaptation* (Cheltenham, UK, and Northampton, Mass.: Edward Elgar, 2003), 3.

25 William Ashworth, *Ogallala Blue: Water and Life on the High Plains* (New York: W.W. Norton & Company, 2006), 17, 18.

26 Ashworth, 58, 59.

27 Ashworth, 153.

28 See John R. Vallentyne & David W. Schindler, *The Algal Bowl: Overfertilization of the World's Freshwaters and Estuaries* (Edmonton: University of Alberta Press, 2008).

29 Those with an interest in leading-edge research on climate change feedbacks in the Arctic may wish to familiarize themselves with the work being done as part of IP3 in Canada. IP3 stands for " Improved Processes and Parameterisation for Prediction in Cold Regions." Among the many projects in this major undertaking is a study of the rate of loss of permafrost in the Northwest Territories just 4 km from the proposed route of the Mackenzie oil pipeline. The research the present chapter refers to was conducted by Dr. William Quinton of Wilfrid Laurier University and can be found at www.usask.ca/ip3/.

30 See John P. Smol & Marianne S.V. Douglas, "Crossing the Final Ecological Threshold in High Arctic Ponds," *Proceedings of the* [US] *National Academy of Sciences* 104, no. 30 (July 24, 2007).

31 See James Garvey, *The Ethics of Climate Change: Right and Wrong in a Warming World* (London & New York: Continuum International Publishing Group, 2008).

32 See Council of Canadian Academies Expert Panel on Groundwater, "The Sustainable Management of Groundwater in Canada" (Ottawa: Council of Canadian Academies, May 2009), accessed 20090625 at www.scienceadvice.ca/groundwater.html.

33 See Ger Bergkamp & Claudia W. Sadoff, "Water in a Sustainable Economy," ch. 8 in *2008 State of the World: Innovations for a Sustainable Economy*, 25th Anniversary ed., edited by Gary T. Gardner, Thomas Prugh, Linda Starke & Worldwatch Institute (New York, London: W.W. Norton, 2008), 107–122.

34 See Peter Annin, *The Great Lakes Water Wars* (Washington, DC: Island Press, 2006).

35 See Environment Canada and US Environmental Protection Agency, "State of the Great Lakes 2009 Highlights," accessed 20090815 at http://binational.net/solec/sogl2009_e.html and www.epa.gov/solec.

36 Annin, 13.

37 See Nicholas Stern, *The Global Deal: Climate Change and the Creation of a New Era of Progress and Prosperity*, (New York: Public Affairs, 2009), 9.

38 See Lauren Farrell, Donald Haley, Michael D'Andrea & William J. Snodgrass, "Storm of August 19, 2005: A Catalyst for Change from Reactive to Adaptive Urban Flood Management in Toronto, Ontario, Canada," International Symposium on Flood Defence, Toronto, May 6–8, 2008.

39 For more on the "Perfect Storm" concept, see David Brooks, Oliver Brandes & Stephen Gurman, eds., "Avoiding the Perfect Storm: Weathering Climate Change by Following Its Effects on Water Resources" in *Making the Most of the Water We Have: The Soft Path Approach to Water Management* (Sterling, Va.: Earthscan, 2009), 23–34.

40 See www.ncdc.noaa.gov/oa/satellite/satelliteseye/cyclones/pfctstorm91/pfctstorm.html

41 See Ken Conca, *Governing Water: Contentious Transnational Politics and Global Institution Building* (Cambridge, Mass.: MIT Press, 2006): xi, xii.

42 See Helen Ingram, "Beyond Universal Remedies for Good Water Governance: A Political and Contextual Approach," presented at the Sixth Biennial Rosenberg International Forum on Water Policy, Zaragoza, Spain, 2008, accessed 20090725 at http://rosenberg.ucanr.org/documents/Ingram.pdf.

43 See Thomas Berry, *The Great Work: Our Way into the Future* (New York: Harmony/Bell Tower, 2000).

BIBLIOGRAPHY

Annin, Peter. *The Great Lakes Water Wars*. Washington, DC: Island Press, 2006.

Ashworth, William. *Ogallala Blue: Water and Life on the High Plains*. New York: W.W. Norton & Co., 2006.

Barghouti, Shawki. "Water Productivity: Challenges Facing Agricultural Development," presented in absentia at the Sixth Biennial Rosenberg International Forum on Water Policy, Zaragoza, Spain, 2008. Accessed 20090725 at http://rosenberg.ucanr.org/documents/III Barghouti.pdf.

Bazerman, Max H., & Michael D. Watkins. *Predictable Surprises: The Disasters You Should Have Seen Coming and How To Prevent Them*. Boston: Harvard Business School Press, 2004.

Bergkamp, Ger, & Claudia W. Sadoff, "Water in a Sustainable Economy," ch. 8 in *2008 State of the World: Innovations for a Sustainable Economy*. 25th Anniversary ed., edited by Gary T. Gardner, Thomas Prugh, Linda Starke & Worldwatch Institute. New York, London: W.W. Norton, 2008.

Berry, Thomas. *The Great Work: Our Way into the Future*. New York: Harmony/Bell Tower, 2000.

Brooks, David, Oliver Brandes & Stephen Gurman, eds. "Avoiding the Perfect Storm: Weathering Climate Change by Following Its Effects on Water Resources" in *Making the Most of the Water We Have: The Soft Path Approach to Water Management*. Sterling, Va.: Earthscan, 2009.

Conca, Ken. *Governing Water: Contentious Transnational Politics and Global Institution Building*. Cambridge, Mass.: MIT Press, 2006.

Council of Canadian Academies Expert Panel on Groundwater. "The Sustainable Management of Groundwater in Canada." Ottawa: Council of Canadian Academies, May 2009. Accessed 20090625 at www.scienceadvice.ca/groundwater.html.

Craik, Wendy, & James Cleaver. "Modern Agriculture under Stress: Lessons from the Murray-Darling." MDBC Publication no. 46/08. Canberra: Murray-Darling Basin Commission, 2008. Accessed 20090625 at www.mdbc.gov.au/__data/page/15/Modern_Agriculture_Under_Stress_-_Lessons_form_the_Murray-Darling.pdf [NB: URL is valid only with the typo 'form' for 'from.']

Diaz, Henry F., & Jon K. Eischeid. "Disappearing 'Alpine Tundra' Köppen Climatic Type in the Western United States." *Geophysical Research Letters* 34, L18707 (September 27, 2007).

El-Ashry, Mohamed T., & Diana Gibbons, eds. *Water and Arid Lands of the Western United States*. UK: Cambridge University Press, 1988.

Environment Canada and US Environmental Protection Agency, "State of the Great Lakes 2009 Highlights," accessed 20090815 at http://binational.net/solec/sogl2009_e.html and www.epa.gov/solec.

Farrell, Lauren, Donald Haley, Michael D'Andrea & William J. Snodgrass. "Storm of August 19, 2005: A Catalyst for Change from Reactive to Adaptive Urban Flood Management in Toronto, Ontario, Canada." International Symposium on Flood Defence, Toronto, May 6–8, 2008.

Garvey, James. *The Ethics of Climate Change: Right and Wrong in a Warming World*. London & New York: Continuum International Publishing Group, 2008.

Giupponi, Carlo, & Mordechai Shechter, eds. *Climate Change in the Mediterranean: Socio-Economic Perspectives of Impacts, Vulnerability and Adaptation*. Cheltenham, UK, and Northampton, Mass.: Edward Elgar, 2003.

Heal, Geoffrey, et al. *Valuing Ecosystem Services: Toward Better Environmental Decision-Making*. Washington, DC: National Academies Press, 2005.

Ingram, Helen. "Beyond Universal Remedies for Good Water Governance: A Political and Contextual Approach," presented at the Sixth Biennial Rosenberg International Forum on Water Policy, Zaragoza, Spain, 2008. Accessed 20090725 at http://rosenberg.ucanr.org/documents/Ingram.pdf.

"It's about People: Changing Perspectives on Dryness, a Report to Government by an Expert Social Panel." Canberra: Commonwealth of Australia, 2008. Accessed 20090625 at www.daff.gov.au/agriculture-food/drought/national_review_of_drought_policy/social_assessment/dryness-report.

Jackson, Wes. *Becoming Native to this Place*. The Blazer Lectures for 1991. Lexington: University Press of Kentucky, 1994.

Jones, David C., *Empire of Dust*. Edmonton: University of Alberta Press, 1987.

Junger, Sebastian. *The Perfect Storm: A True Story of Men against the Sea*. New York: Norton, 1997.

Kahrl, William. *Water and Power: The Conflict over Los Angeles' Water Supply in the Owens Valley*. Berkeley: University of California Press, 1982.

Los Angeles Department of Water & Power. "Securing LA's Water Supply," May 2008. Accessed 20090725 at www.ladwp.com/ladwp/cms/ladwp010588.jsp.

Luckman, Brian, & Trudy Kavanagh. "Impact of Climate Fluctuations on Mountain Environments in the Canadian Rockies." *Ambio* 29, no. 7 (November 2000).

Ponting, Clive. *A Green History of the World: The Environment and the Collapse of Great Civilizations.* Rev. ed. New York: Penguin, 2007.

Smol, John P., & Marianne S.V. Douglas. "Crossing the Final Ecological Threshold in High Arctic Ponds." *Proceedings of the [US] National Academy of Sciences* 104, no. 30 (July 24, 2007).

Spence, C., S. Hamilton, P.H. Whitfield, M.N. Demuth, D. Harvey, D. Hutchinson, B. Davison, T.B.M.J. Ouarda, H. Goertz, J.W. Pomeroy & P. Marsh. "Invited Commentary: A Framework for Integrated Research & Monitoring (FIRM)." *Canadian Water Resources Journal,* 34, no. 1 (Spring 2009).

Stegner, Wallace. Introduction to *Report on the Lands of the Arid Region of the United States, with a More Detailed Account of the Lands of Utah,* by John Wesley Powell (1878). Cambridge, Mass.: Belknap Press, Harvard University Press, 1962.

Stern, Nicholas. *The Global Deal: Climate Change and the Creation of a New Era of Progress and Prosperity.* New York: BBS Public Affairs, 2009.

Vallentyne, John R., & David W. Schindler. *The Algal Bowl: Overfertilization of the World's Freshwaters and Estuaries.* Edmonton: University of Alberta Press, 2008.

Wilhite, Donald A., ed. "Drought as a Natural Hazard," in *Drought: A Global Assessment.* Routledge Hazards & Disasters Series vol. 1. New York: Routledge, 2000.

Worster, Donald. *Dust Bowl: The Southern Plains in the 1930s.* 25th Anniversary ed. New York: Oxford University Press, 2004.

———. *Rivers of Empire: Water, Aridity and the Growth of the American West.* New York : Pantheon Books, 1985.

———. *Under Western Skies: Nature and History in the American West.* New York and Oxford: Oxford University Press, 1992.